# DESSERTS
## LaBelle

# DESSERTS
# LaBelle

*Soulful Sweets to Sing About*

# Patti LaBelle

### Laura Randolph Lancaster

*with* Rick Rodgers

GRAND CENTRAL
Life & Style

NEW YORK • BOSTON

Grand Central Life & Style
Hachette Book Group
1290 Avenue of the Americas, New York, NY 10104

grandcentrallifeandstyle.com
twitter.com/grandcentralpub

First Edition: April 2017

Grand Central Life & Style is an imprint of Grand Central Publishing. The Grand Central
Life & Style name and logo are trademarks of Hachette Book Group, Inc.

The publisher is not responsible for websites (or their content) that are not
owned by the publisher.

The Hachette Speakers Bureau provides a wide range of authors for speaking events.
To find out more, go to www.hachettespeakersbureau.com or call (866) 376-6591.

Photo on page ix is by Melanie Dunea. Photos on pages xvi, 14, 48, 55, 62, 90, 112, 114,
124, 129, 133, 152, 190, 216, 228, and 234 are by Amy Roth. Photos on pages xii, xiii, xv,
21, 24, 39, 57, 94, 131, 142, 144, 145, 146, 147, 165, 170, 181, and 182 are from Patti
LaBelle's personal collection. All other photos are by Steve Legato.

Print book interior design by Gary Tooth / Empire Design Studio

Library of Congress Cataloging-in-Publication Data

Names: LaBelle, Patti.

Title: Desserts LaBelle : soulful sweets to sing about / Patti LaBelle, Laura
Randolph Lancaster with Rick Rodgers.

Description: First edition. | New York : Life & Style, 2017. | Includes index.

Identifiers: LCCN 2016054255| ISBN 9781455543403 (hardcover) |
ISBN 9781455543410 (ebook)

Subjects: LCSH: Desserts. | LCGFT: Cookbooks.

Classification: LCC TX773 .L25 2017 | DDC 641.86--dc23 LC record available at
https://lccn.loc.gov/2016054255

ISBNs: 978-1-4555-4340-3 (hardcover); 978-1-4555-4341-0 (ebook)

Printed in the United States of America

Q-MA

10  9  8  7  6  5  4  3  2  1

This book is dedicated to the women whose recipes molded my cooking identity and whose wisdom molded my core identity: my mother, Bertha "Chubby" Holte, and my aunts, Hattie Mae Sibley and Joshia Mae James. From them I learned the secrets to baking rich and fulfilling soulful desserts…and the keys to living a rich and fulfilling soul-filled life. May they continue to watch over and guide me as I pass down their timeless wisdom to the youngest descendant of the Holte women family tree: my beautiful granddaughter, Gia.

# Contents

# Sweet Talk from Patti

I know what you're thinking: A dessert cookbook from *me*? Patti LaBelle? The woman who, for the better part of two decades, has been telling anyone who will listen she is diabetic? The one who lost her mother to diabetes-related complications long before her time? *The woman who served as spokesperson for the American Diabetes Association?* Yes, yes, and yes. I've got some sweet recipes I need to share. Sweet stories I need to tell. And what better time to share them than right now? Right here.

One story in particular provides the perfect launch.

I call it the Patti Pie Phenomenon—the PPP for short. It happened a few years ago, when a fan purchased one of my sweet potato pies from Walmart, then posted a review on YouTube singing its praises. Literally. His passionate performance immediately went viral. (James Wright Chanel, you know you can sing!) *Twenty million* views later, everyone was rushing out to get their hands on one of my sweet potato pies. In 48 hours, every single one of those pies sold out...at *every single Walmart store*. And that was just the beginning. When word leaked that no one at the store knew when the pies would be restocked, the would-be pie scalpers started a now-famous resale market. Before the PPP was all over, my sweet potato pies—which cost $3.48 at Walmart—were selling on eBay for $45. I knew something *really* serious was happening when people started auctioning them off with bid prices ranging from $50 to $12,000.

What was happening, I have come to realize, was not one phenomenon, but two. The first I don't really, or I should say fully, understand; the second I'm pretty sure I do. The phenomenon I don't fully understand is the one I just described: the PPP. Since it happened, I've gone from wondering if I have some kind of mystical/spiritual/ancestral connection to sweet potatoes to being convinced that I do. There's just no other way to explain it.

My girlfriend Cassie went to school with a woman who would know just what I mean. Cassie doesn't remember her name, so I'm going to call her "Annie," in honor of Ann Lowe, the African American designer who made Jackie Kennedy's wedding dress. Cassie says that from the moment Annie sat down at her mother's rickety old Singer, she could make any outfit you could dream up, draw, or describe. (Think: the red carpet gowns worn at the Met Gala.) Not only did Annie *sew* like a professional dressmaker from the get-go, Cassie says, she also quilted and embroidered like nobody's business. And she did it all without ever taking so much as a single home economics class, never mind formal sewing lessons. Here's what I believe deep in my soul: Annie had something special that no class, no school, no formal sewing lessons, could provide: her grandmother's genes. Annie's grandmother was a master seamstress.

Which brings me back to the PPP. (For the full story—and all the delicious details [pun intended]—check out the story behind Gia's

sweet potato flan on pages 181–183.) I'm pretty sure my grandmother Tempie had a hand in it. Her homemade breads in general, and sweet potato biscuits in particular, are the stuff of legend. For reasons unrelated to baking skill, I think my sister Barbara had something to do with it, too. (I stayed up all night cooking her favorite foods and baked a dozen of her much-loved sweet potato pies for her wedding…and for her funeral.) I *know* my aunts and my mother were heavily involved in the PPP, and by heavily involved I mean they probably orchestrated the whole thing. Anyone who knew Aunt Hattie Mae, Aunt Joshia Mae, and Chubby—that's what everybody called my mother—will tell you they were sweet potato sorceresses. They did things to sweet potatoes, magic things, that made grown men cry. And I am the grateful beneficiary of the unexpected blessings that brings.

Every sweet potato pie I make, in fact, is a version of Chubby's. No two ways about it: Her sweet potato pie is the OG. Not only is my Walmart sweet potato pie recipe based on it; it's also the inspiration for my dear friend Norma's black bottom sweet potato pie recipe (readily available online and in my first cook-book, *LaBelle Cuisine*). Ditto the sweet potato pie recipe in this book (page 132).

So that's the (mystical/spiritual/magical) phenomenon I believe in but can't really explain. Since it happened, when it comes to the mystic, here's what I've decided: You can question its existence, or you can let it free you from some-thing, something inexplicable but deeply reassuring, too. Put it this way. I have embraced what the London-based artist Robert Montgom-ery says: "The people you love become ghosts inside of you, and like this you keep them alive."

I believe the recipes you love become part of something inside of you, too. Something spiritual;

something sacred. Because those recipes bring the people who originally cooked them for you into your consciousness as well as your kitchen again, and, as Mr. Montgomery says, like this you keep them alive. Like this you keep them ever close. It says everything that my mother's sweet potato pie is responsible for the PPP, which, in turn, is responsible for the gazillion requests I received to write a cookbook filled with my favorite desserts.

I won't lie: When my son Zuri (he's also my manager) first raised the idea, I dismissed it out of hand. (Shout-out to my cooking buddy, Rick Rodgers, for putting the bug in his ear.) I believe my exact words to my son were, "Child, have you lost your natural mind?" Let's face it, as a diabetic, cooking and eating high-carb / high-sugar *anything*—never mind down-home, go-tell-it-on-the-mountain-good Southern desserts—isn't high on my list of Daily Healthy Kitchen Activities. But then, everywhere I went—the airport, the grocery store, backstage at my concerts—people started telling me the *stories* of their best-loved desserts, stories that were every bit as important to them as the desserts' deliciosity. (If that's not a word, it should be.)

Like the young bride whose grandmother shared her top-secret peach cobbler recipe as a wedding gift: Even though her grandmother had debilitating arthritis in *both* her hands, Girlfriend told me her grandmother gift-wrapped that recipe in the finest, most delicate tissue and ribbons. Is it any wonder that the moment she lifted it out of the box she knew how very much she was loved? (Both sides of the family had been pestering her grandmother for that recipe for years.) She said, "Ms. LaBelle, I wouldn't trade that recipe—or the tissue paper it was wrapped in—for all the money in the world." And I believe her. Like I said, soulful sweets to sing about.

Since the PPP, I've learned that the rich and connected know the power of soulful sweets, too. Ann Romney, for example, wife of the gazillion-aire former presidential candidate Mitt Romney, did something five years ago for her husband that blew my mind. The morning after he conceded defeat in the 2012 presidential campaign, she came home and made him her grandmother Pottinger's pancakes. With all her money, Girl-friend could have done *anything* to comfort her husband, anything to ease the pain of that loss: buy him some fabulous luxury vehicle (the Romneys have an elevator for their *cars*...yep, you heard me right). Take him on a first-class trip around the world (they have the kind of cash that makes it easy to follow the stay-at-the-Ritz-or-stay-at-home directive).

You name it, Ann Romney could have hooked it up. But Girlfriend knew the power of those pancakes: In a much happier, much simpler time, when she and Mitt were first married and going to college in Utah, she used to make them for him all the time. Comfort food. Loving food. Soulful sweets to sing about. (As her own children were growing up, Ann Romney made her grandmother Pottinger's pancakes for them on weekends and special occasions. See why I say recipes can connect generations across time and space?)

Lest you think this pancake story is a fluke, let me give you another example of the comfort food / loving food and powerful people connec-tion. (Bonus: It explains why I believe with all my heart that President Obama would under-stand just how much those precious pancakes meant to Mitt Romney.) Nobody knows better than Barack Obama the perks of power. When you're the leader of the free world, you learn quick, fast, and in a hurry that you can give your family just about anything their hearts desire, even when they don't ask for it.

Perfect example: On their first night in the White House, while their parents partied at the inaugural balls, Sasha and Malia got a surprise visit (and a private concert) from one of the hottest boy bands in the country. At the height of JoBro mania, none other than Kevin, Joe, and Nick—aka the Jonas Brothers—treated the First Daughters and several of their BFFs to one of those dreamy, fairy-tale nights no preteen girl ever forgets. (Sasha was seven and Malia was ten. Somebody tell me, where did the time go?) I hope they sang "Hello Beautiful." And that Nick and Joe took turns on lead. And that all three of the guys took pictures with every single tween at the party, though that might just be the tween in me talking.

Oops, sorry. I got waaay off track. What can I tell you? I've always been a sucker for a White House performance, even if I'm not singing in it. Where was I? Oh, right: I was giving you another example of how strongly the rich and powerful are connected to comfort food / loving food. And, of course, the kinds of soulful sweets that are in this book. As I said earlier, it also explains why I'm so sure President Obama could relate to the importance of sitting down and sharing a simple meal with the person (or the people) you love—just like Mitt Romney and his wife cherished the simple act of sharing those pancakes. *Because that's what he did almost every night of his presidency.* Not the pancakes part; the sitting down with his family and eating part.

No matter how busy he was, the president honored and preserved the family dinnertime. Almost every evening between 6:30 p.m. and 7:30 p.m., President Obama left the Oval Office, walked to the residence, and sat himself down to dinner with Michelle and the girls. Just how do I happen to know the precise time the president headed over to the Executive Residence?

I have the best of sources, I assure you. Make that the ultimate source: Michelle. (Since my granddaughter, Gia, was born, I've told this story so many times that Zuri now gets up and leaves the room whenever anyone mentions the White House, even in passing.) I don't know what about my visits to the Obama White House I'll remember more: that dinner story, or Michelle introducing me as her "other mother."

Because I know for a fact that President Obama has a serious sweet tooth—he has a *major* thing for pie—I'm willing to bet that, Michelle's famous veggie garden aside, more than a few of those family dinners included dessert. And that plenty of *them* were soulful sweets. Case in point: Last year, President Obama posted a picture of himself eating sweet potato bourbon pecan pie in the Oval Office private dining room. It looked so much like Chubby's, I had to go to bed before the sun went down to stop myself from calling the White House and inviting myself over for a slice. I kid you not.

Given these kinds of stories, you can see why, since the PPP, I have come to believe in the second phenomenon: the *SSP*—the Soulful Sweets Phenomenon—the one that flows from the original PPP. The one I think I understand. Here's what it comes down to, really: At the milestone moments of our lives—the birthdays, graduations, christenings, weddings, anniversaries, even the funerals—there is always a sweet dish—a cake, a cobbler, a pie, a pudding—that helps us mark it. Memorize it. Memorialize it. (The perfect example: the top layer of the wedding cake that every bride freezes, hoping it will be, if not as moist and delicious as it was on the day she said "I do," at least fresh enough to eat a few bites of on her first anniversary.)

Like year-old wedding cakes and Ann Romney's pancakes and the peach cobbler recipe-cum-wedding-gift from the grandmother whose name I wish I knew, desserts—and the traditions that surround them—touch our souls as much as our stomachs. Maybe even more. Since Gia was born, for example, my family has started a new tradition: We always sing "Happy Birthday" to her in three-part harmony. I do the melody, her grandfather, my ex-husband, Armstead, does the low harmony, and her parents, Zuri and Lona, come in on the high parts. Judging from the performances at Gia's last party, nobody's going to be quitting their day job anytime soon. But off-key or in perfect pitch, singing "Happy Birthday" to Gia in three-part harmony is our family tradition, and it's the perfect one for us.

So of course I had to write a dessert cookbook, and of course I had to share my favorite family recipes and stories. (Hey Z: You were right. But don't get used to hearing me say *that*!)

Before we get to the fabulous recipes, though, let me offer some equally good food for thought—seven lessons I've learned in my more than 50 years of watching the great bakers in my family whip up amazing desserts, lessons I hope will make your baking experiences every bit as wonderful as mine:

1. Don't mention weight at the table; that's just a land mine waiting to be stepped on.

2. Remember—and heed—the sage advice of the late newspaper columnist Harriet Van Horne: *Cooking is like love—it should be entered into with abandon or not at all.* Because that goes double for baking.

3. When it comes to family dessert traditions, there are no hard-and-fast rules. You have to create the ones that suit *your* family's needs. The fact that I am diabetic means I have to plan my "treat moments" carefully and in advance…and that's just fine with me. So whether you're starting a family dessert tradition or strengthening one, just freestyle it, and, as Zuri would say, "do you."

4. Load up on the memories, not the calories.

5. Speaking of calories, I have a theory about the ones that are in our most beloved desserts. It came to me when I heard about the findings of a (surprising!) study on the way vacations affect our happiness. (My personal thanks to the journal *Applied Research in Quality of Life* for publishing them, hence giving me something scholarly and science-y to show my diabetes doctor.) Turns out that the mere act of *planning* their vacation trip makes people happy. Happier, oftentimes, than actually taking the trip! Which brings me to my theory: I say the same concept should/would apply to the soulful sweets we love and so often crave. (Hello, food researchers; this is soooo worth studying.) Of course, if I'm right—and where dessert is concerned I usually am—that means just *planning to* bake, say, the monkey bread on page 201 or the Strawberry Moon shortcake on page 140, will give you a lot of the joy (and none of the calories) you'd get from actually eating them!

6. It's no accident that *desserts* is *stressed* spelled backward.

And last but not least:

7. When it comes to dessert recipes and traditions, well, I'll quote the Old Testament (Joel 1:3) because nothing says it better:

> *Tell it to your children,*
> *And let your children tell it to their children,*
> *And their children to the next generation.*

Now, grab your apron, Sugar, and let's do some baking, Patti-style.

*Hanging with baby Gia. Comedian Jim Gaffigan is sooo right: Babies should be classified as an antidepressant.*

## Patti's Desserts... And Yours, Too!

Let me tell you a little about how to use this book. These scrumptious recipes were collected from my friends and family, and I think of them as enduring all-American classics. You may have a recipe for chocolate cake—good enough. But I want you to have the very best chocolate cake recipe that is worthy to add to your recipe box (which may be in your computer).

These are the desserts that bring memories of good times at barbecues, weddings, baptisms, family reunions, birthday parties, and other get-togethers with my loved ones. With very few exceptions, I am not sharing sweets from restaurants I've enjoyed on the road or on vacation. These are the down-home, so-good-you-could-slap-your-mama cakes, cobblers, pies, and more that have shaped my life. I didn't go to Le Cordon Bleu, but this girl loves to bake!

Some of these recipes are easy and anyone can make them. Others require some skill (you just don't make Cousin Patricia's yellow-chocolate cake, or *any* layer cake for that matter, without setting aside some time), but I still like to think that I have written them so anyone who can follow directions can make them. I have also included a couple of recipes that are at the opposite end of the "from scratch" menu and use convenience products. They are perfect for when you have to feed a crowd but just don't have the time the way our grandmothers did.

The book starts with chapter 1, "Patti's Kitchen." In it, I talk about the ingredients, tools, and utensils you'll need for baking these recipes. I also outline some of the basic techniques that we all need to master. This way, newbies have a general overview and more experienced bakers have a refresher course before getting started.

At the end of the book, I've given a mini cooking class on each of the chapter subjects, from fancy layer cakes right through to breakfast treats. And when a recipe has a special tip that would help you, I've added it at the end of the recipe, and I've called these Patti's Pointers.

As I said earlier, these recipes have been handed down from my dearest friends and relatives. Should some of them become your family's favorites, well, like the desserts themselves, that would be something to sing about.

*Kitchen chemistry. Me and my best friend, Norma, have always had it. Like this Bundt Pound Cake (see page 59), our 50-plus years of friendship were made with love.*

# 1 ) *Patti's Kitchen*

It's no secret that a baker needs to be set up with the right equipment and good ingredients for success. So please take a few minutes to look this section over because the information below applies to all of the recipes in this book.

I'm a self-taught baker. Or I should say a Chubby-Daddy-Aunt-Hattie-and-Aunt-Josh-taught baker. Until I wrote this book, I never really thought much about the science of baking, how the chemistry of it works. So I asked my cooking buddy, Rick Rodgers (he's a master baker), to give me the 411 on the whys and hows of baking. Questions like "Why does shortening make flaky piecrust and butter a crisp crust?" And "What is the difference between baking powder and baking soda, anyway?" His answers and my observations follow.

# Ingredients

I use very good ingredients, and I pride myself on knowing that I can be a good baker without having to shop all over town. You will find all of these groceries at your local supermarket and natural food store.

### CHOCOLATE AND COCOA

If you look at chocolate bar labels, you might see something like "70% cacao." The basic ingredients in chocolate are cacao (sometimes called cocoa), sugar, vanilla (natural or synthetic), and lecithin (an emulsifier), which add up to 100 percent of the bar. Therefore, the higher the cacao content, the lower the sugar content and the more bitter the chocolate's flavor. Some people like very bitter chocolate, but for baking, I take a middle-of-the-road approach. These recipes all use standard semisweet chocolate (like Baker's, Lindt, or Callebaut, sold at supermarkets or natural food stores) with an average cacao content of 55 percent. Don't use chocolate with a cacao content of more than 62 percent, or the recipe may not turn out as good because of the reduced amount of sugar.

Cocoa is processed in two ways, natural and Dutch processed. **Natural cocoa** is simply roasted and pulverized cacao beans. Hershey's is the most common brand. **Dutch-processed cocoa** (Droste is found in many supermarkets) has been treated with alkali to reduce its acidity and darken its color. The two are not always interchangeable. I use only natural cocoa in these recipes. (See **baking soda**, on page 4, for more on Dutch-processed cocoa.)

### DAIRY PRODUCTS

**Milk** is the preferred liquid to add flavor and structure to cake batters. Always use whole-fat milk, half-and-half, and sour cream. With **yogurt**, low-fat yogurt is fine (there is typically plenty of other fat in the recipe), but not nonfat, unless specified. There is a texture difference between thick **Greek yogurt** and standard yogurt, so be sure to use the one called for in the recipe.

**Buttermilk** is a favorite ingredient with bakers because its acidity tenderizes the flour and makes for very light-textured cakes. It's not easy to find full-fat buttermilk, so just use the low-fat kind sold at every supermarket. Buttermilk can be refrigerated for a few weeks after opening, and if you don't drink it or use it in your baking, consider making ranch salad dressing with the leftovers. If you want a substitute, mix equal parts standard (not thick Greek) low-fat plain yogurt and whole milk. This is a better alternative than the typical substitution of 1 cup whole milk with 1 teaspoon vinegar or lemon juice, because the consistency of the yogurt version resembles the thickness of buttermilk.

It is a good idea to have the milk for the recipe at room temperature to avoid curdling the batter, which can happen if any of the ingredients (such as milk or eggs) are too cold. If necessary, microwave the milk or buttermilk in its measuring cup (which is likely to be glass and microwave-safe) until it loses its chill, about 20 seconds on high (100%) power for 1 cup. (You can adjust the time for more or less milk.) Or heat it in a small saucepan over low heat, stirring almost constantly. Use your finger to check the milk's temperature. Do not heat the milk to where it is actually lukewarm, or you could melt the butter when adding it to the batter.

### DECORATIONS

I don't do a lot of fancy decorating with a pastry tube and tips. If you have that talent…you go! Instead, I get a lot of bang for the buck from multicolored **sprinkles** and the tiny colored sugar balls called **nonpareils.**

## EGGS

Use large eggs—not extra-large, jumbo, or any other size. This is important, especially in recipes that call for a lot of eggs, because you can easily throw off the dry-to-liquid ratio by changing the egg size.

It is important to use room-temperature eggs in cake batters and cookie doughs. Of course, the easiest way is to simply let the eggs stand out of the refrigerator for 30 to 45 minutes. But if you forget to do this, there is an easy fix. Just put the uncracked eggs in a bowl of hot tap water. Let them stand for 3 to 5 minutes, long enough for them to lose their chill. Then crack the eggs and proceed with the recipe.

**To separate eggs,** use chilled eggs, as the yolks and whites stay distinct better if they are cold. Have two bowls ready—a very clean, grease-free larger bowl for holding the whites, and a smaller bowl for the yolks. Even a speck of fat—such as butter, oil, or even a bit of the egg yolk—will keep the whites from whipping into peaks, so the cleanliness of the bowl and the mixer beaters is very important.

Crack the eggshell in half with a rap on the side of the larger bowl. At this stage, you may have seen cooks hold the egg over the larger bowl, transferring the egg back and forth to let the white drip over the shells to eventually end up with the yolk cupped in an eggshell half. You can do it that way. Or you can simply hold one hand (be sure it is clean and grease-free and has no sharp rings that can get in the way) with your fingers cupped together over the larger bowl and put the insides of the cracked egg in the cupped fingers. Separate your fingers a little so the white drains through them into the bowl, but leave the yolk in your hand. You can quickly separate

eggs that way and you don't have to worry about breaking the yolk on a sharp eggshell edge.

Sometimes a recipe calls for egg whites alone. Whole eggs are easier to separate if they are cold, but the whites will whip best if they are warm. In that case, separate the chilled eggs, putting the whites in a heatproof bowl. Put the bowl of whites in a larger bowl of hot tap water and let stand, stirring occasionally, until they don't feel cold anymore (test with a clean finger). This should take only a couple of minutes. Remember, you aren't actually heating the whites, just getting rid of the chill.

## FATS

These are an important ingredient in baking, providing bulk, tenderness, moisture, and, depending on the particular fat, flavor. By far, butter is the favorite fat of most bakers. (Let's pretend that margarine doesn't even exist. It tastes greasy and salty, and its healthy benefits have proven to be unfounded.)

I prefer **unsalted butter** because then you have control over the amount of salt in the recipe. Use the best—that means Grade A. Look for sales at the supermarket, buy a few extra pounds, and freeze them for later use. That is a great way to save money, especially during the busy holiday baking season. The frozen butter will thaw quickly (in about an hour) at room temperature. For tips on creaming butter and sugar (an essential step in many recipes), see page 11.

**Vegetable shortening,** which has a very mild flavor, is used in some recipes, but mainly as an ingredient for flaky pie dough. Why use shortening instead of butter? When flour gets wet, gluten forms. (Gluten is the stuff in flour that makes dough tough or tender, depending on how much the dough is mixed, among other factors.) Because shortening has very little water, the dough doesn't tend to toughen as much, and the baked crust stays flaky.

Butter has a higher water content than shortening, so the dough starts to toughen as soon as the butter and the flour are combined. All-butter pie dough bakes up crisp, like a cookie. To get the best of both worlds, I like to use butter-flavored vegetable shortening in my pie dough.

## FLAVORINGS

The great bakers in my family are never without the Holy Trinity of Extracts: **vanilla**, **lemon**, and **almond**. I buy the pure versions of these flavorings. However, there are people who swear they cannot tell the difference between the pure and the imitation extracts. So the choice is yours. If you want to use vanilla seeds from the bean and freshly grated lemon zest, more power to you. In general, the seeds from one vanilla bean equal 1 teaspoon vanilla extract, and the grated zest from 1 medium lemon equals 1 teaspoon lemon extract.

## FLOUR

I use **unbleached all-purpose flour** for these recipes. These days, with all the talk about gluten-free foods, we are more aware of the role that gluten plays in wheat flour. Basically, in traditional baking, you need to know that when flour is moistened, gluten creates an invisible network that strengthens the dough. The bleaching process (which increases the flour's shelf life) reduces the gluten's strength, too. Unbleached all-purpose flour contains a moderate amount of protein (about 12 percent) to make tender cakes, cookies, and pies, but also enough for a yeast dough that needs sufficient gluten to sustain kneading. Butter and sugar both will tenderize rich doughs and batters, too. Unbleached flour has more flavor than bleached all-purpose flour, which has less protein (about 10 percent) and gluten. I use supermarket brands like Pillsbury and Gold Medal. King Arthur is a good brand, too, but it is a bit "stronger," with more protein than the other two. A few recipes call for **cake flour**, which has a very low protein content (about 7 percent) and makes an especially tender cake crumb. Comparing the gluten contents, you can see that it is not a good idea to switch flours.

## FRUIT

I can't tell you how important it is to use wonderful, delicious fruit at the peak of its season. This is surely one of the reasons why some of my family's recipes became such favorites—the cooks would pick raspberries at just the right time. Flavorless, sour fruit will not taste any better with sugar and butter on it. In some cases, you can use frozen berries (and my cherry pie uses canned or bottled sour cherries), but fresh and flavorful is always best.

If you are diabetic, consider that the carbohydrates in fresh fruit come from natural, not refined sugars; plus, you are taking in fiber, too. But they are still carbs and must be counted in your daily intake.

## LEAVENINGS

In many baked goods (think cakes and cookies), butter and sugar are creamed together to create tiny air bubbles in the mixture. (See page 11 for tips on creaming butter and sugar.) Then leavenings take over, making the cake rise from there.

The two major leavenings are baking soda and baking powder. Although they both have "baking" in their names, they are very different.

**Baking soda** (bicarbonate of soda) is alkaline and needs acidic ingredients (such as natural cocoa, brown sugar, molasses, or buttermilk) to create the chemical reaction that inflates the air bubbles. (Remember that old science experiment in school that mixed baking soda and vinegar to make fake volcanic foam? It's that kind of reaction that makes your cake rise.) For this reason, if you use Dutch-processed cocoa in a recipe that calls for natural cocoa and baking soda, it may not work because this cocoa has had its acidity reduced with an alkali treatment.

**Baking powder** is a combination of a dry acid (cream of tartar) and baking soda, so it will leaven a batter or dough without any concern for acidic ingredients.

### SALT

Use basic table salt (either plain or iodized, regular or sea salt) with fine crystals in these recipes because it dissolves easily in the batter or dough. Reserve coarse/crystal/kosher salt for savory foods. That's just my opinion. If another cookbook wants you to use kosher salt, go ahead.

### SUGAR

Sugar plays many roles in baking. It tenderizes flour, adds bulk, helps the food brown in the oven, and, of course, acts as a sweetener. I use pure cane sugar. Be sure it says cane sugar on the label, because beet sugar does not act the same as cane sugar in some recipes—especially when it is cooked into syrup.

There are many different kinds of sugar, and they have different uses. **Granulated sugar** is the workhorse of the baker's kitchen, with a versatile sweetness that works in all kinds of recipes. **Confectioners' sugar** has a powdery texture and is used for making frostings and as a garnish. **Brown sugar** is granulated sugar that has been sprayed with molasses. It contributes a deeper flavor and color to baked goods, as well

as some extra moisture. **Light brown sugar** has less molasses and a milder flavor than **dark brown sugar**, but they are interchangeable otherwise. **Turbinado sugar** is a kind of brown sugar with coarse, square crystals that don't melt easily, making it a good choice as a decorating sugar. Other **decorating sugars** (sometimes called **sanding sugars**, for their texture) are often colored. **Molasses** is a liquid by-product of the sugar-refining process. Don't use blackstrap molasses, which has been processed so much that it has a bitter flavor.

For information on alternatives to sugar and its cousins, see pages 218–219.

# Appliances

When my relatives were baking on a daily basis, an awful lot of great food was made in a bowl with a spoon (and maybe a handheld eggbeater). We're so busy now (although I wonder how those ladies would react to that statement, considering all of the household chores they did), and we like time-saving appliances. Here are the ones that are most useful to a baker.

### STANDING MIXER

If you don't own one already, you might want to treat yourself and get a standing mixer. The heavy-duty machine is not cheap, but it will save you an awful lot of time. How? Well, you don't hold it, like you do a hand mixer, so your hands are free to do other things while the machine is doing its job. The paddle attachment is used for creaming butter and mixing batters, the whisk whips egg whites and heavy cream like a dream, and the dough hook takes the "grunt" out of kneading. (Although kneading by hand is a nice upper-body workout.)

### ELECTRIC HAND MIXER

Use a hand mixer for mixing or whipping smaller amounts (such as a few egg whites or less than a cup of heavy cream) in small or medium bowls. A hand mixer can't handle heavy-duty jobs like kneading dough or mixing stiff cookie dough, but what it does, it does well.

### BLENDER AND FOOD PROCESSOR

A lot of cooks lean on their food processors for a large range of kitchen jobs, but you really don't need one for basic baking. And to puree ingredients, a blender actually works better because liquid ingredients tend to seep through the central hole in most processors.

# Equipment, Utensils, and Other Basic Tools

Again, good tools make the job go easier. It is a heck of a lot easier to frost a cake on a turntable with a metal spatula than on a platter with a dinner knife! There is no need to break the bank, and you can get just about anything you might need online or at a crafts shop, as they all now carry cake decorating supplies as well as fabric.

### BAKING PANS

Heavy-gauge aluminum baking pans are the best. (Skip the **silicone pans** in pretty colors. They are too floppy and actually make the cake more difficult to unmold. Also, the cakes don't brown as well.)

You can bake a good cake in a supermarket **nonstick pan**, as long as you are aware of a few issues:

- First, the color of the baking pan affects the baking time. Uncoated aluminum pans refract the heat, so the metal is about the same temperature as the oven heat. Dark pans coated with nonstick material soak up the heat and make the baked goods cook more quickly. To compensate for this, if you want to use a dark pan, turn the oven temperature down 25°F, or start testing for doneness about three-quarters of the way through the estimated baking time.

- Read the fine print on some nonstick pans. They guarantee only easy cleanup, not that the cakes won't stick. Always line the bottom of the pan with parchment paper or waxed paper cut to fit. Butter the pan first so the paper sticks, then flour just the sides of the pan. You won't need to flour and butter the paper because it is already nonstick.

I use only **cake pans** with 9-inch diameters and 1½-inch sides for the layer cakes in this book. The **muffin pans** are standard, with cups about 2¾ inches across. The cheesecake cups on page 99 use a **mini-muffin** pan with cups about 1¾ inches across. The **Bundt pan** (also called fluted tube pan) has a 10- to 12-cup capacity and is 10 inches across. It is especially important to butter and flour a Bundt pan, even if it is nonstick. Most of the **loaf pan** recipes in the book call for an 8½ by 4½ by 2½-inch pan. However, the pound cake on page 59 has a large amount of batter and uses a 9 by 5 by 3-inch loaf pan.

For a **rectangular baking pan**, 9 by 13 by 2-inch is a versatile size, but I sometimes use an 11½ by 8-inch pan (also called a **brownie pan**) or an 8-inch square pan. These are all good for bar cookies, which can be a hassle to get out of the pan. In each recipe, I give instructions on how to create handles out of nonstick aluminum foil to make the task much easier (or see the detailed instructions on page 241).

For **pie pans**, I prefer metal or Pyrex. I use a 9-inch pan with 1½-inch sides, no deeper. I like the look of ceramic pie pans, but metal and Pyrex are better conductors of heat and help crisp the crust. Ceramic pie pans are pretty, but they are also deep, and you will have to adjust most American recipes to get the filling and dough to fit.

All professional bakers use **half-sheet pans** at their shops. These large baking sheets measure 18 by 13 inches. (A full-sheet pan measures 18 by 26 inches and fits only commercial ovens.) This pan holds many more cookies than the typical flimsy, small cookie sheet. Its heavy-gauge construction, which evenly absorbs the oven heat, discourages burned baked goods. With rimmed sides, your cookies won't slide off the pan either, and half-sheets make good liners under fruit pies to catch any filling overflow. Half-sheet pans are always uncoated, which is an advantage because it makes them even more versatile. (Nonstick pans have a dark coating that actually encourages scorched cookie bottoms.) If you want a nonstick surface, line the pan with parchment paper or a silicone baking mat. In other words—if you still use thin cookie sheets, upgrade to half-sheet pans. You won't have any desire to go back to the wimpy ones.

## CAKE ROUNDS

When decorating a 9-inch fancy layer cake, it is a good idea to support the bottom with an 8-inch cardboard cake round. (The slightly smaller round will not be seen peeking out from the edges of the larger cake.) The cake round makes the cake much easier to transport, even if it is just around the kitchen to carry it from the work counter to the serving platter, or in and out of the refrigerator. This is another one of those items that you might think you can live without but that will make your baking so much easier. You can also use the metal bottom of a 9-inch tart pan with removable sides.

## CITRUS REAMER

To get the juice out of lemons, limes, and oranges, a citrus reamer does a quick job. If you have the room on your countertop, an inexpensive **electric juicer** is a good thing to have as you will be able to get lots of juice in seconds.

## KITCHEN SCALE

Many serious home bakers swear by weighing their ingredients, especially flour. To each their own! (For more on this controversial subject, see page 10.) But there are times when you really do want to use a scale to confirm an ingredient's weight. There are many inexpensive electric kitchen scales available, and they are useful, so go ahead and pick one up if you don't have one. They are especially good for weighing the batter for even cake layers.

## MEASURING CUPS AND SPOONS

If I had to pick the number one mistake that home bakers make, it would be incorrect measuring. I'm not talking about weighing or not weighing the flour, but using one set of measuring cups for both dry and wet ingredients. There are two specific kinds of cups:

- **Dry-ingredient cups** are usually made from metal or plastic and are squat with stubby handles. The standard set has four cups in ¼-, ⅓-, ½-, and 1-cup sizes. There are larger sets with ⅔- and ¾-cup sizes, but it is very easy to grab the wrong cup because they look so much alike. If you are a dedicated baker, it helps to have two sets of cups so you don't have to keep washing them to keep up with a busy burst of holiday baking.

- **Liquid measuring cups** are clear glass or plastic. With most models, you hold the glass at eye level to check the measurement.

The 1-cup and 2-cup (1-pint) sizes are indispensable, but the 4-cup (1-quart) and 8-cup (2-quart) versions are also useful. If you get the same brand of all cups, they can be stacked inside of each other and take up less room in your kitchen (which is always a good thing).

The most common set of **measuring spoons** (metal spoons are most durable) has ¼-teaspoon, ½-teaspoon, 1-teaspoon, and 1-tablespoon measures. If you get additional sizes, be careful because the ⅛-teaspoon and ¾-teaspoon sizes can be confused with other spoons of a similar measurement.

### PARCHMENT PAPER

Parchment paper, which gives any flat-bottomed pan a nonstick surface, can now be purchased in rolls in any supermarket. It is a fantastic time-saver because it allows the baker to skip buttering and flouring baking sheets for cookies. It is also used to line the bottoms of cake and loaf pans to keep the cakes from sticking when unmolded. (You can use waxed paper for lining cake pans, but not for baking cookies. On a baking sheet, the exposed coating will melt in the oven, while the waxed paper is completely covered by the batter in the cake pan.)

The only problem is that the rolled parchment paper can curl. There are two ways to deal with this. First, spread a dab of butter or shortening in each corner of the baking sheet (or grease the entire cake or loaf pan) to hold the paper. But the easiest solution is to buy packages of flat parchment paper, sold online and at baking supply shops. If you bake a lot of layer cakes, you can buy precut rounds so you don't have to cut the parchment paper to fit the pans.

Some bakers prefer reusable **silicone baking mats**, sized to fit half-sheet pans, over the disposable parchment paper. The choice is yours.

### PASTRY BLENDER

This metal tool, with three or more curved blades held together by a handle, is used to cut the chilled fat into flour when making pie dough. You also can use two knives, pulled through the mixture in a crisscross fashion; and some people even get the job done by rubbing the fat between their fingertips. But the pastry blender is the most efficient and keeps your hands relatively clean.

### PASTRY BRUSH

I don't use one too often, but when I need to apply a glaze or thin icing, a medium brush about 1 inch wide does the trick. For baking, a bristle brush works better than the silicone model, which is mainly for slathering sauce on barbecued meats. Always wash the brush well with dish soap and rinse it well after each use. (I know this applies to all utensils, but the bristles need a bit of extra TLC.)

### PIE WEIGHTS

Made from metal or ceramic, these weigh down the pie dough in a pie pan to hold it in place when prebaking the crust. If not supported with a liner of aluminum foil and the weights, the crust can slump. You can substitute dried beans or raw rice to do the same job, but these eventually go rancid and will have to be changed.

### PORTION SCOOP

Every single professional baker uses a spring-loaded portion scoop to fill muffin cups with batter. See more about this essential muffin tool on pages 239–240.

## ROLLING PIN

Rolling pins are not created equal. Some are shaped like big dowels, and others have tapered ends. I like a big, heavy rolling pin with ball bearings and handles. A large pin weighs down the dough better for easier rolling. When the pin is too short (say, 12 inches), the edges can cut into the dough. Most pins are constructed of wood or even plastic, but the new silicone-coated ones are great because they don't stick to the dough.

## SPATULAS

There are two kinds of spatulas in the baker's kitchen. **Flexible spatulas** are used for scraping down the sides of the bowl during mixing. Heatproof (silicone) spatulas are best because they can be used for stirring hot foods on the stove. **Metal spatulas** are used to frost cakes. An offset metal spatula is considered essential by many bakers, as it allows the cook to access places on a cake that would otherwise be awkward to reach.

## THERMOMETERS

An **instant-read thermometer** can be used to accurately check the temperature of custard mixtures (if they go beyond 190°F, they will curdle) and candy syrups. An instant-read thermometer is easier to use than a bulky candy thermometer, which has to be clipped onto the side of the saucepan. Frankly, I don't need a thermometer that much in my baking because there are visual ways to check when the mixtures are done. However, it is good to have for other jobs like checking the internal temperature of meat and so on.

An **oven thermometer** is not a "nice to have" item but rather an essential tool. You've heard it before, and it's true: Every oven has its quirks, and the only way to check the true temperature is with a thermometer.

## TIMERS

Every smartphone has a timer these days, so you don't even have to buy a dedicated kitchen timer, unless you want one.

## TURNTABLE, DECORATING

A decorating table rotates to give you easy access to all sides of a cake when applying the frosting. A serious baker who frosts a lot of cakes will want one. However, there is an alternative. Choose a wide-bottomed bowl and turn it over on your work counter. You can now place the cake (preferably on a cake round or tart pan, but a platter will work, too) on the bowl bottom, and turn the cake as needed. It's not quite as stable and professional as the turntable, but it works.

## WHISKS

The wire construction of a whisk mainly serves to incorporate more air into egg whites and heavy cream during whipping. But a whisk is also good for quickly mixing dry ingredients (although sifting is better) and for combining ingredients in a saucepan during cooking. There is not a one-size-fits-all whisk, unfortunately. You should have at least two: a thin-wired balloon whisk for whipping ingredients, and a smaller, narrow whisk for mixing and cooking lemon curd and similar mixtures.

## WIRE RACKS

Ideally, you need at least two **wire cooling racks** for cooling cake layers and cookies. You will be glad you have more than one rack if you have to cool dozens of cookies during the holidays. A **round wire rack** is good for holding an unmolded cake as it comes out of the pan. Flip the cake over and transfer it to a larger rack to cool completely.

### WIRE SIEVES

Of course, wire sieves are made for draining foods from liquid. But in the baking world, they do double duty as sifters for dry ingredients.

### ZESTERS

Finely grated citrus zest adds a spark of fruit flavor to many baked goods. The trick is to use only the colored zest from the peel, and not the bitter white pith underneath. The best tool for this job is a Microplane zester, which has very small teeth that won't dig into the pith. (Microplane is a brand, but the name is now used generically to describe this kind of zester.) An alternative to grating the zest is to use the smallest holes on a box shredder, as long as you are careful to avoid the pith.

# Baking Basics

Baking uses the same techniques over and over again. I learned how to bake from watching my mother, father, and aunts cook day in and day out, so many of these things are second nature to me now. Nowadays you can watch cooking clips on YouTube. But regardless of where you learn them, these are the building blocks of great desserts.

### PREHEATING THE OVEN

The first order of business is to heat the oven to the optimum temperature for the recipe. Arrange the racks in their proper positions before turning on the heat. For some pies, you might want to have the rack in the lower third so it gets a little extra heat refracted off the oven floor to help the bottom crust get crisp. For cakes, the center position is needed for even browning. With cookies, you can sometimes use the top third so you can bake two sheets of cookies at a time, but be sure to switch the sheets halfway through baking or the upper sheet may get too brown (from the refracted heat from the top of the oven this time).

On average, it takes 15 to 20 minutes for most ovens to reach the baking temperature. Always set the oven to preheat before you start making the batter or dough (unless, of course, the dough needs to rest for more than 20 minutes before baking). Some batters don't like to wait around and will deflate if they don't go into the oven right away.

Every great baker has an oven thermometer to double-check the temperature. They are inexpensive and a great cheap investment.

### MEASURING AND SIFTING FLOUR

This has become a big deal in the last few years. When I learned how to bake, there was only one way to measure flour—stir up the flour, dip in the measuring cup, use a knife to sweep off the excess level with the edge of the cup, and use it. I don't think I have ever had a recipe fail because I didn't measure the flour the "right" way.

Now, many good bakers I respect insist on weighing out the flour on a scale. The reasoning is that everyone has a unique way of packing (or not) the flour into the cup, so you can get quite a difference in measurements. One person's cup of flour can be heavier or lighter than another person's. This is because flour settles in its container. Other ingredients, such as sugar and cornmeal, aren't as powdery, so they don't pose the same problem. However, most professional bakers weigh every-thing, including the water.

If you like to weigh your flour, go ahead. But you need to know how I measure my flour and how much is in the average cup. **I use the dip-and-sweep method** I mentioned above, and my 1 cup of flour weighs in at 140 grams/5 ounces.

Sifting may seem like a pain in the neck,

but it serves a purpose. If you want a light cake, then it makes sense to aerate the flour before adding it to the batter. Some people think that whisking the dry ingredients together is enough to combine and aerate them, but it is not nearly as good as sifting. Also, sifting will break up any clumps of leavening—many a chocolate cake as been ruined when someone bit into a piece with a pellet of undissolved baking soda. So…sift. It's no big deal.

You do not have to buy a single-purpose flour sifter to store in some cluttered cabinet—a standard medium-mesh wire sieve can do double duty as a sifter. A really fine-wire sieve should be reserved for straining out the tiny seeds from berry purees; the mesh is so small that the flour can't pass through.

## CREAMING BUTTER AND SUGAR

Not every recipe for baked goods requires creaming the butter with sugar, but it is a very important technique to master for the ones that do. During this process, air is beaten into the butter. When leavenings are added (such as baking powder or baking soda), a chemical reaction adds carbon dioxide, inflating these little air bubbles like so many tiny balloons—and that's what makes the cake rise. So if the butter is too soft, the bubbles won't form. Or if you underbeat the butter and sugar mixture, too few bubbles will form. And then you could overbeat the mixture and collapse the bubbles.

I hope I didn't scare you, because this is not a hard technique! Here are some simple tips:

- The butter should be close to room temperature, but not softened to the point where it is shiny or squishy. Just cut the butter into tablespoon-sized chunks, put them in the mixing bowl (you do not have to use a standing mixer), and let them stand for

15 to 30 minutes, depending on the ambient heat in your kitchen. This is usually the same amount of time it will take you to preheat the oven thoroughly and gather, measure, and prep the remaining ingredients. Press the butter with a finger, and if it leaves an impression, the butter is ready. The friction of the beaters is going to warm and soften the butter a bit, too.

- If you forget to take the butter out of the refrigerator and you are really in a hurry to get mixing, shred the stick on the large holes of a box shredder.

- Never soften butter in the microwave. No matter how hard you try to get it right, it will probably get too soft or melt.

- Beat the butter with the electric mixer set on high speed. Gradually add the sugar and continue beating, occasionally scraping down the sides of the bowl with a flexible spatula, until the mixture is smooth and homogeneous, about 3 minutes with a standing mixer. The mixture will look pale yellow and have a lighter texture (if not downright fluffy, a description you may often see in recipes) from the air you have beaten into it.

## ADDING EGGS

There is a reason why the eggs added to the creamed butter mixture should be at room temperature. Have you ever seen a batter break and look curdled when you added the eggs? Sometimes the batter comes together when you add flour, and sometimes not, and the cake doesn't rise well. What happened?

A cake batter is an **emulsion**, where very different ingredients (in this case, flour, eggs, and butter) are blended together in a way that the liquid is suspended in the fat (butter) and doesn't separate out. A vinaigrette salad dressing is an emulsion, as the vinegar (liquid) is suspended in the oil (fat).

One reason a batter breaks is dramatic differences in temperature. If the creamed butter and sugar are at room temperature, and refrigerator-cold eggs or milk is added, the butter starts to chill—and the batter breaks. If the eggs are at room temperature, the problem will be averted. The eggs also help the cake rise, and they will accept more air during beating if they are at room temperature. For ways to bring eggs to room temperature, see page 3.

Generally, add the eggs **one at a time** to the creamed mixture. Beat each egg for 10 to 15 seconds after each addition to be sure it is thoroughly absorbed into the batter before adding the next egg. (And don't crack the egg on the side of the bowl and add it to the batter—that's a sure way of getting bits of eggshell in the cake. Instead, crack the eggs into a separate bowl first and discard any bits of shell that show up. It may seem like extra work, but the first time you get shells in your cake, you'll change your tune.)

## WHIPPING EGG WHITES

Beaten egg whites are used in some batters to give the cake an even lighter, fluffier texture. Perfectly whipped egg whites are not hard to achieve. However, some bakers overdo it. They just don't want to believe that once the whites are shiny and stand up in a pointed peak when the beaters are lifted, they are done. So they continue beating until the whites break down from the perfect stage to a somewhat lumpy state where the whites look more like cottony clouds than peaks. Here's how to do it the right way:

- There are two important things to remember when whipping whites. First, the whites must be at room temperature. (See page 3 for directions on separating whites.) Second, the bowl and beaters must be very clean and free of any grease. I hear you thinking, *My bowls are not dirty or greasy!*—but you would be surprised how fats can linger on bowls that you think you have cleaned well.

- Put the egg whites in a medium or large bowl (allowing space for the whites to triple in volume with some headroom) and start whipping with an electric mixer set on high speed. Occasionally stop the mixer and lift the beaters to check the whites. The soft peak stage occurs when the whites form shiny but distinct mounds with tips that droop over. Stiff peaks happen when the peaks form points that stand up vertically with very little droop. The whites are now ready for folding into the batter. In some cases, such as a meringue, the stiff peak stage is when you would beat in the sugar, beating until the mixture is very glossy and resembles old-fashioned aerosol shaving cream. Always use whipped egg whites immediately, before they get a chance to deflate.

# 2 ) Fancy Cakes

I admit, you won't make one of these beauties in a few minutes, but it is cakes like these that make the memories that last forever. Picture a photo in an album labeled "Baby's First Birthday," with your little girl in a high chair blowing out her first candle. Or "Ellington's Graduation," with the smiling graduate in his mortarboard cap cutting into a gorgeous cake. You'll find some of my family's most treasured recipes here—the pound cake of your dreams, the perfect yellow layer cake with an outrageous chocolate fudge icing, and truly luscious blackberry cake with both fresh berries and jam. So get out your prettiest cake stand and get baking! But before you do, take a few minutes and read through the tips and techniques on pages 236–238.

# Jammin' Blackberry Jam Cake with Caramel Icing

Every Southern cook has a recipe for jam cake somewhere in his or her culinary past. I have a Bundt pan version in another one of my books. But this recipe is for a spicy layer cake that is even more suitable for special occasions. The fruit flavor isn't very strong, so to play up the berries more, I add fresh ones between the layers. It is topped with a caramel icing that is another old-time favorite.

Makes 12 to 16 servings

### JAM CAKE

Softened butter and flour, for the pans

2 cups unbleached all-purpose flour

1 teaspoon baking soda

½ teaspoon ground cinnamon

½ teaspoon ground allspice

½ teaspoon freshly grated or ground nutmeg

½ teaspoon ground cloves

½ teaspoon salt

1 cup (2 sticks) unsalted butter, at room temperature

1 cup granulated sugar

3 large eggs, at room temperature

1 cup blackberry or elderberry preserves (one 12-ounce jar)

¾ cup buttermilk

½ cup coarsely chopped pecans

½ cup seedless dark raisins

### BERRY FILLING

12 ounces (about 2⅔ cups) fresh blackberries or blueberries

½ cup blackberry or elderberry preserves (see Patti's Pointers)

### CARAMEL ICING

1 cup packed dark or light brown sugar

½ cup heavy cream

¼ cup (½ stick) unsalted butter, thinly sliced

2 tablespoons light corn syrup

2 cups confectioners' sugar

1 teaspoon vanilla extract

1. **To make the cake:** Position a rack in the center of the oven and preheat the oven to 350°F. Butter the insides of two 9 by 1½-inch round cake pans. Line the bottoms with waxed paper rounds. Dust the pan sides with flour and tap out the excess flour.

2. Sift the flour, baking soda, cinnamon, allspice, nutmeg, cloves, and salt together. Beat the butter in a large bowl with an electric mixer set on high speed until creamy, about 1 minute. Gradually beat in the granulated sugar. Continue beating until the mixture is

light in color and texture, about 3 minutes. One at a time, beat in the eggs, beating well after each addition. Beat in the preserves. Reduce the mixer speed to low. In thirds, beat in the flour mixture, alternating with two equal additions of buttermilk, scraping down the sides of the bowl as needed with a rubber spatula, and mix just until smooth. Fold in the pecans and raisins. Divide the batter equally among the pans and spread it evenly.

3.  Bake until a wooden toothpick inserted into the centers of the cakes comes out clean and they have slightly pulled away from the sides of the pans, 30 to 35 minutes. Transfer to wire racks and cool for 10 minutes. Run a dinner knife around the inside of each pan to release the cakes. Invert and unmold the cakes onto the racks and discard the paper. Using a wide spatula, turn the cakes right side up and cool completely.

4.  Place one cake layer, upside down, on a 9-inch cardboard cake round or the removable bottom of a 9-inch tart pan.

5.  **To make the filling:** Gently toss the berries with the preserves in a small bowl. Arrange the coated berries in a single layer on the cake layer. Cover with the second cake layer, top side up. Place the cake on a wire rack set over a baking sheet.

6.  **To make the icing:** Do not make the icing until the cake is assembled. Bring the brown sugar, cream, butter, and corn syrup to a boil in a medium saucepan over medium heat, whisking almost constantly. Reduce the heat to medium-low. Let the mixture cook at a low boil, without stirring, for 2 minutes (use a timer). Remove from the heat. Whisk in the confectioners' sugar and vanilla and mix until smooth. Place the bowl in a larger bowl of iced water and stir just until the icing cools a bit and thickens slightly but is still pourable, about 30 seconds.

7.  Using a rubber spatula, immediately scrape and pour the warm icing over the top of the cake. Using an offset spatula, smooth the icing over the cake top, coaxing the excess icing down the sides and letting it drip randomly. Let the icing set. (The cake can be stored at room temperature, covered with a tall cake dome, for about 8 hours.) Slice the cake with a thin, long knife dipped into hot water between slices, and serve.

**Patti's Pointers:** *You can use just about any kind of berry preserves for this recipe. Even though the recipe title says jam, preserves have a little less sugar and work well. Do not use jelly.*

*Country cooks would make preserves from wild fruit, with blackberries and elderberries topping the list. You can buy elderberry preserves at specialty markets. But be aware that raw elderberries are toxic.*

Caramel icing is delicious, but tricky. Some people make a double batch and use it to frost the sides of the cake with a wet icing spatula, but you have to work very quickly before it sets up. It really isn't worth the trouble, and the dripping icing and exposed berry filling look very cool. The texture of the icing is like pralines—that is, a little firm and sugary, almost a candy.

# Patti's Perfect Pouilly-Fuissé Cake

Here's my idea of the perfect Sunday afternoon: I get up around noon, throw on some cozy but fabulous lounge-around-the-house drag, and head downstairs to a picture-perfect kitchen. In my world, that means two things: (1) The kitchen is squeaky-clean—countertops are gleaming, cabinets are glistening, and the floor is so spotless you could eat the wine cake I'm going to bake right off of it; and (2) the fridge is fully stocked. Depending on how I feel, I may or may not drop by my favorite farmers' market and pick up some just-laid eggs. Either way, I'm in no hurry to decide because the day is wide open: I've got no calls to take, no meetings to attend, no planes to catch. And, best of all, nobody is coming over I don't feel like seeing!

After watching a little television (I'm a food TV fanatic), I eat a low-carb/low-calorie breakfast because, before the afternoon is over, I'll be treating myself to something sweet. Often, that means this Pouilly-Fuissé cake because, not only is it delicious; I usually sip some of the wine I use in it while it's baking. Before anyone freaks out, let me say this: Whether I do or don't indulge (in Pouilly-Fuissé cake or any other treat) depends entirely on my sugar level. And when I do indulge, I never let my sweet tooth become a sweet fang.

Just the other day, Gia's other grandmother, Ro, asked me how I could stay on the eat-right track *and* bake such fabulous goodies. I told her the same thing I tell my family, my doctors, and now, what I'm about to tell you: I'm *always*, always, mindful of what I put in my body, even when—*especially* when—I allow myself a little

treat. And *little* is the right word here. I don't do portion distortion. Which means my cake slice will be on the skinny side. Ditto my cookie quota or cobbler cut.

Now, back to the Pouilly-Fuissé cake. A big reason I wanted to include it in this book is because its inspiration is my grandmother Ellen. She made the best wine cake I have ever tasted. Between her jam cake and her wine cake, I'm hard-pressed to say which one I loved more. They were both made from elderberries, which grew all over Grandmother Ellen's Florida farm. And when I say all over, I mean *everywhere*. Her farm was close to the St. Martin River, which Grandmother Ellen said fed the soil with all kinds of minerals that made elderberries grow. Uncle Dave—that's what I called my grandfather, don't ask me why—said it had nothing to do with the river, but that Grandmother Ellen knew—and practiced—some kind of voodoo that made elderberries grow.

I don't know if it was the minerals in the river or the magic in Grandmother Ellen, but it was *something*. By summer's end, there were more elderberries growing on that farm than Grandmother Ellen knew what to do with. But she never let a single one go to waste. Not after she'd spent all day picking them in the hot sun. Grandmother Ellen made elderberry *everything*: elderberry jelly, elderberry syrup, elderberry dumplings, elderberry pie, and, of course, her famous elderberry jam cake (see page 17). Her favorite thing to make with elderberries, however, was wine.

In August, when Grandmother Ellen said the elderberries were at their sweetest, she

*My grandmother
Ellen Robertson.*

stomped them by the bucketful. Sometimes for hours at a time. The only time I ever saw her take a break was when she disappeared into the kitchen for more chewing tobacco or into the outhouse for, well, you know what for. When I close my eyes, I can still see her standing in the yard, smiling and laughing and stomping and singing as she smashed those elderberries like there was no tomorrow. Even though they stained her feet bright purple, Grandmother Ellen *never* crushed them with her hands. She said using your hands did something to the seeds that made your wine bitter. And sweet wine was worth walking around with purple feet.

I hope that kind of joy is hereditary because, along with her recipes, I want my grandkids, Gia and Ellington, to inherit it. I don't think I've ever seen anyone as happy and as free as Grandmother Ellen when she was stomping elderberries. I'm no shrink, but I'm pretty sure that's a big reason I love Elton John's song "Elderberry Wine." That, and because I really love *him*. Elton and I go way back—back to the early '70s when he was playing piano for Sarah, Nona, and me as we were morphing from Patti LaBelle and the Bluebelles into Labelle. Hanging out with Elton in London is one of my happiest memories of those long-ago days. Especially the times we stayed up all night sharing our worries (he wondered if he'd ever make it in the music business; I wondered if we'd ever make it as Labelle) and sharing our meals. (Elton *loved* my cooking. He was the first person to tell me my macaroni and cheese was addictive—his word, not mine.)

Now, excuse me; I have an irresistible urge to get started with my Pouilly-Fuissé cake…and sing along with Elton to "Elderberry Wine."

# Patti's Perfect Pouilly-Fuissé Cake

Grandmother Ellen loved elderberry wine, but I'm a white wine girl. I have a special fondness for Pouilly-Fuissé (repeat after me: *poo-yee fwee-SAY*), a famous French Chardonnay known for its dry but rich flavor. At about $20 a bottle, it's an affordable treat, but sometimes I have leftovers that I might not feel like drinking. That's when I mix up this cake. It's a cake-mix recipe, and one that I can make with my eyes closed—although I don't recommend that! Actually, while this is super easy, I have learned a few tips over the decades that I've been making it, so read Patti's Pointers before you start.

Makes 12 servings

Softened butter and dried bread crumbs (or flour), for the pan

One 15.25-ounce box yellow cake mix

One 5.1-ounce box instant vanilla pudding mix

⅓ cup unbleached all-purpose flour

¾ cup Chardonnay, preferably Pouilly-Fuissé

¾ cup grapeseed oil or any vegetable oil

4 large eggs, at room temperature

⅓ cup water

1 teaspoon imitation butter flavoring (optional)

Confectioners' sugar, for garnish

1. Position a rack in the center of the oven and preheat the oven to 350°F. Butter the inside of a 10- to 12-cup Bundt (fluted tube) pan, preferably nonstick. Sprinkle in the bread crumbs, rotate the pan to coat, and tap out the excess crumbs.

2. Whisk the cake mix, pudding mix, and flour together in a large bowl. Make a well in the center of the dry ingredients and add the wine, oil, eggs, water, and butter flavoring, if using. Using a handheld electric mixer, mix on medium speed for 2 minutes, scraping down the sides of the bowl as needed. Pour into the prepared pan and smooth the top.

3. Bake until a wooden toothpick inserted into the cake comes out clean, about 50 minutes. Let cool in the pan on a wire rack for 10 to 15 minutes. Run a knife around the inside of the pan to loosen the cake. Invert and unmold the cake onto the rack and let it cool completely.

4. Sift confectioners' sugar over the top of the cake. Slice and serve.

**Patti's Pointers:** *A few years ago, all of the cake-mix manufacturers downsized the box size a full 3 ounces, from 18.25 to 15.25 ounces. To compensate, I now add ⅓ cup flour to the recipe. You can use this trick with any cake-box recipe with the same issue.*

*Be sure to buy the large 5.1-ounce box of instant (not "Cook & Serve" or sugar-free) pudding. It is easy to accidentally grab the smaller 3.4-ounce box or the wrong type, so double-check.*

*I prefer the pale green color and light flavor of grapeseed oil for this cake because I think it complements the wine. But you can use canola oil if you prefer. I haven't tried it, but I bet regular (not extra-virgin) olive oil would be good, too.*

*Any good Chardonnay, American or French, works for this recipe. It's just that Pouilly-Fuissé is our "house white," and I happen to have that on hand most often. Chardonnay is good because it's nice and dry and balances the sugar in the batter. Stay away from sweeter wines, such as Riesling. And never cook with a wine that you would not drink!*

*The butter flavoring can be found with the other extracts in well-stocked supermarkets. Because the cake is made with oil and not butter, I do like to add the flavoring to the batter, but it is entirely optional.*

# Somebody Loves You, Baby, Hummingbird Layer Cake

When my granddaughter, Gia, turned one, I bought her a chocolate cupcake from a local bakery. I know what you're thinking: *A cupcake, Patti, really? A store-bought cupcake? Have you no shame?* Allow me to explain. I *wanted* to bake the perfect birthday cake for my only granddaughter—a big, over-the-top buttery confection. But I couldn't. I was in the middle of a sold-out tour and my hotel suite didn't have a kitchen. (Note to Zuri: See why in-room kitchens are so important?) Still, I couldn't let Gia's first birthday pass without doing *something*.

*I know I'm her glammother, but isn't Gia darling? That's her favorite tee shirt. She loves ice cream cones almost as much as my cakes! Look really close. That's a hummingbird pin she's wearing. Yep, birthday lessons (see next page) have begun.*

So I did what any good glamma would. I improvised. To my no-kitchen suite, I invited three of Gia's favorite people: her mom, her dad, and her aunt Norma. (Her dad, Zuri, is my son/manager; her mom, Lona, is my daughter-in-law/makeup artist; and her aunt Norma is my best friend/wardrobe consultant, so all three are part of my road crew.) Once everyone was settled in, I passed out party hats, stuck a candle in the cupcake, and sang "Happy Birthday" to my granddaughter like I was singing "Over the Rainbow" at Carnegie Hall.

I'm not going to front: It wasn't a Beyoncé-and-Blue-Ivy-dropped-by-and-the-Muppets-passed-out-presents-while-the-Power-Rangers-helped-the-birthday-girl-blow-out-her-candle kind of affair. But it didn't matter. Because the whole time I was singing "Happy Birthday," Gia was laughing and Zuri and Lona were crying and Norma was clapping and there was so much love in that room I knew no party could have been more perfect because no child could have been more loved.

After everyone left, I scrubbed chocolate icing out of my hair (don't ask), then went to bed dreaming of the kind of birthday cake I was going to bake Gia when I got back home. By the time we landed in Philly, I knew it would be a hummingbird cake. For Gia's first birthday, no other kind would do. Not because it's so off-the-chain delicious, though it is. But because it's named for the hummingbird. And the flight of the hummingbird is filled with life lessons I want to pass along to my (amazing, wonderful, brilliant, beautiful) granddaughter.

I've spent a fair amount of time at my kitchen table silently rehearsing what I'm going to say:

*You know, Boo, the hummingbird flies backward as well as forward.* (Lesson #1: Take time to look into your past. Not to dwell in it, but to find what's important and enduring.)

*And it can change direction instantly, no matter how fast it's flying.* (Lesson #2: Change is part of life; never fear it. Correct your course the moment you recognize you're not following your path…or your heart.)

*But the hummingbird reserves its flyest trick (pun intended) for when it hovers in midair. And guess what it does then, Boo? It flutters its wings in a figure eight. The pattern of the infinity symbol. The symbol of eternity, of perpetuity, of continuity.* (Lesson #3: You are, always and forever, connected to something larger than yourself.)

I haven't figured out exactly how I'm going to work in *all* of these life lessons while we're baking her birthday cake. I do, however, know this: The wise words of my favorite philosopher will have to be part of lesson #2: "Be yourself. No one can tell you you're doing it wrong." That's what Snoopy says, and what kid doesn't listen to him?

All kidding aside, I know that the eternal wisdom of Gia's great-grandmothers Bertha "Chubby" Holte and Anna Edwards will have to be part of lesson #3. So will the sweet spirit of my father, Henry Holte Jr., and his sisters, Hattie Mae Sibley and Joshia Mae James. And I'll *have* to find a way to tell her about the brave-in-the-face-of-death strength and grace of my sisters, her great-aunts Vivian, Barbara, and Jackie, all snatched away by cancer far too soon.

And I know this, too: While Gia's birthday cake is baking, "Black Gold" will be playing in my kitchen. And I'm going to sing along with Esperanza Spalding when she gets to the part that says:

Think of all the strength you have in you
From the blood you carry within you

But there's plenty of time for me to get it all figured out. Gia's only two, and whenever I bake a cake, the only thing she cares about is whether or not I'm going to let her lick the icing off the spatula. Here's where I have to pause and drop some knowledge on some of you because somebody had to drop it on me. Once upon a time, I would have let Gia lick the bowl, just like Chubby let me, and Grandmother Ellen let her. But since last year, when the Food and Drug Administration said eating raw batter could make kids seriously sick, I don't let her near it.

Lest you think I'm just being an over-protective glamma, you should know this: The don't-let-your-kids-lick-the-bowl warning is not just due to the raw egg–salmonella thing. The *flour* in the batter is also a problem. (Because the grain it comes from isn't always treated to kill bacteria, it can contain all kinds of disease-causing nasties. Without going into a bunch of details I don't understand, I'll just say E. coli and leave it at that.)

The good news is that Gia loves licking the icing off of the spatula every bit as much as licking the batter out of the bowl. As I tell all the glammothers I know, cake icing is to kids what blazing-fast Wi-Fi is to millennials: *utterly irresistible.* Which means grandbabies are always up for a trip to the house that has it. #Glammother advice.

Hey Zuri, can you say, "Over the river and through the woods to Glammother's house we go"?

# Somebody Loves You, Baby, Hummingbird Layer Cake with Cream Cheese Frosting

This cream cheese frosting is Gia's favorite. The cake itself isn't all that ancient and dates back only a couple of decades to a recipe in *Southern Living* magazine, but it quickly became a staple in the Southern dessert repertoire. Hummingbird cake is unashamed of its sweetness and has a kitchen-sink list of such ingredients as coconut, pecans, pineapple, and bananas. As for all banana cakes, be sure that the fruit is good and ripe or the flavor will be flat. Cream cheese frosting is the traditional icing, but you might also like the Simple Buttercream Frosting on page 47.

Makes 8 to 10 servings

### HUMMINGBIRD CAKE

Softened butter and flour, for the pans

2¼ cups unbleached all-purpose flour

1½ cups granulated sugar

¾ teaspoon ground cinnamon

¾ teaspoon baking soda

½ teaspoon salt

1½ cups mashed ripe bananas
 (from 3 medium bananas)

3 large eggs, at room temperature

¾ cup vegetable oil

1½ teaspoons vanilla extract

One 20-ounce can crushed pineapple,
 well drained (1 cup)

¾ cup (3 ounces) finely chopped pecans

¾ cup finely chopped sweetened
 coconut flakes

### CREAM CHEESE FROSTING

One 8-ounce package cream cheese,
 at room temperature

½ cup (1 stick) unsalted butter, at room
 temperature

2 teaspoons vanilla extract

4 cups confectioners' sugar

About 24 pecan halves, for garnish

1. **To make the cake:** Position a rack in the center of the oven and preheat the oven to 350°F. Butter the insides of two 9 by 1½-inch round cake pans. Line the bottoms with waxed paper rounds. Dust the sides with flour and tap out the excess flour.

2. Sift the flour, granulated sugar, cinnamon, baking soda, and salt into a medium bowl. Whisk the bananas, eggs, oil, and vanilla well in another bowl, pour into the flour mixture, and stir just until combined. Mix in the drained pineapple, pecans, and coconut. Divide the batter equally among the pans and spread it evenly.

3. Bake until the cakes are golden brown and a wooden toothpick inserted into the

centers comes out clean, about 30 minutes. Transfer to wire racks and cool for 10 minutes. Run a dinner knife around the inside of each pan to release the cakes. Invert and unmold the cakes onto the racks and discard the paper. Using a wide spatula, turn the cakes right side up and cool completely.

4.  **To make the frosting:** Beat the cream cheese, butter, and vanilla together with an electric mixer set on high speed in a large bowl. Reduce the speed to low. Gradually beat in the confectioners' sugar. Return the speed to high and beat until the frosting is light and fluffy, about 1 minute.

5.  Spread a dab of the frosting on the serving platter. Place one cake, smooth side up, on the platter. Slip strips of waxed paper under the cake to protect the platter from the frosting. Spread the top with about ½ cup of the frosting. Repeat with the second cake layer. Frost the top and then the sides of the cake with a thin layer of frosting. Refrigerate until the frosting sets, about 15 minutes.

6.  Frost the cake with the remaining frosting. Press a row of pecan halves into the frosting around the top edge of the cake. Slip out and discard the waxed paper. (The cake can be refrigerated for up to 2 days. This cake can be served cold, but it is better if allowed to stand at room temperature for 1 hour before slicing.)

# Jackie's Redemptive
# Red Velvet Marble Cake

I call this redemptive red velvet cake because, in a way, it redeemed me. Not in a religious, born again, come-to-Jesus way. But in ways both meaningful and spiritual, ways I believe were divinely inspired. More than most, I know the formidable, sometimes mystical, power that food can have over people. I've seen it for myself—up close and personal. Whether it was my great-grandmother Mariah's pound cake tempting rich folks out of rubies (page 59) or my mother's fried chicken making people speak in tongues (page 213), I *know* food has the power to make people do unusual things.

So you'd think I would have been the first person to acknowledge the sway that red velvet cake holds over me. But I didn't. Not for a long time. Not until my best friend, Norma, pointed out the way it lifts me out of a funk when nothing else can. And I don't even have to eat it to get the feel-good effect. Just the *smell* of red velvet cake baking in the oven gives me a rush. Actually, it's more than a rush. It's a natural high. To paraphrase Frankie Beverly, soul master and fellow Philly native: *From deep in my soul, it gives me happy feelings.*

Like I said, it was Norma who solved the mystery. As she correctly deduced, the red velvet cake / happy feelings thing was all about my baby sister, Jackie. Jackie loved all my desserts. My red velvet cake, however, was one of her all-time favorites. It was Jackie's love of my red velvet cake, in fact, that ended a particularly nasty fight between us, as Norma reminded me a few years ago when I couldn't stop craving it. It was the

craziest thing. When the cravings started, I hadn't made red velvet cake in a year, maybe more. With one exception—I went to the bakery with a friend who was buying one for her husband's birthday—I hadn't even laid eyes on a red velvet cake in I can't remember how long. But after that trip to the bakery, I couldn't stop craving it. I even *dreamed* about red velvet cake. So much so, I thought I was going crazy.

As I learned when I was writing this book, crazy I was not. As it turns out, my reaction to red velvet cake in general and to its smell in particular has a medical/clinical explanation, the details of which are way beyond my ability to explain. It's complicated and science-y, but here's the gist of it: Smells are powerful triggers of specific memories. They're so powerful, in fact, they're often used in therapy to recover lost memories. A number of studies have even shown that memories triggered by smells tend to be clearer, more specific, and more emotional. Clearly, my trip to the bakery triggered some very specific, *very* emotional memories of Jackie. Beginning with The Fight in Atlantic City.

Like most of our arguments, it started over something stupid. I was performing at one of the big hotels and Jackie wanted to sell souvenir tee shirts in the lobby before the show. She'd been doing it for months, but for some reason that night I said no. Why did I do that? My feisty little sister—Jackie weighed 90 pounds soaking wet—told me to stick it where the sun don't shine; that she was selling her tee shirts no matter what I said. Those of you who knew Jackie know where this story's headed. I said, "Over my dead body"; Jackie said, "If that's how you want it"; and before you could say, "Call security!" we were going at each other like Ali vs. Frazier. Thank God for Norma. When security showed up, she managed to convince them that everything was under control…without opening the door. And things *were* under control—as soon as Norma stopped me from strangling Jackie with the bra strap I had wrapped around her neck.

Jackie and I had had other fights, lots of them, but this one was different. We usually made up in a few days—a week or two tops. But after the drama in Atlantic City, Jackie didn't speak to me for months. I knew things were serious when she asked a friend who worked at the phone company if there was any way to have my calls permanently blocked. There's no getting around it; I was as wrong as a karaoke cover band at Carnegie Hall. But with Jackie refusing to take my calls, I was between a rock and a hard place. I couldn't get her to listen to my apology (I really was sorry) or my explanation (I really was PMS-ing, which, trust me, has nothing on hot flashes and night sweats).

This is where the red velvet cake comes in. The cake, and a little bit of divine intervention/ inspiration. As Jackie and I were heading into our third month of silence, my friend Diane asked me to bake a red velvet cake for her, which she'd offered to donate to a charity bake sale. Why did Diane do that? She's a pretty good cook, but a baker, not so much. So, despite the short notice, I said yes, figuring (a) it was for a good cause; and (b) it was for a good friend.

Imagine my surprise when, the day after the bake sale, Diane showed up at my door, red velvet cake in hand. "I told the organizers I'd pay double if they saved me the best dessert so I could give it to you as a thank-you gift," she explained.

They charged Diane fifty bucks and sent her home with—you guessed it—my red velvet cake. To this day, we laugh about it. But as I tell Diane all the time, she got off easy. That cake was worth a hundred bucks easy.

Looking back, I believe that cake came back to me for a reason: to make it, if not easy, at least not so hard to keep trying to get through to Jackie. Apologizing to somebody more than once is a lot harder than you think. At least it is for me. I don't do rejection well…Okay, fine: I don't do it at all. But that red velvet cake made me want to keep reaching out. Crazy as it sounds, that cake gave me the courage—and a couple of really good reasons—to give an apology another shot. For one thing, I thought it would soften Jackie's heart. (Homemade desserts, like long-stemmed roses, tend to have that effect.) For another, I was doing really well on a low-carb diet that I didn't want to blow. (Just keeping it real.)

It worked! Two days after my nephew dropped that red velvet cake off at her house, Jackie and I were cool again. And we stayed that way for the better part of a year, which, as anyone who knew us both can tell you, was a minor miracle. I tell Norma all the time how glad I am that she made the Jackie / red velvet cake / happy feelings connection because, as I said earlier, in some ways it redeemed me. Until then, every time I thought about Jackie my mind went straight to the fried egg sandwich.

I've shared the story a million times, but, on the off chance there's someone who hasn't heard it, here's everything you need to know: I didn't grant Jackie's last wish, which was that I make her a fried egg sandwich. When she called me from the hospital where she was undergoing treatment for brain cancer, I told her I was tired. That I would make it for her later. Only later never came. As I was about to head to the hospital to take it to her, Aunt Hattie called and said, "Don't rush, Patsy. It's too late." Jackie died before I got to do the last thing she ever asked of me.

Whenever I think about Jackie, I think about the fried egg sandwich. With all my heart I wish I'd taken it to the hospital the day she called and asked me to make it for her. But I think about the red velvet cake, too. Not just how much Jackie loved it but, unlike the fried egg sandwich, the many times I made it for her

when she asked: Her birthday. Her friends' birthdays. (Jackie always told everybody she baked it.) Sometimes on an I-just-want-a-piece-of-red-velvet-cake Tuesday. It doesn't eliminate the guilt, but it sure does ease it. Because it reminds me of all the good times Jackie and I shared, times no amount of bad memories can ever erase.

The next time you need to take a dish to a bake sale, give this recipe a try. Better yet, make it for someone you love as much as I loved Jackie.

# Jackie's Redemptive Red Velvet Marble Cake with Boiled Frosting

It's easy to take familiar red velvet cake and give it a twist (literally) by marbleizing red and white batters. This cake has one of the most tender, melt-in-your-mouth textures around, but its main flavor is vanilla—the cocoa is in the batter only to darken the red color. Some people see the cocoa in the cake and think it is going to taste like chocolate—not. The boiled frosting may be new to you, although it has been around for years and is basically a sweet paste beaten into butter. The end result is smooth and creamy.

Makes 8 to 10 servings

**RED VELVET MARBLE CAKE**

Softened butter and flour, for the pans

2½ cups cake flour (not self-rising)

1 teaspoon baking soda

1 teaspoon salt

½ cup (1 stick) unsalted butter, at room temperature

1½ cups granulated sugar

2 large eggs, at room temperature

2 teaspoons vanilla extract

1 cup low-fat buttermilk

1 tablespoon natural unsweetened cocoa powder, such as Hershey's

Red food coloring, preferably paste or gel (see Patti's Pointers)

**BOILED FROSTING**

1 cup granulated sugar

⅓ cup unbleached all-purpose flour

1 cup whole milk

1 cup (2 sticks) unsalted butter, at room temperature

1 teaspoon vanilla extract

Red decorating sugar, for sprinkling

1. **To make the cake:** Position a rack in the center of the oven and preheat the oven to 350°F. Butter the insides of two 9 by 1½-inch round cake pans. Line the bottoms with waxed paper rounds. Dust the pan sides with flour and tap out the excess flour.

2. Sift the flour, baking soda, and salt together. Beat the butter and granulated sugar together in a large bowl with an electric mixer set on high speed, occasionally scraping down the sides of the bowl with a rubber spatula, until the mixture is pale and gritty (it won't get fluffy), about 3 minutes. One at a time, beat in the eggs, beating well after each addition, then add the vanilla. Reduce the mixer speed to low. In thirds, add the flour mixture, alternating with two equal additions of the buttermilk, scraping down the sides of the bowl with a rubber spatula as needed, and mix just until smooth.

*Continued on page 34*

3. Pour half of the batter into a medium bowl. Sift the cocoa powder into the batter (sifting keeps it from clumping) and stir it in. Tint this batter bright red with the food coloring. (The amount depends on your desired shade and the kind of coloring used. You will probably use only 2 drops of paste, slightly more gel, or 1 to 2 tablespoons liquid.)

4. For each pan, spoon in one-fourth-sized dollops of the red batter, placing the batter at the 12 and 6 o'clock positions. Fill the empty spaces in the pan (at the 3 and 9 o'clock positions) with one-fourth-sized dollops of the plain batter. Run a dinner knife through the batter a few times to marbleize the batters together.

5. Bake until the cakes begin to shrink from the sides of the pans and a wooden toothpick inserted into the centers comes out clean, about 25 minutes. Transfer to wire racks and cool for 10 minutes. Run a dinner knife around the inside of each pan to release the cakes. Invert and unmold the cakes onto the racks and discard the paper. Using a wide spatula, turn the cakes right side up and cool completely.

6. **To make the frosting:** Whisk the granulated sugar and flour together in a medium heavy saucepan. Gradually whisk in the milk. Bring to a boil over medium heat, whisking often, to make a thick paste. Transfer to a small bowl and press plastic wrap directly onto the surface to keep a skin from forming. Using a small sharp knife, pierce a few holes in the plastic to allow the steam to escape. Let cool completely, at least 1 hour. (Or place the bowl in a larger bowl filled about halfway with iced water to speed the cooling.)

7. Beat the butter in a medium bowl with an electric mixer set at high speed until the butter is creamy and fluffy, about 1 minute. Gradually beat in the cooled paste. Beat in the vanilla.

8. Dab a tablespoon of the frosting on the serving platter. Place one cake, upside down, on the platter. Slip strips of waxed paper under the cake to protect the platter from the frosting. Spread the cake top with about ½ cup of the frosting. Repeat with the second cake layer, smooth side down. Frost the top and then the sides of the cake with a thin layer of frosting. Refrigerate until the frosting sets, about 15 minutes.

9. Frost the cake with the remaining frosting. Sprinkle with the decorating sugar. Slip out and discard the waxed paper. (The cake can be refrigerated for up to 1 day. Let the cake stand at room temperature for 1 hour before slicing.) Slice and serve.

**Patti's Pointers:** *Red food paste gives the truest, darkest red color. It is sold at hobby and craft shops and online. It is very intensely colored, so use it by the drop. If you use gel or liquid food coloring, expect to add more to get the right hue. Food coloring paste and gel are often sold in small plastic squeeze bottles to apply by the drop. Otherwise, dip a wooden toothpick into the coloring and add it to the food being colored one speck or dab at a time. Remember that you can always add more coloring, but once it is too dark, you can't reverse the process.*

# Chocolate Cake with Fudge Frosting

It's sometimes nice to have a cake that is a "project." But it is just as good to bake a layer cake that is super easy but tastes like it took hours to put together. The simple, stir-it-up batter for this moist and tender cake is so quick and easy that it will be ready before the oven is preheated! The recipe was invented during World War II when eggs and milk were rationed, but you'll never miss them here. And the frosting matches the cake, bite for bite, with chocolate flavor. This cake is so full of chocolaty flavor that it doesn't really need any garnish. Sometimes I substitute cold brewed coffee (not dark roast) for the water in the cake. You won't taste the coffee at all, but it pumps up the cocoa flavor.

Makes 10 to 12 servings

### EASY CHOCOLATE CAKE

Softened butter and flour, for the pans

3 cups unbleached all-purpose flour

2 cups granulated sugar

½ cup natural unsweetened cocoa powder, such as Hershey's

2 teaspoons baking soda

¼ teaspoon salt

2 cups cold water

¾ cup vegetable oil

2 tablespoons white distilled or cider vinegar

2 teaspoons vanilla extract

### CHOCOLATE FUDGE FROSTING

½ cup (1 stick) unsalted butter

4 ounces unsweetened chocolate, coarsely chopped

3 cups confectioners' sugar

½ cup natural unsweetened cocoa powder, such as Hershey's

½ cup whole milk, as needed

1 teaspoon vanilla extract

1. **To make the cake:** Position a rack in the center of the oven and preheat the oven to 350°F. Butter the insides of two 9 by 1½-inch round cake pans. Line the bottoms with waxed paper rounds. Dust the pan sides with flour and tap out the excess flour.

2. Sift the flour, granulated sugar, cocoa, baking soda, and salt into a large bowl. Pour in the water, oil, vinegar, and vanilla. Mix with an electric mixer set on low speed, scraping down the sides of the bowl often, just until the batter is smooth. Divide evenly among the prepared pans and smooth the tops.

3. Bake until the tops spring back when pressed lightly in the center and the cakes are beginning to shrink from the pan sides, 30 to 35 minutes. Transfer to wire racks and

cool for 10 minutes. Run a dinner knife around the inside of each pan to release the cakes. Invert and unmold the cakes onto the racks and discard the paper. Using a wide spatula, turn the cakes right side up and cool completely.

4.  **To make the frosting:** Melt the butter in a small saucepan over low heat. Remove from the heat. Add the chopped chocolate and let stand until softened, about 3 minutes. Whisk until the chocolate is melted and the mixture is smooth. Transfer to a medium bowl. Add the confectioners' sugar, cocoa, about ⅓ cup of the milk, and the vanilla. Mix with an electric mixer on low speed until combined. Increase the speed to high and mix, adding more milk as needed, occasionally scraping down the sides of the bowl, until the mixture is very smooth and fluffy, about 1 minute.

5.  Spread a dab of the frosting on the serving platter. Place one cake, upside down, on the platter. Slip strips of waxed paper under the cake to protect the platter from the frosting. Spread the top with about ¾ cup of the frosting. Top with the other layer, right side up. Frost the top and then the sides of the cake with a thin layer of the frosting. Refrigerate until the frosting is set, about 15 minutes. Frost the cake with the remaining frosting. Let the frosting set, about 1 hour. (The cake can be loosely covered and stored at room temperature for up to 1 day.) Slice and serve.

# Cousin Patricia's Pass-It-On Party Cake

*A party without cake is just a meeting.*

Julia Child said that, and every time I bake a cake for one of Zuri's parties or meetings, I know one thing for certain and two things for sure: (1) Julia wasn't just a smart cook—she was a smart cookie; and (2) the women in my family knew how to party. Especially Aunt Joshia Mae. Aunt Josh didn't just love a good party; she was often the life of it. "Every now and then, you have to go out and shake a leg," she used to say, breaking into her signature dance, which I can describe only as a cross between the Charleston and the Lindy… with a Harlem Shake edge. Oh yeah, Aunt Josh had moves. Who do you think I was channeling on *Dancing with the Stars*?

There were some parties, however, where Aunt Josh refused to shake so much as her little pinky: those that didn't have good food. And she was seriously picky about what qualified as "good." Remember, Aunt Josh and Aunt Hattie grew up eating Great-Grandmother Mariah's old-fashioned pound cake (page 59), the cake that was worth its weight in rubies, so she knew good food when she tasted it. As my cousin Patricia reminded me when she gave me this recipe, her mother's definition of a good party didn't include good food; it *was* good food. And if your party didn't have it, Aunt Josh was out of there. Everything else could be kicking—the music, the setting, the people. But if the food wasn't happening, Aunt Josh would start asking Aunt Hattie Mae to take her home 15 minutes after the party started.

You couldn't be mad at her, though. Because Aunt Josh didn't just talk the talk; she walked the walk. Whenever Patricia was invited to a party or a potluck, Aunt Josh would always bake her something fabulous for the table. This cake is one of Patricia's favorites. Aunt Josh named it Pass-It-On Party Cake because that's what she always told Patricia to do: Pass it on. Share the love. And, of course, the food. As both of my aunts used to say, they're usually the same thing.

*My beloved aunt Hattie and aunt Josh.*

# Cousin Patricia's Pass-It-On Party Cake

There are few old-school desserts more beloved than tender and buttery yellow cake layered with swirls of homemade chocolate frosting. Sometimes, for a very big party, our family will double the recipe and stack it all into a towering four-layer cake, in which case it is best served in very thin slices. No matter how you make it, you will want to have a big glass of ice-cold milk to drink with your portion.

Makes 8 to 10 servings

**SIMPLE YELLOW CAKE**

Softened butter and flour, for the pans

2 cups cake flour (not self-rising)

1½ cups granulated sugar

1 tablespoon baking powder

1 teaspoon salt

½ cup (1 stick) unsalted butter, cut into tablespoons, at room temperature

3 large eggs, at room temperature

¾ cup whole milk

1 tablespoon vanilla extract

1 batch Chocolate Fudge Frosting (page 37)

Multicolored cake decorating nonpareils or sprinkles (jimmies), for decoration (optional)

1.  **To make the cake layers:** Position a rack in the center of the oven and preheat the oven to 350°F. Butter the insides of two 9 by 1½-inch round cake pans. Line the bottoms with waxed paper rounds. Dust the pan sides with flour and tap out the excess flour.

2.  Sift the flour, sugar, baking powder, and salt in a large bowl. Add the butter, eggs, milk, and vanilla. Using an electric mixer set on low speed, mix just until the mixture is combined. Increase the speed to medium-high and mix for 2 minutes (use a timer), scraping down the sides of the bowl as needed. Divide the batter among the pans and smooth the tops.

3.  Bake until the cakes begin to shrink from the sides of the pans and a wooden toothpick inserted into the centers comes out clean, about 25 minutes. Transfer to wire racks and cool for 10 minutes. Run a dinner knife around the inside of each pan to release the cakes. Invert and unmold the cakes onto the racks and discard the paper. Using a wide spatula, turn the cakes right side up and cool completely.

4.  Dab a tablespoon of the frosting onto the serving platter. Place one cake, upside down, on the platter. Slip strips of waxed paper under the cake to protect the platter from the frosting. Spread about ¾ cup of the frosting on top of the layer. Top with the second layer, bottom side down. Frost the top and then the sides of the cake with the remaining frosting. Sprinkle the jimmies over the edge of the cake, patting them gently to adhere. Slip out and discard the waxed paper. (The cake can be refrigerated for up to 1 day. Let stand at room temperature for 1 hour before slicing.) Slice and serve.

# Lemon Meringue Cake

You've heard of lemon meringue pie...but why not lemon meringue cake? This beautiful cake is a fantastic dessert for winter when so many fresh fruits except citrus are out of season. With its brown-tinged meringue frosting, it is a real showstopper, and the flavor lives up to the cake's visual promise. Because this isn't the easiest cake in the world (but worth the effort), it might be best to build the cake without the meringue, then frost with the meringue and brown it a couple of hours before serving, and let it stand at room temperature for the big reveal. Avoid making it when the weather is humid, as the meringue could shrink. For an optional garnish, use a special citrus zester (sometimes called a channel knife) to remove a few thin strips from one of the lemons, and use the strips to decorate the top of the cake.

Makes 10 servings

**LEMON FILLING**

2 to 3 large lemons

½ cup sugar

2½ teaspoons cornstarch

Pinch of salt

1 large egg plus 2 large egg yolks, beaten together (save the whites for the meringue)

2 tablespoons unsalted butter

**LEMON BUTTER CAKE**

Softened butter and all-purpose flour, for the pans

3 cups cake flour (not self-rising)

2 teaspoons baking powder

1 teaspoon salt

1 cup whole milk

1 teaspoon vanilla extract

1 teaspoon lemon extract

1 cup (2 sticks) unsalted butter, at room temperature

2 cups sugar

4 large eggs, at room temperature, separated

**LEMONADE SYRUP**

½ cup sugar

½ cup water

3 tablespoons fresh lemon juice

**MERINGUE**

⅔ cup sugar

5 large egg whites

½ teaspoon vanilla extract

1. **To make the lemon filling:** Finely grate the zest from 1 lemon. Juice all of the lemons; measure ½ cup lemon juice.

2. Place a wire sieve over a bowl near the stove. Whisk the sugar, cornstarch, and salt together in a small heavy saucepan. Whisk in the lemon juice, followed by the egg and yolks. Cook over medium-low heat, whisking constantly, until the mixture thickens and begins to bubble, 3 to 5 minutes. Let bubble for 30 seconds. Strain the

filling through the sieve into a bowl to remove any bits of cooked egg white. Add the butter and lemon zest and stir until the butter is incorporated into the filling. Cover with a piece of plastic wrap pressed directly onto the surface. Pierce a few holes in the wrap with a sharp knife. Let cool to room temperature. Refrigerate until chilled and set, at least 2 hours.

3. **To make the cake:** Preheat the oven to 350°F. Lightly butter the insides of two 9 by 1½-inch round cake pans. Line the bottoms with waxed paper rounds. Dust the insides of the pans with flour and shake out the excess.

4. Sift the flour, baking powder, and salt into a medium bowl. Mix the milk, vanilla, and lemon extract in a glass measuring cup. Beat the butter and sugar together in a large mixing bowl with an electric mixer at high speed until the mixture is light in color and texture, about 3 minutes. One at a time, beat in the egg yolks, beating well after each addition. Reduce the mixer speed to low. In thirds, add the flour mixture, alternating with two equal additions of the milk mixture, scraping down the sides of the bowl with a rubber spatula as needed, and mix just until smooth.

5. Using very clean beaters, beat the 4 egg whites in a medium bowl until they form stiff but not dry peaks. Using a large rubber spatula, stir about one-fourth of the whites into the batter, then fold in the remaining whites. Spread evenly in the pans.

6. Bake until the tops spring back when pressed gently in the center, 30 to 35 minutes. Transfer to wire racks and cool for 10 minutes. Run a dinner knife around the inside of each pan to release the cakes. Invert and unmold the cakes onto the racks and discard the paper. Using a wide spatula, turn the cakes right side up and cool completely.

7. **To make the syrup:** Bring the sugar and water to a full boil in a small saucepan over high heat, stirring to dissolve the sugar. Remove from the heat and stir in the lemon juice. Pour into a small bowl and let cool completely. (The syrup can be covered and refrigerated for up to 3 days.)

8. Place one cake layer upside down on a tart pan bottom that you are sure is ovenproof. Place the cake on a cake turntable or an overturned bowl with a wide bottom. Brush and drizzle half of the syrup over the cake. Spread the filling over the cake, leaving a ½-inch border around the edge. Top with the second layer, top side up, and brush it with the remaining syrup. Set the cake aside.

9. **To make the meringue:** Position a rack in the lower third of the oven and reheat the oven to 400°F.

10. Choose a large saucepan that will snugly fit a large mixing bowl or the bowl of a heavy-duty standing mixer. Bring an inch of water to a boil over high heat in the saucepan, and then turn the heat to very low. Whisk the sugar and the 5 egg whites together in the bowl. Place the bowl over the hot water and stir with the whisk, scraping down any splashes on the side of the bowl, until the mixture is warm, turns whiter, and the sugar dissolves, 2 to 3 minutes. (Rub a bit of the mixture between your thumb and forefinger to feel for undissolved sugar.) Beat the egg white mixture with a handheld mixer or the whisk attachment on the mixer on high speed until the meringue forms stiff, shiny peaks. Beat in the vanilla.

11. Spackle the space between the cake layers with the meringue to seal in the curd. Generously frost the entire cake with the remaining meringue, decoratively swirling the meringue. Place on a rimless baking sheet (or use a rimmed sheet, with the edge facing down, as it is easier to slide the cake from the sheet that way). Bake until the meringue is tinged with brown, about 5 minutes. (The cake can be stored, uncovered, for up to 2 hours. If you refrigerate it, let the cake stand at room temperature for 1 hour before serving or the cake layers will be too firm.) To serve, slice the cake with a long, thin knife dipped into a tall glass of hot water between slices.

# Sprinkle Celebration Cake

In 1996, I became *Dr.* Patti.

I was sitting at my kitchen table when I learned Boston's internationally famous Berklee College of Music was awarding me an honorary doctorate in music. Forget Cloud 9; after that call, I was on Cloud 900! Especially since I know how selective the school is about the people to whom they give this honor. As Berklee explains it:

> There is a select group of performing and recording artists, educators and contributors to today's professional music who are recipients of the honorary doctorate degree from Berklee College of Music. Their contributions have the enduring qualities that define the musical era in which they played a leading role.

And I was about to become a member of that select group! No two ways about it: When you're about to join the likes of Duke Ellington, Dizzy Gillespie, Tony Bennett, Sarah Vaughan, James Taylor, and Quincy Jones, that's a celebration moment if ever there was one. And since for the past two weeks I'd been having an insatiable cake-and-icing jones—a jones that, let the record show, I had *not* indulged—I decided to bake myself a cake that would satisfy my desire for all three: the celebration, the cake, and the buttercream icing!

When you have something truly fabulous to celebrate, you won't find a better dessert. And check out the cake's photo; it's as cute as it is delicious!

# Sprinkle Celebration Cake with Simple Buttercream Frosting

There are some times when only a tender white cake, uncolored by egg yolks, will do. The picture on page 48 shows off flecks of colored sprinkles in the batter. And you won't believe how easy and good the buttercream is—it uses marshmallow cream as its base! For a shower, you might want to use blue or pink (or a combination) sprinkles, or green and red for Christmas, or...well, you get the idea. (Sprinkles are easy to find at cake decorating and hobby stores, or online at amazon.com.) But multicolored ones for a birthday seem to declare "Happy Birthday!"

Makes 10 to 12 servings

### WHITE CAKE

Softened butter and flour, for the pans

2 cups unbleached all-purpose flour

1½ cups sugar

1 tablespoon baking powder

½ teaspoon salt

¼ cup (½ stick) unsalted butter, cut into tablespoons, well softened

¼ cup vegetable shortening, cut into tablespoons, at room temperature

1 cup whole milk, divided

4 large egg whites (½ cup), at room temperature

1 teaspoon vanilla extract

⅓ cup multicolored cake decorating sprinkles (jimmies)

### SIMPLE BUTTERCREAM FROSTING

One 7-ounce jar marshmallow cream (1 heaping cup)

1½ cups (3 sticks) unsalted butter, at room temperature, cut into tablespoons

1 teaspoon vanilla extract

½ cup multicolored cake decorating sprinkles (jimmies), as needed, for decorating

1. **To make the cake:** Position a rack in the center of the oven and preheat the oven to 350°F. Butter the insides of two 9 by 1½-inch round cake pans. Line the bottoms with waxed paper rounds. Dust the pan sides with flour and tap out the excess flour.

2. Whisk the flour, sugar, baking powder, and salt together in a large bowl. Add the butter, shortening, and ⅔ cup of the milk. Mix with an electric mixer on low speed for 30 seconds (use a timer). Add the egg whites, the remaining ⅓ cup milk, and the vanilla. Beat on high speed, scraping down the sides of the bowl often with a rubber

spatula, for 2 minutes (use a timer). Fold in the sprinkles. Divide the batter evenly among the prepared pans and smooth the tops.

3.  Bake until the cakes are golden brown and beginning to shrink from the pan sides, about 30 minutes. Transfer to wire racks and cool for 10 minutes. Run a dinner knife around the inside of each pan to release the cakes. Invert and unmold the cakes onto the racks and discard the paper. Using a wide spatula, turn the cakes right side up and cool completely.

4.  **To make the frosting:** Beating the marshmallow cream in a medium bowl with an electric mixer set at medium-high speed, add the butter, one tablespoon at a time, beating well after each addition. When all of the butter has been added, continue beating until the frosting is very smooth, pale, and fluffy, 1 to 2 minutes more. Beat in the vanilla.

5.  Spread a dab of the frosting on the serving platter. Place one cake, upside down, on the platter. Slip strips of waxed paper under the cake to protect the platter from the frosting. Spread the top with about ¾ cup of the frosting. Top with the other layer, right side up. Frost the top and then the sides of the cake with the frosting. Place the cake on a rimmed baking sheet to catch any falling sprinkles. Scatter the sprinkles over the top of the cake. If desired, use your cupped hand to press more sprinkles onto the sides of the cake. Let the frosting set, about 1 hour. (The cake can be loosely covered and stored at room temperature for up to 1 day.) Discard the waxed paper strips. Slice and serve.

# Lemon–Poppy Seed Chiffon Cake

It is the goal of every baker that each cake be mouthwateringly moist…
no one likes a dry, heavy cake. The chiffon family of cakes is made with oil,
not butter, and the extra liquid gives the dessert its wonderful texture. The
cake can look a little plain, but with one bite, you'll be a goner.

Makes 12 to 14 servings

**CHIFFON CAKE**

2¼ cups cake flour (not self-rising)

1½ cups granulated sugar

1 tablespoon baking powder

1 teaspoon salt

½ cup canola or vegetable oil

5 large eggs, separated, plus
  3 large egg whites, at room
  temperature

Finely grated zest of 1 lemon

¼ cup fresh lemon juice

½ cup water

1 teaspoon vanilla extract

3 tablespoons poppy seeds

**LEMON ICING**

2 cups confectioners' sugar

Finely grated zest of 1 lemon

⅓ cup fresh lemon juice, as needed

2 tablespoons unsalted butter,
  melted

Water, if needed

1. **To make the cake:** Position an oven rack in the center of the oven and preheat the
   oven to 350°F.

2. Whisk the flour, sugar, baking powder, and salt together in a large bowl. In this order,
   add the oil, 5 egg yolks, lemon zest, lemon juice, water, and vanilla. Beat with an
   electric mixer set at medium speed, scraping down the sides of the bowl as needed,
   until the batter is smooth, about 1 minute. Fold in the poppy seeds.

3. Using an electric mixer with clean beaters in another large bowl, beat the 8 egg whites
   on high speed until they form stiff, shiny peaks. Using a rubber spatula, stir one-fourth
   of the whites into the batter to lighten the batter. Fold in the remaining whites. Pour
   the batter into an ungreased 10-inch-diameter tube pan (preferably without nonstick
   coating) with a removable bottom. (This is commonly called an angel-food cake pan.)
   Smooth the top of the batter.

4. Bake until a long wooden skewer inserted into the cake comes out clean, about
   50 minutes. Turn the pan upside down and balance it on its inner tube on a work surface.
   (If necessary, balance the pan on upside-down ramekins to lift the pan above the
   work surface.) Let the cake cool completely.

5.  Run a long metal spatula or thin knife around the inside of the pan and tube to loosen the cake. Remove the cake from the pan, and gently pull the bottom of the cake away from the tube insert. Place the cake, flat side down, on a wire rack set over a rimmed baking sheet.

6.  **To make the icing:** Whisk the confectioners' sugar, lemon zest and juice, and melted butter in a medium bowl until smooth and the consistency of thick heavy cream. If necessary, add water, a teaspoon at a time, to the icing to reach the desired consistency. Pour the icing over the cake and smooth it with a metal spatula, letting the excess glaze run down the sides of the cake. Let the cake stand until the glaze is set, about 1 hour. Slice with a serrated knife and serve. (The cake can be stored at room temperature, tightly covered with plastic wrap, for up to 3 days.)

# Bourbon Chocolate Cake

I don't want to hear any cracks about baking with booze—it is a great idea because the alcohol does a chemical trick to bring out the flavors in the other ingredients. The bourbon is terrific with the chocolate in this cake, but if you are a teetotaler, you can use cold coffee instead. Use a good, moderately priced whiskey, and save the sippin' bourbon for juleps.

Makes 12 to 14 servings

**CAKE**

Softened butter and flour, for the pan

2 cups granulated sugar

1¾ cups unbleached all-purpose flour

¾ cup natural unsweetened cocoa powder, such as Hershey's

2 tablespoons cornstarch

2 teaspoons baking soda

1 teaspoon baking powder

1 teaspoon salt

1 cup sour cream

½ cup canola or vegetable oil

½ cup plus 2 tablespoons bourbon or cool brewed coffee (not dark roast)

½ cup water

2 large eggs

2 teaspoons vanilla extract

**CHOCOLATE GLAZE**

½ cup heavy cream

4 ounces semisweet chocolate, finely chopped

**WHITE CHOCOLATE DRIZZLE**

2 tablespoons heavy cream

2 ounces white chocolate, finely chopped

1. **To make the cake:** Position a rack in the center of the oven and preheat the oven to 350°F. Butter and flour the inside of a 12-cup Bundt (fluted tube) pan (preferably nonstick) and tap out the excess flour.

2. Sift the sugar, flour, cocoa, cornstarch, baking soda, baking powder, and salt together into a large bowl. Whisk the sour cream, oil, ½ cup of the bourbon, the water, eggs, and vanilla together in another bowl. Pour over the dry ingredients and whisk until smooth. Pour into the pan and smooth the top.

3. Bake until a wooden toothpick inserted into the center of the cake comes out clean and the cake has begun to shrink from the sides of the pan, about 1 hour. Let the cake cool on a wire rack for 15 minutes. Drizzle the remaining 2 tablespoons bourbon over the warm cake and let stand for 5 minutes. Invert and unmold the cake onto the rack and let cool completely.

4. **To make the glaze:** Bring the cream to a simmer in a small saucepan over medium heat. Remove from the heat. Add the semisweet chocolate and let stand until the chocolate softens, about 3 minutes. Whisk until the glaze is smooth. Let the glaze cool and thicken slightly, about 10 minutes.

5. Place the cake on the rack over a baking sheet. Pour the glaze around the top of the cake, letting the excess glaze drip down the sides. Scrape up the glaze from the baking sheet and spoon it over the top of the cake again. Let the glaze set until it no longer looks wet, about 30 minutes.

**To make the drizzle:** Bring the cream to a simmer in a small saucepan over medium heat. Remove from the heat. Add the white chocolate and let stand until the chocolate softens, about 3 minutes. Whisk until the mixture is smooth. Let the mixture cool and thicken slightly, about 10 minutes.

6. Using a dessert spoon, drizzle the white chocolate mixture over the chocolate glaze. Transfer the cake to a serving platter and refrigerate to set the glaze and drizzle, about 30 minutes. (The cake can be loosely covered with plastic wrap and stored at room temperature for up to 1 day.) Slice and serve.

# Irish Cream Cheesecake

I've had a lot of outrageous desserts in my life—the kind where your eyes roll back in your head and you start to make strange noises that you can't explain to the people around you. This is one of those desserts. It is especially fun at a party with a bunch of ladies (a shower or a bachelorette party), because there are very few women who don't love Baileys. So skip the "Magic Mike" hire and serve this instead.

Makes 12 servings

**GRAHAM CRACKER CRUST**

1¼ cups graham cracker crumbs (see Patti's Pointers, at right)

¼ cup sugar

4 tablespoons (½ stick) unsalted butter, melted

**FILLING**

2 pounds cream cheese, at soft room temperature (see Patti's Pointers, page 100)

1 cup sugar

4 large eggs, at room temperature, beaten

1 cup Irish cream liqueur, such as Baileys or Carolans

2 tablespoons cornstarch

1.  Position a rack in the center of the oven and preheat the oven to 375°F. Lightly butter a 9-inch springform pan.

2.  **To make the crust:** Mix the crumbs, sugar, and butter in a small bowl. Press firmly and evenly onto the bottom and ½ inch up the sides of the pan. Bake until the crust smells lightly toasted, about 10 minutes.

3.  **To make the filling:** Mix the cream cheese and sugar in a heavy-duty mixer fitted with a paddle blade on medium speed, just until smooth. Occasionally scrape down the sides of the bowl, and do NOT overmix. Gradually mix in the eggs, again being carefully not to overmix. Mix in the liqueur and cornstarch. You can use a hand mixer, if you prefer. Pour into the crust and smooth the top.

4.  Place the cheesecake in the oven and immediately reduce the oven temperature to 325°F. Bake until the sides are puffed (the very center may seem slightly unset) and beginning to brown, about 45 minutes. Transfer to a wire cake rack. Run a thin sharp knife around the inside of the pan to release the cake. Cool completely in the pan.

5.  Remove the sides of the pan and wrap the cheesecake in plastic wrap. Chill at least 6 hours or overnight. Serve chilled, sliced with a thin knife dipped into hot water before cutting each slice.

**Patti's Pointers:** *One sleeve of graham crackers, with 9 whole crackers, is just enough to make 1¼ cups of crumbs. The easiest method for crushing them into crumbs is to process the crackers in a food processor. Or place the crackers in a large plastic bag and smash them with a rolling pin.*

# Great-Grandmother Mariah's
# Old-Fashioned Pound Cake

It's one of life's defining moments. The kind no mother ever forgets. The kind every mom I know clearly remembers for the rest of her life. No, I'm not talking about the moment a young mother brings her baby home from the hospital for the very first time. I'm talking about the moment an older mother learns her baby is going to have a baby. That she is going to be a grandma. Or, as I like to call it, a *glamma*. (I would be remiss if I did not pause and give a shout-out to Sir Richard Branson, the self-made billionaire and Virgin Records cofounder. According to my sources, Sir Richard prefers *granddude* to *granddad*. A man after my own heart.)

For me, the moment came a few minutes before I was heading out to do a big photo shoot. I was sitting in the makeup chair and Lona was putting the finishing touches on my lipstick and lashes. Part of the reason I hired Lona as my makeup artist is because I'd heard she could roll with the punches of life on the fly—and the road—both of which perfectly describe mine. And one bedbug scare and two national tours later, I knew the intel I'd gotten on Lona was spot-on. From day one, she was Ms. Mellow—cool and unflappable. And I'm not just saying that because she's my daughter-in-law; I hired Lona *before* she married Zuri. This particular week, however, Ms. Mellow was Ms. Moody. I assumed it was because we'd been on the road a lot and she was exhausted and sick of sleeping in hotels. I assumed right—Lona was exhausted. But not for the reason I thought. It was because she was pregnant!

To this day, I don't know who was happier about the baby, Lona or me. I was pushing 70, and my Grandmother Clock (see below) had never been louder. When Lona told me the news, I burst into tears of joy. I cried so hard, I had to go to the photo shoot without my false eyelashes. As anyone in my Glam Squad can tell you, that's a serious no-no. At photo shoots, false lashes—like Spanx and stilettos—are mandatory. That day, however, I would have posed for the cover of this book without any of them. (Okay, fine, maybe not my five-inch pumps. As a stylist once told me, heels + anything = everything.)

When the shoot was over, Lona made me promise I'd keep her secret until her second trimester. While I assured her my lips were sealed, I knew the only way I'd be able to keep my promise was if I: (1) stayed off the phone; and (2) didn't talk to Armstead. With the possible exception of Zuri, my ex-husband knew more than anyone how desperate I was for Lona to have a baby…because he was, too. I'm always telling Zuri that his father is an unindicted coconspirator because, as quiet as Armstead likes to keep it, he was every bit as desperate as I was for Lona and Zuri to have a kid!

And *desperate* is the right word here. From the day they announced their engagement, I bugged Lona and Zuri about their baby-making plans every day of the week and twice on Sundays. In my defense, you should know that I'd been hearing the ticking of the Grandmother Clock for *years*. Long before Lona and Zuri got married. When my son Stanley and his wife, Aki, had

*Me and baby Gia—they grow up so fast . . . I remember holding Zuri close to my heart, and now I can relive those moments with Gia.*

Ellington, it quieted for a while. But a month or two later, it was back—even louder.

What in the Sam Hill, you're probably wondering, is the Grandmother Clock? (All you wannabe grandmothers who've never heard of it can thank me later.) The Grandmother Clock is the reason women of a certain age bug their kids to have kids. Plenty of researchers believe moms-

to-be aren't the only ones who have a biological clock; many say one is ticking for wannabe grandmas, too. (I knew I wasn't crazy!)

If you think about it, the theory makes perfect sense. Just as you can be too old to have a child, you can be too old to take care of one. You can definitely be too old to chase a toddler around the house, as I learn every time Gia and Ellington are in mine at the same time. And, depending on your health and fitness level, you can also be too old and—how can I put this?— "forgetful" to be left in charge of a child not your own for the weekend. Citing her never-tempt-fate rule, a friend who recently became a grandmother refuses to even *say* what she calls "the A words": arthritis, Alzheimer's, and assisted living.

I'm not *that* freaked out about aging; 70 is the new 50, I always say. (Two words: Tony Bennett.) Besides, I'm with Springsteen. As he sings in "No Surrender," "I'm ready to grow young again." But I won't lie: Every time I hear a knee pop or a joint crack, I know my days of playing Twister with Gia and Ellington are numbered. What can I say? It is what it is. Like it or not, vibrancy, like fertility, isn't forever.

To Zuri and Lona's credit, neither ever told me to stop sticking my nose where it didn't belong. Never pointed out that their baby-making plans were their business, not mine. Of course, Zuri pretty much *had* to put up with all the hinting and the badgering—he's my kid, what's he going to do? But Lona had other options. Lots of them. She could have ignored my calls. Or skipped Sunday dinners. Or, God forbid, told Zuri she wanted to move out of the state.

Because Lona did none of those things— and because she told her mother and me the news before almost everyone else!—I wanted to say *thankyouthankyouthankyou.* And I knew exactly how I wanted to say it. The way the great Southern cooks in my family have said it for generations:

With something baked from scratch, something amazing. And nothing is more amazing than my great-grandmother Mariah's old-fashioned pound cake. The more I thought about it, the more I knew it was the perfect thank-you gift. Not because it's so delicious, though it is. But because it's so full of family history, a history I wanted to pass down to Lona and, one day, to the child she was carrying.

According to Aunt Hattie Mae, Great-Grandmother Mariah's pound cake was worth its weight in rubies. Literally. Aunt Hattie *swore* there was "a city woman," a woman who "had more money than sense," who used to come from Savannah to visit Great-Grandmother Mariah in Pin Point. (Yes, that's a real place in Georgia.) Aunt Hattie said every time the woman from Savannah came to the farm, she *begged* my great-grandmother for her pound cake recipe. Now, my great-grandmother hardly ever shared her recipes, and never with anyone who wasn't family. So all that begging didn't move Great-Grandmother Mariah one bit. And then one day the woman from Savannah showed up with a ruby necklace...which she offered to give my great-grandmother in exchange for the recipe.

Aunt Hattie never could finish telling the story without cracking up. "Patsy," she used to say, laughing so hard her whole body shook, "if Miss Moneybags knew Grandmother Mariah mixed her batter in the family washpot, I don't know if she would have been so anxious to part with those rubies." Aunt Hattie's gone now, and Great-Grandmother Mariah died before I got to meet her. But every time I bake this pound cake, they feel so close.

That's a big reason I love "the ruby recipe," as Aunt Hattie and Aunt Josh always called it, so very much. That, and because, like the pancakes Ann Romney makes for her family à la Grandmother Pottinger (see story on page xi), it's the best evidence I know for how food in general and recipes in particular connect generations across time and space. (To start your own pancake tradition, give the ones on page 208 a try.)

Aunt Hattie never would tell me whether Great-Grandmother Mariah ever gave the woman from Savannah the recipe (and got the ruby necklace!), and I guess it really doesn't matter. Because she gave it to Aunt Hattie and Aunt Hattie gave it to me.

I hope you love it as much as I do.

# Great-Grandmother Mariah's Old-Fashioned Pound Cake

Pound cake is glorious in a classic, time-honored, old-school way—the cake equivalent of the once-in-a-generation voice of Mahalia Jackson. Many vintage pound cake recipes don't include either vanilla or baking powder. I have altered this recipe a little for current tastes, but it still is a cake that Great-Grandmother Mariah could be proud of. Be sure to use an electric mixer (either the hand or standing variety) to beat plenty of air into the creamed butter. Just follow the recipe and you will get pound cake the way it is supposed to be. I probably don't have to tell you that it makes a great shortcake with juicy berries or peaches, or that you can put ice cream on it or simply serve it plain with a cold glass of milk.

Makes 8 servings

Softened butter and flour, for the pan

2 cups unbleached all-purpose flour

1 teaspoon baking powder

½ teaspoon salt

⅓ cup whole milk, at room temperature

1 teaspoon vanilla extract

1 teaspoon lemon extract

1 cup (2 sticks) unsalted butter, at room temperature

1½ cups sugar

3 large eggs, at room temperature

1. Position a rack in the center of the oven and preheat the oven to 350°F. Butter the inside of 9 by 5-inch loaf pan (see Patti's Pointers), preferably an uncoated aluminum pan. Line the bottom with waxed paper. Dust the inside of the pan with flour and tap out the excess flour.

2. Sift the flour, baking powder, and salt into a medium bowl. Mix the milk, vanilla, and lemon extract together in a liquid measuring cup. Beat the butter in a large bowl with an electric mixer set on high speed until the butter is a shade paler and smooth, about 1 minute. Gradually beat in the sugar and continue beating until the mixture is pale yellow and has a fluffy texture, about 3 minutes. One at a time, beat in the eggs, beating for 15 seconds after each addition and scraping down the bowl as needed. With the machine on low speed, add the flour mixture in thirds, alternating with two equal additions of the milk mixture, mixing just until smooth after each addition and scraping the bowl down as needed. Transfer to the prepared pan and smooth the top.

*Continued on page 61*

3. Bake until the top of the cake is a deep golden brown and a wooden toothpick inserted into the center comes out clean, about 1 hour and 10 minutes. Let cool in the pan on a wire rack for 10 minutes.

4. Run a knife around the inside of the pan to loosen the cake. Unmold the cake onto the rack and discard the paper. Turn the cake right side up and let cool completely.

**Bundt Pound Cake:** *This cake also makes a lovely Bundt cake, iced with a thick white glaze. Substitute a 10- to 12-inch fluted Bundt (tube) pan for the 9 by 5-inch loaf pan. Butter the pan, but coat it with dried plain bread crumbs and tap out the excess crumbs. Fill the pan and smooth the top. Bake until a wooden toothpick inserted in the center of the cake comes out clean, 50 minutes to 1 hour. Let it cool in the pan on a wire cake rack for 15 minutes before unmolding.*

*To make the icing, sift 1 cup confectioners' sugar into a bowl. Add 1/2 teaspoon vanilla extract. Gradually stir in about 1 tablespoon whole milk to make a thick but pourable icing. The icing should be opaque, so don't add too much milk. With the cake on the cake rack set over a plate to catch the drippings, pour the icing over the top of the cake, letting the excess run down the sides. Let the cake stand until the icing sets, at least 1 hour.*

**Patti's Pointers:** *This pound cake has a large amount of batter and should be made in a 9 by 5-inch loaf pan; otherwise, it won't cook through properly. If you have to use a smaller pan, fill it only three-quarters full and discard the remaining batter. Do not try to cram it all into the smaller pan.*

# 3 ) *Make It Quick...Breads, Muffins, and More*

Some people think of muffins as breakfast food. They are great served in the morning, but they also shine in the afternoon when you want a little something to go with your coffee break. Muffins and their cousins, quick breads, are fast and easy to make because, for the most part, they don't call for creaming butter and sugar, and they rarely need frosting. Muffins are small, bake quickly, and can be eaten warm for instant gratification. These quick breads and muffins have ingredients that celebrate flavors for the entire calendar and run from apples to zucchini. While these quick breads are simply prepared, it still might do you some good to glance over the tips and techniques on pages 239—240.

# Apple Crumb Muffins

These truly awesome muffins have a coffee cake–like texture and flavor, making them a great choice for when you want to serve something sweet as an afternoon treat. Or make them for breakfast and fill your kitchen with apple pie–like aromas. Use any apple variety that bakes up firm, such as Granny Smith, Golden Delicious, or Empire, but skip Red Delicious and McIntosh, which fall apart when heated.

Makes 8 muffins

Nonstick cooking oil spray, for the pan

**CRUMB TOPPING**

¼ cup unbleached all-purpose flour

2 tablespoons sugar

¼ teaspoon pumpkin pie spice or ground cinnamon

2 tablespoons unsalted butter, melted

**MUFFINS**

1¼ cups unbleached all-purpose flour

⅔ cup sugar

2 teaspoons baking powder

1 teaspoon pumpkin pie spice (or use ½ teaspoon ground cinnamon, ¼ teaspoon ground ginger, and ¼ teaspoon freshly grated or ground nutmeg)

½ teaspoon salt

½ cup whole milk

½ cup canola or vegetable oil

1 large egg

1 teaspoon vanilla extract

1 firm apple, such as Granny Smith, Golden Delicious, or Empire, peeled and cut into ⅓-inch dice (about 1 cup packed diced apple)

1. Position a rack in the center of the oven and preheat the oven to 400°F. Line 8 standard muffin cups with paper liners. Lightly spray the top of the muffin pan with the oil.

2. **To make the topping:** Mix the flour, sugar, and pumpkin pie spice together in a small bowl. Add the butter and stir until the mixture is crumbly. Work the mixture between your fingers to form coarse crumbs.

3. **To make the muffins:** Sift the flour, sugar, baking powder, pumpkin pie spice, and salt together into a large bowl. Whisk the milk, oil, egg, and vanilla together in another bowl. Make a well in the center of the dry ingredients, pour in the liquid mixture, and stir just until the batter is combined. Fold in the diced apple.

4. Using a ⅓-cup-capacity spring-loaded portion scoop, transfer the batter to the cups, being sure each portion forms a mound that rises just above the edge of the cup. Divide the topping evenly over the muffins, gently pressing the topping to help it adhere. Bake until the muffins are golden brown and a wooden toothpick inserted into the center of a muffin comes out clean, 20 to 25 minutes. (The crumb topping gets in the way of the "pressing the muffin top" test for doneness.) Let cool in the pan for 10 minutes. Remove the muffins from the pan and serve warm or cooled to room temperature.

# Banana Nut Muffins

If you like banana bread, you will love these muffins, which really taste like the fruit. They cook in much less time than a loaf, and they take no time to stir up. The bananas must be ripe with lots of brown spots, but not necessarily squishy—that's rotten, not ripe!

Makes 8 muffins

Nonstick cooking oil spray, for the pan

1½ cups unbleached all-purpose flour

1 teaspoon baking soda

½ teaspoon ground cinnamon

½ teaspoon salt

1 cup packed light brown sugar

1 cup mashed ripe bananas (from about 3 bananas)

5 tablespoons unsalted butter, melted and cooled slightly

1 large egg, beaten

1 teaspoon vanilla extract

½ cup coarsely chopped walnuts

1. Position a rack in the center of the oven and preheat the oven to 400°F. Line 8 standard muffin cups with paper liners. Lightly spray the top of the muffin pan with the cooking oil.

2. Sift the flour, baking soda, cinnamon, and salt together into a large bowl. Add the brown sugar and mix well, being sure the sugar is well crumbled. Make a well in the center of the dry ingredients. Mix the bananas, melted butter, egg, and vanilla together in a bowl, add to the well, and stir just until the batter is combined. Fold in the walnuts.

3. Using a ⅓-cup-capacity spring-loaded portion scoop, transfer the batter to the cups, being sure each portion forms a mound that rises just above the edge of the cup. Bake until the muffins are golden brown and the tops spring back when lightly pressed with a fingertip, about 20 minutes. Let cool in the pan for 10 minutes. Remove the muffins from the pan and serve warm or cooled to room temperature.

# Aunt Joshia Mae's Blue-Ribbon Blueberry Muffins

✳

On the subject of cooking, here's a list of all the things my aunts, Joshia Mae and Hattie Mae, agreed on: (1) Hellman's is the only mayonnaise good cooks use; (2) Aunt Hattie made the best raspberry pie (page 124); and (3) Aunt Josh made the best blueberry muffins.

Everything else was a fierce debate. Aunt Josh, for example, said you should never mix cake batter more than 50 or 60 times; Aunt Hattie said 60 to 70 was the better range. Once, at Thanksgiving dinner, they almost came to blows over, of all things, *salt*. Aunt Josh insisted you sprinkled it in your baked goods to hide bitter tastes; Aunt Hattie said you added it to make the dough more elastic.

Their biggest fights by far, however, were over who was the better cook. With the exception of these blueberry muffins, Aunt Hattie went to her grave swearing anything Aunt Josh could cook she could cook better. "Joshia Mae," she always said, "I could outcook you with both eyes closed and one hand tied behind my back."

Aunt Josh always laughed out loud at that. She knew that when Aunt Hattie started the *serious* trash talk, it meant she had gotten under Aunt Hattie's skin, usually by reminding Aunt Hattie it was *her* blueberry muffins that took the blue ribbon at the church bake-off. Me? I didn't want to get a frying pan upside the head, so I never took sides; I always stayed neutral.

For the record, you shouldn't take the epic nature of their culinary competitions to mean my aunts couldn't come together when they needed to. Aunt Josh and Aunt Hattie cooked their family's holiday dinners together for more than half a century—long past the time their kids thought they should be lifting 20-pound turkeys for 30-plus family members, never mind handling heavy, smoking-hot cast-iron pans. And they didn't come together just for their own families. In their community, Aunt Hattie and Aunt Josh were the go-to sisters: Whenever a neighbor, a friend, or a fellow church member had a need or faced a crisis, they were the first to lend a helping hand. Or I should say four helping hands.

My favorite story about their coming together, however, involves President Dwight D. Eisenhower. I shared it in *LaBelle Cuisine*, but when I was writing this book, I learned I knew only half the story. I knew that on a trip to the South, President Eisenhower stopped to visit the family Aunt Josh was working for. I also knew that when he decided to spend the night, Aunt Josh was hell-bent on cooking him breakfast the next morning. And not just any breakfast. A breakfast that would, as Aunt Josh put it, "knock Ike's socks off."

But I didn't know *why*. Or I should say I didn't know all the reasons why. For a long time, I thought the reason Aunt Josh was so insistent on cooking the president breakfast was as plain as it was simple: She wanted bragging rights. "Did you know I made pancakes for the president?" Aunt Josh would ask sweetly whenever she wanted a plum assignment at the church bake sale.

And she did want bragging rights. But as her daughter, Patricia, told me when I was writing this book, that wasn't the only reason Aunt Josh wanted to cook breakfast for the president. It wasn't even the *main* one. The main reason Aunt Josh wanted to cook President Eisenhower breakfast was because she really admired the way he handled the Little Rock school desegregation thing. That really touched her heart. See how family recipes really can teach us about our families? Even when, maybe *especially* when, we think there's nothing left to learn.

So cooking pancakes for the president was exactly what Aunt Josh did. After Ike retired for the evening, Aunt Josh called Aunt Hattie and the two of them stayed up all night cooking a soul food feast: hogshead bacon, sausage scrapple, grits and redeye gravy, pancakes and waffles, Grandmother Tempie's famous biscuits, Aunt Hattie's sweet tater bread, and, of course, Aunt Josh's blue-ribbon blueberry muffins. Both my aunts said President Eisenhower mopped his plate clean. Aunt Josh, however, said he did a whole lot more than that. "Patsy," she told me,

"that man ate second helpings of everything… and he took a bag of my blueberry muffins to go!"

I wouldn't be mad at him if he took *ten* bags of muffins, especially if what Aunt Josh told me is true. Aunt Josh said her sources told her that the president didn't get to eat a whole lot of home cooking. She said Mamie Eisenhower was from a seriously wealthy family and she had it on good authority that from the time she was a little kid, Mrs. Eisenhower's mother told her not to learn her way around a kitchen or people would expect her to cook all the time. But after Aunt Josh found out that the First Lady strongly approved of the decision to invite Marian Anderson to sing the national anthem at the president's inaugural ceremony, she said she didn't care if the First Lady couldn't boil water!

How much of this story is true I don't know. I do, however, know this: Aunt Josh's blueberry muffins are so scrumptious, there's not a person on earth who would blame the president if he took a suitcase full of them back to Washington, whoever was doing the cooking in the White House.

# Aunt Joshia Mae's Blue-Ribbon Blueberry Muffins

Bake these, and you just might become as famous for your blueberry muffins as Aunt Joshia Mae. A little lemon extract gives them an additional hint of home-baked flavor. (Today's cooks might use fresh lemon zest, but my aunts were never without a bottle of lemon extract in their kitchens.) They really are pretty much the perfect blueberry muffins—easy to make, but tender and studded with juicy berries. Aunt Joshia Mae sprinkled plain sugar over her muffins, but the large-crystal turbinado or regular decorator sugar (aka sanding sugar, the kind used for cookies) looks nice, too. If you have extra blueberries, top each muffin with a few more before baking.

Makes 8 muffins

Nonstick cooking oil spray, for the pan

One 6-ounce container (about 1⅓ cups) fresh blueberries

2 cups plus 1 tablespoon unbleached all-purpose flour

¾ cup granulated sugar

2 teaspoons baking powder

½ teaspoon salt

¾ cup whole milk

2 large eggs

¼ cup (½ stick) unsalted butter, melted and cooled slightly

1 teaspoon vanilla extract

½ teaspoon lemon extract; or finely grated zest of ½ lemon

1 tablespoon turbinado, white decorator, or more granulated sugar, for sprinkling (optional)

1. Position a rack in the center of the oven and preheat the oven to 400°F. Line 8 standard muffin cups with paper liners. Lightly spray the top of the muffin pan with the oil.

2. Toss the blueberries in 1 tablespoon of the flour. Place them in a medium-mesh sieve and shake off all of the excess flour. Set the blueberries aside.

3. Sift the remaining 2 cups flour, the granulated sugar, baking powder, and salt together into a large bowl. Whisk the milk, eggs, melted butter, vanilla, and lemon extract together in another bowl. Make a well in the center of the dry ingredients and add the milk mixture. Stir just until the batter is combined. Fold in the floured blueberries.

4. Using a ⅓-cup-capacity spring-loaded portion scoop, transfer heaping portions of the batter to the cups, being sure each portion forms a mound that rises just above the edge of the cup. Sprinkle the turbinado sugar over the muffins, if using.

5. Bake until the muffins are golden brown and a wooden toothpick inserted into the center of a muffin comes out clean, 20 to 25 minutes. Remove from the oven. Let cool in the pan for 10 minutes. Remove the muffins from the pan and serve them warm or cooled to room temperature.

# Blackberry Corn Muffins

Now, you might think, *Why do we need two berry muffin recipes in this book?* Because this one is so good that I couldn't stand to pass it up. It uses Greek yogurt, which makes the muffins extra tender, but be sure to use the low-fat and not the nonfat variety. This batter is also wonderful with blueberries instead of blackberries.

Makes 8 large muffins

Nonstick cooking oil spray, for the pan

1¼ cups unbleached all-purpose flour

1 cup yellow cornmeal, preferably stone-ground

⅓ cup plus 1 tablespoon sugar

1 teaspoon baking soda

1 teaspoon baking powder

½ teaspoon salt

1¼ cups plain low-fat Greek yogurt

½ cup whole milk

¼ cup (½ stick) unsalted butter, melted

1 large egg

½ teaspoon vanilla extract

One 6-ounce container (about 1⅓ cups) fresh blackberries or blueberries

1. Position a rack in the center of the oven and preheat the oven to 400°F. Line 8 standard muffin cups with paper liners. Lightly spray the top of the muffin pan with the oil.

2. Sift the flour, cornmeal, sugar, baking soda, baking powder, and salt together into a large bowl. Whisk the yogurt, milk, butter, egg, and vanilla together in another bowl. Make a well in the center of the dry ingredients, pour in the liquid mixture, and stir just until the batter is combined. Fold in the blackberries.

3. Using a ⅓-cup-capacity spring-loaded portion scoop, transfer the batter to the cups, being sure each portion forms a mound that rises just above the edge of the cup. Bake until the muffins are golden brown and the tops spring back when lightly pressed with a fingertip, about 25 minutes. Let cool in the pan for 10 minutes. Remove the muffins from the pan and serve warm or cooled to room temperature.

# Good Morning Muffins

These are muffins that think they are carrot cake, but they also have apple, oatmeal, and coconut flakes to make them not only high in flavor, but high in fiber as well. If you can't decide what muffin to bake, you might as well make these because they have everything in them anyway! You may be tempted to put some cream cheese frosting on top, but then they would be cupcakes and not muffins.

Makes 8 muffins

Nonstick cooking oil spray

1 cup unbleached all-purpose flour

1 teaspoon baking soda

1 teaspoon ground cinnamon

½ teaspoon fine salt

¾ cup packed light brown sugar

¾ cup canola oil

2 large eggs

1 cup coarsely grated carrots (use the large holes on a box grater)

½ cup coarsely grated tart (such as Granny Smith) apple (use the large holes on a box grater)

½ cup chopped walnuts or pecans

⅓ cup seedless raisins

⅓ cup old-fashioned (not instant) oatmeal

⅓ cup sweetened coconut flakes

1. Position a rack in the center of the oven and preheat the oven to 400°F. Line 8 standard muffin cups with paper liners. Lightly spray the top of the muffin pan with the oil.

2. Sift the flour, baking soda, cinnamon, and salt together into a large bowl. Whisk the brown sugar, oil, and eggs together in another bowl. Make a well in the center of the dry ingredients, pour in the liquid mixture, and stir just until the batter is moistened. Add the carrots, apple, walnuts, raisins, oatmeal, and coconut and mix to combine.

3. Using a ⅓-cup-capacity spring-loaded portion scoop, transfer the batter to the cups, being sure each portion forms a mound that rises just above the edge of the cup. Bake until the muffins are golden brown and the tops spring back when lightly pressed with a fingertip, 20 to 25 minutes. Let cool in the pan for 10 minutes. Remove the muffins from the pan and serve warm or cooled to room temperature.

**Good Morning Hawaii Muffins:** *Add one 8-ounce can crushed pineapple, very well drained (about ½ cup after draining) to the batter with the carrots and other final additions. The muffins may take an extra few minutes to bake.*

# Lemon Pistachio Muffins

The secret to the melting texture of these muffins is heavy cream, and they get extra citrus flavor from some lemon syrup after they come out of the oven. These are really a treat, especially with a hot cup of tea. Shelled pistachios are easy to find these days at the supermarket.

Makes 8 muffins

**MUFFINS**

Nonstick cooking oil spray

1½ cups unbleached all-purpose flour

1 cup granulated sugar

1 teaspoon baking powder

½ teaspoon salt

2 large eggs

¾ cup heavy cream

¼ cup canola or vegetable oil

Finely grated zest of 1 lemon

½ cup coarsely chopped pistachios

**SYRUP**

¼ cup fresh lemon juice

¼ cup confectioners' sugar

1. **To make the muffins:** Position a rack in the center of the oven and preheat the oven to 400°F. Line 8 standard muffin cups with paper liners. Lightly spray the top of the muffin pan with the oil.

2. Sift the flour, granulated sugar, baking powder, and salt together into a large bowl. Whisk the eggs, cream, oil, and lemon zest together in another bowl. Make a well in the center of the dry ingredients and add the egg mixture. Stir just until the batter is combined. Fold in the pistachios.

3. Using a ⅓-cup-capacity spring-loaded portion scoop, transfer the batter to the cups, being sure each portion forms a mound that rises just above the edge of the cup. Bake until the muffins are golden brown and a wooden toothpick inserted into the center of a muffin comes out clean, about 25 minutes. Remove from the oven.

4. **To make the syrup:** Whisk the lemon juice and confectioners' sugar together in a small bowl to dissolve the sugar. Drizzle and brush the glaze over the hot muffins. Let cool in the pan for 10 minutes. Remove the muffins from the pan and serve them warm or cooled to room temperature.

# Cranberry Orange Scones

Scones are supposed to be triangular, which is one way to tell them from biscuits. They are also on the sweet and rich side, as this recipe will show. Dried cranberries pair nicely with the orange, but currants are good, too. Another time, try them with coarsely chopped dried cherries.

Makes 6 scones

Finely grated zest of ½ orange

4 tablespoons fresh orange juice, divided

⅔ cup heavy cream, plus more for brushing

½ cup coarsely chopped dried cranberries

2 cups unbleached all-purpose flour, plus more for patting out the dough

3 tablespoons granulated sugar

1 tablespoon baking powder

½ teaspoon salt

6 tablespoons (¾ stick) cold unsalted butter, thinly sliced

2 teaspoons turbinado (raw) sugar (see Patti's Pointers), for topping

1. Position a rack in the center of the oven and preheat the oven to 375°F.

2. Combine the orange zest, 2 tablespoons of the orange juice, and the heavy cream in a liquid measuring cup. Toss the dried cranberries and the remaining 2 tablespoons orange juice in a small bowl. Set aside for 10 minutes.

3. Whisk the flour, granulated sugar, baking powder, and salt in a large bowl. Add the butter. Using a pastry blender or two knives, cut the butter into the flour mixture until the mixture is mostly crumbly with some pea-sized pieces of butter. Add the heavy cream mixture and stir just until moistened. Add the cranberries with their juice and stir until the dough comes together.

   Turn out the dough onto a lightly floured work surface. Pat the dough into a 7-inch round about ¾ inch thick. Using a large knife, cut the dough into 6 equal triangles. Brush very lightly with additional heavy cream and sprinkle with the turbinado sugar. Arrange the scones on an ungreased baking sheet.

4. Bake until the scones are golden brown, 20 to 25 minutes. Let cool for 10 minutes and serve warm or at room temperature.

**Patti's Pointers:** *If you don't have the turbinado sugar, just use sanding sugar (the kind for cookies) or even plain granulated sugar for the topping.*

# Pumpkin Cranberry Muffins

These hearty muffins will make you think of a crisp autumn morning with the leaves blowing around outside—just the kind of day to putter around the kitchen and bake up a batch of something delicious. It's a recipe that gives you another good reason to always have a can of pumpkin in the pantry. There will be leftover pumpkin from the can, so just freeze it for another use.

Makes 9 muffins

Nonstick cooking oil spray

1¾ cups unbleached all-purpose flour

1¾ teaspoons pumpkin pie spice (or use
   1 teaspoon ground cinnamon,
   ½ teaspoon ground ginger,
   ¼ teaspoon freshly grated or ground
   nutmeg, and ⅛ teaspoon ground
   cloves)

1 teaspoon baking soda

½ teaspoon salt

¾ cup granulated sugar

½ cup packed light brown sugar

1 cup canned pure pumpkin
   (not pumpkin pie mix)

2 large eggs, beaten to blend

¼ cup canola or vegetable oil

¼ cup water

¾ cup dried cranberries

1 tablespoon unsalted hulled
   pumpkin seeds (pepitas)

1. Position a rack in the center of the oven and preheat the oven to 400°F. Line 9 standard muffin cups with paper liners. Lightly spray the top of the muffin pan with the oil.

2. Sift the flour, pumpkin pie spice, baking soda, and salt together into a large bowl. Add the granulated and brown sugars and mix well, being sure that the brown sugar isn't lumpy. Make a well in the center of the dry ingredients and add the pumpkin, eggs, oil, and water. Stir just until the batter is combined. Fold in the cranberries.

3. Using a ⅓-cup-capacity spring-loaded portion scoop, transfer the batter to the cups, being sure each portion forms a mound that rises just above the edge of the cup. Sprinkle the pumpkin seeds onto the muffin tops.

4. Bake until the muffins are golden brown and a wooden toothpick inserted into the center of a muffin comes out clean, about 25 minutes. Let cool in the pan for 10 minutes. Remove the muffins from the pan and serve them warm or cooled to room temperature.

# Cheddar and Jalapeño Cornbread

Sometimes you want something savory for breakfast, and that's the time to make this cornbread. The creamed butter makes it a bit more cake-like than other versions, so if you like that kind of cornbread, this is the one. You can use just about any kind of corn you have on hand—cut fresh from the cob, canned, or thawed frozen.

Makes 9 servings

2 strips bacon

1 cup unbleached all-purpose flour

1 cup yellow cornmeal, preferably stone-ground

2 teaspoons baking powder

½ teaspoon salt

6 tablespoons (¾ stick) unsalted butter, at room temperature

2 tablespoons sugar

2 large eggs, at room temperature

¾ cup whole milk

½ cup plus 2 tablespoons fresh or thawed frozen corn kernels, divided

½ cup plus 2 tablespoons shredded Cheddar cheese, divided

2 teaspoons minced seeded jalapeño

1. Cook the bacon in a large skillet over medium heat, turning occasionally, until crisp and browned, 8 to 10 minutes. Transfer the bacon to paper towels to drain, reserving the bacon fat. Coarsely chop the bacon.

2. Meanwhile, position a rack in the center of the oven and preheat the oven to 400°F.

3. Whisk the flour, cornmeal, baking powder, and salt together in a medium bowl. Beat the butter and sugar together in another medium bowl with an electric mixer set on high speed until the mixture is pale, about 2 minutes. Reduce the mixer speed to low. One at a time, beat in the eggs. In thirds, alternating with two equal additions of milk, add the flour mixture, scraping down the sides of the bowl as needed. Stir in ½ cup of the corn, ½ cup of the Cheddar, the chopped bacon, and the jalapeño.

4. Pour 1 tablespoon of the bacon fat into an 8-inch square baking pan and tilt the pan to coat the bottom with the fat. Discard the remaining fat. Place the pan in the oven and bake until the pan is very hot, about 2 minutes. Spread the batter in the pan and sprinkle with the remaining Cheddar and corn.

5. Bake until the cornbread is golden brown and a wooden toothpick inserted into the center comes out clean, 25 to 30 minutes. Cool for 15 to 20 minutes. (You can cut the cornbread before this waiting period has passed, but it will crumble.) Cut into squares and serve warm or cooled to room temperature.

# Date-Walnut Bread

You can talk about fancy restaurants all you want...but in my world, nothing satisfies like the old favorites. Date nut bread—who makes that anymore? But that doesn't mean it isn't good! It is best to use fresh, soft dates here and not the pre-chopped ones. The soaking step may seem odd, but the baking soda softens the tough date skins. Coffee will not give the cake a mocha flavor but serves to give the loaf its proper dark color.

Makes 8 servings

Softened butter and flour, for the pan

1 cup pitted and diced (½-inch) dates (use a large oiled knife for chopping)

¾ cup hot brewed coffee (not dark roast)

1½ teaspoons baking soda

2 large eggs

¼ cup (½ stick) unsalted butter, melted and cooled

1¾ cups unbleached all-purpose flour

¾ cup packed light brown sugar

½ teaspoon salt

½ cup coarsely chopped walnuts

1. Position a rack in the center of the oven and preheat the oven to 350°F. Butter the inside of an 8½ by 4½-inch loaf pan. Line the bottom with waxed paper. Dust the inside of the pan with flour and tap out the excess flour.

2. Mix the dates, hot coffee, and baking soda together in a small bowl. Let the mixture stand, stirring occasionally, until completely cooled, 20 to 30 minutes. Add the eggs and melted butter and mix to combine.

3. Sift the flour, brown sugar, and salt together through a medium sieve, rubbing the sugar through the sieve to be sure the sugar is well crumbled. Add the date mixture and stir just to moisten. Fold in the walnuts. Scrape the batter into the prepared pan and smooth the top.

4. Bake until a wooden toothpick inserted into the top crack near the center of the loaf comes out clean, 50 to 60 minutes. (The dates make this quick bread moist, so it is best to test the cake in one of the top cracks for doneness, as that is the last place to bake.) Let cool on a wire rack for 15 minutes. Invert the cake onto the rack and discard the waxed paper. Turn the cake right side up and let cool completely. (The bread can be wrapped in plastic wrap and stored at room temperature for up to 3 days. In fact, it is even better if a day or two old.)

# Old-Fashioned Gingerbread with Warm Apple Compote

When the weather is chilly, few desserts are as satisfying as a chunk of warm gingerbread right from the oven. This is a classic recipe baked in an oblong pan (although a Bundt pan looks nice, too), deliciously moist and filled with the flavors of spice and molasses. It makes a large gingerbread, so you might want to keep it in mind for a party. Although it is fantastic plain (perhaps topped with ice cream or whipped cream), I like to gild the lily with warm sautéed apples.

Makes 12 servings

### GINGERBREAD

Softened butter and flour, for the pan

2½ cups unbleached all-purpose flour

2 teaspoons baking soda

2 teaspoons ground ginger

1½ teaspoons ground cinnamon

½ teaspoon ground cloves

½ teaspoon salt

½ cup (1 stick) unsalted butter, at room temperature

1 cup granulated sugar

1 cup molasses (not blackstrap)

2 large eggs, at room temperature

1 cup boiling water (see Patti's Pointers)

### APPLE COMPOTE

1 tablespoon unsalted butter

3 Golden Delicious or other cooking apples, peeled, cored, and cut into ½-inch wedges

2 tablespoons light brown sugar

2 tablespoons water

¼ teaspoon ground cinnamon

Whipped Cream (page 132), for serving

1. **To make the gingerbread:** Position a rack in the center of the oven and preheat the oven to 350°F. Butter and flour a 9 by 13-inch baking pan, tapping out the excess flour.

2. Sift the flour, baking soda, ginger, cinnamon, cloves, and salt together. Beat the butter and granulated sugar together in a large bowl with an electric mixer set at high speed until the mixture is light in color and texture, about 3 minutes. Gradually beat in the molasses. One at a time, beat in the eggs, beating well after each addition. In thirds, with the mixer on low speed, add the flour mixture, alternating with two additions of the boiling water. Pour the batter into the prepared pan.

3. Bake until a wooden toothpick inserted into the center of the gingerbread comes out clean, 35 to 40 minutes. Let cool in the pan on a wire cake rack for 15 minutes.

4. **While the gingerbread is baking, make the compote:** Melt the butter in a large skillet over medium-high heat. Add the apples and cook, stirring only occasionally, until they are lightly browned and crisp-tender, about 4 minutes. Sprinkle in the brown sugar and the 2 tablespoons water, and mix well until the sugar is melted. Stir in the cinnamon. Remove from the heat and set aside to cool for 15 to 30 minutes. The compote should be warm, not piping hot. Transfer to a serving bowl.

5. Cut the gingerbread into serving pieces and transfer to dessert plates. Top each with a spoonful of the compote and a scoop of whipped cream and serve.

**Gingerbread Bundt Cake:** *The batter can also be baked in a 10- to 12-cup decorative Bundt (fluted tube) pan for 50 minutes to 1 hour. Be sure to butter the pan well, and sprinkle the inside with dried plain bread crumbs. (Do not use flour.) This special crumb pan coating guarantees that the sticky cake will come out of the pan.*

**Patti's Pointers:** *Why does this gingerbread (and other antique recipes) call for boiling water? Back in the day, the baking soda was not pulverized well, and the hot liquid helped it to dissolve. These days, you can really get away with hot tap water.*

# Chocolate Zucchini Bread

If you've ever grown zucchini, you know that there comes a point in the summer when you think you will never use it all up. Surely this recipe was born from that necessity, but...surprise! It's really good, and not just an excuse to use zucchini. Go ahead and make the small amount of chocolate glaze to top it, or simply dust it with confectioners' sugar.

Makes 8 servings

### ZUCCHINI BREAD

Softened butter and flour, for the pan

1 ounce unsweetened chocolate, finely chopped

2 cups unbleached all-purpose flour

½ teaspoon baking soda

¼ teaspoon baking powder

½ teaspoon salt

2 large eggs, at room temperature

1 cup sugar

1 teaspoon vanilla extract

½ cup canola or vegetable oil

1⅓ cups shredded zucchini (use the large holes of a box shredder)

½ cup coarsely chopped nuts

### CHOCOLATE GLAZE

⅓ cup plus 1 tablespoon heavy cream

½ cup semisweet chocolate chips

1. **To make the bread:** Position a rack in the center of the oven and preheat the oven to 350°F. Butter the inside of an 8½ by 4½-inch loaf pan. Line the bottom with waxed paper. Dust the inside of the pan with flour and tap out the excess flour.

2. Place the chocolate in a small ramekin or custard cup. Melt the chocolate in a microwave oven set at 50% (medium) power in 30-second intervals, stirring after each interval, until smooth and melted. Or place the ramekin in a small skillet with ½ inch of barely simmering water and melt, stirring occasionally, being sure not to splash any water into the chocolate. Let the chocolate cool slightly.

3. Sift the flour, baking soda, baking powder, and salt together. Beat the eggs and sugar in a large bowl with an electric mixer set on high speed until the mixture is thick and pale yellow, about 2 minutes. Beat in the vanilla. Gradually beat in the oil, followed by the zucchini and melted chocolate. Add the flour mixture and mix just until combined. Do not overmix. Fold in the nuts. Scrape the batter (it will be thick) into the prepared pan.

4. Bake until a wooden toothpick inserted into the top crack near the center of the loaf comes out clean, 50 to 60 minutes. Let cool on a wire rack for 15 minutes. Invert the cake onto the rack and discard the waxed paper. Turn the loaf right side up and let cool completely.

5. **To make the glaze:** Bring the cream to a simmer into a small saucepan over low heat. Remove from the heat and add the chocolate chips. Let stand until the chips soften, about 3 minutes. Stir well until smooth. Place the loaf on a wire rack set over a baking sheet. Pour the glaze over the loaf. Using a metal spatula, smooth the glaze over the loaf, letting extra glaze run down the sides. Scrape up the glaze on the baking sheet and drizzle it over the loaf, this time smoothing it over the sides. Let the glaze cool. (The loaf can be wrapped in plastic wrap and stored at room temperature for up to 3 days.)

# 4 ) The Cookie Jar

In my neighborhood growing up, lucky households had a cookie jar full of treats—and the same can be said of today's families. As a kid, you often never knew what kind of treasures might be awaiting you inside the jar—would there be chewy ginger cookies, fruity jam-filled bars, or chocolatey brownies? One of the many good things about cookies is that they are in individual, bite-sized (or a little more) portions. Sometimes if I have a craving for something sweet, a single, really good homemade cookie does the trick. Of course, you have to have the willpower to not eat a dozen of them, but knowing that you ate something homemade makes up for a lot. In this chapter, I've put together some of my cookie favorites, and believe me…it was hard to narrow it down to just the ones here. There is something for everyone, be you a caramel or a chocolate lover, a fan of chocolate chip cookies, or on the search for the best lemon squares that you ever wrapped your lips around. Before making these cookies, give yourself a refresher course by reading over the tips and techniques on pages 240—242.

# Two-Fruit Almond Crumble Bars

These bar cookies are easy enough to make anytime, but pretty enough to be on your best holiday cookie platter. I make them with just one kind of fruit preserves, but here's a little trick from me to you: If you use two flavors, spread on opposite sides of the crust, you'll end up with two kinds of cookies for variety. And you'll look as if you spent twice as much time in the kitchen! This recipe uses raspberry and apricot, but try apricot and strawberry, or two different berries. If you want them to look a bit more almond-y, insert a sliced almond into the top of each baked bar.

Makes 16 bars

Softened butter and flour, for the pan

1½ cups unbleached all-purpose flour

½ cup almond meal or almond flour (see Patti's Pointers)

½ cup packed light brown sugar

¼ teaspoon salt

1 cup (2 sticks) cold unsalted butter, cut into ½-inch cubes

1 teaspoon vanilla extract

½ teaspoon almond extract

½ cup red raspberry preserves

½ cup apricot preserves

1. Position a rack in the center of the oven and preheat the oven to 350°F. Lightly butter the bottom and sides of an 8-inch square baking pan (preferably nonstick for this recipe). Fold a 14-inch-long strip of aluminum foil (preferably nonstick) lengthwise to fit into the bottom and up two sides of the pan, letting the excess foil hang over the sides as "handles." Dust the exposed sides of the pan with flour and tap out the excess.

2. Whisk the flour, almond meal, brown sugar, and salt together in a large bowl (preferably the bowl of a standing heavy-duty mixer). Add the butter and mix to coat with the flour. Blend, with the mixer set on low speed (use the paddle attachment of the standing mixer), until the mixture is combined and begins to clump, adding the vanilla and almond extracts just at the end of mixing. Set aside 1 cup of the dough.

3. Press the remaining dough evenly into the prepared pan. Spread the raspberry preserves on one half of the dough. Repeat with the apricot preserves on the opposite side. Crumble the reserved dough over the top of the preserves, letting some of the preserves peek through.

*Continued*

4. Bake until the preserves are bubbling in the center of the pan and the top is lightly browned, about 45 minutes. Let cool for a few minutes until the filling stops bubbling.

5. Run a small sharp knife around the inside of the pan to release the pastry from the sides of the pan. Let cool completely on a wire rack. Cut into 16 bars. Lift up on the foil handles to remove the bars. (The bars can be stored at room temperature in an airtight container for up to 3 days.)

**Patti's Pointers:** *More and more recipes are calling for almond meal these days, so it is not as exotic an ingredient as it used to be. You can find almond meal or almond flour at just about every supermarket. Either the brown meal (ground with the skins) or the white "flour" (made from blanched almonds) will work in this recipe. Store the almond meal in the freezer or refrigerator to keep it from turning rancid. If you prefer, grind ½ cup natural sliced almonds with ½ cup of the flour from the recipe in a food processor (or in batches in an electric coffee grinder) until it is powdery but not ground into a paste.*

*Lona and Zuri eating the cookies I baked to bribe them to let me keep Gia for the weekend.*

# Chocolate Bourbon Balls

When holiday baking time comes around, bourbon balls show up on many folks' must-have lists. One of their many positive qualities is that they are not baked. The downside is that they are best after aging for a day, so you really should wait before nibbling. Many bourbon ball recipes call for vanilla or chocolate wafers, but try chocolate grahams (which are much easier to find than chocolate wafers—and cheaper, too). Roll them in confectioners' sugar or decorate them with colored jimmies, whatever you have time for. These look especially nice in paper candy cups.

Makes about 3½ dozen balls

2¼ cups finely crushed chocolate graham crackers (from about 18 whole crackers)

1 cup very finely chopped pecans (see Patti's Pointers)

¾ cup confectioners' sugar, plus more for rolling, if desired

3 tablespoons natural unsweetened cocoa powder, such as Hershey's

3 tablespoons unsalted butter, well softened

3 tablespoons light corn syrup or honey, plus more as needed for decorating (optional)

⅓ cup plus 1 tablespoon bourbon, dark rum, or cool brewed coffee, as needed

Colored cake decorating sprinkles (jimmies), for decorating (optional)

1. With your hands, mix the cracker crumbs, pecans, confectioners' sugar, cocoa, butter, and corn syrup together in a large bowl with your hands until combined. The mixture will be sticky. Pour in enough of the bourbon to make a moist mass that holds together when rolled into a ball.

2. Dust your hands with confectioners' sugar to keep the balls from sticking. Using a level tablespoon for each, roll the mixture into balls. A few at a time, roll the balls in sifted confectioners' sugar.  Or brush each ball lightly with corn syrup or honey and then coat with the sprinkles.

Patti's Pointers: *If you have a food processor, use it to crush the crackers and chop the pecans. The pecans should be very fine but not chopped into a paste. An old-fashioned rotary nut grinder works well, too. But people have been making bourbon balls for decades by hand-chopping the pecans, so don't worry too much about this.*

# Ginger Crinkles

I love spices—especially cinnamon and ginger. If I could, I would put them in everything I bake. These cookies have crinkly tops and chewy insides. They are shaped into balls before baking—not rolled and cut into gingerbread cookies; the dough is too soft for that. In fact, be sure to chill the dough in the refrigerator before baking so it is easier to form into balls.

Makes about 3 dozen cookies

2¼ cups unbleached all-purpose flour

2 teaspoons ground ginger

1 teaspoon ground cinnamon

½ teaspoon baking powder

½ teaspoon baking soda

½ teaspoon salt

¼ teaspoon ground cloves

¾ cup (1½ sticks) unsalted butter, at room temperature

1¼ cups sugar, divided

1 large egg, at room temperature

¼ cup molasses (not blackstrap)

1. Sift the flour, ginger, cinnamon, baking powder, baking soda, salt, and cloves together. Beat the butter and 1 cup of the sugar in a large bowl with an electric mixer set at medium-high speed just until the mixture is smooth, about 2 minutes. Do not overbeat. Beat in the egg, followed by the molasses. With the mixer on low speed, gradually beat in the flour mixture. Cover the bowl and refrigerate until chilled and firm, at least 2 hours or up to 8 hours.

2. Position racks in the top third and center of the oven and preheat the oven to 350°F.

3. Using about 1 tablespoon for each, roll the dough into 1-inch balls. Put the remaining ¼ cup sugar in a small bowl and roll the balls in the sugar to coat. Place the balls about 2 inches apart on two ungreased rimmed baking sheets. (For easier cleanup, line the cookie sheets with parchment paper.) Bake, switching the positions of the cookie sheets from top to bottom and rotating front to back halfway through baking, until the cookies are lightly browned but still slightly soft when pressed in the centers, about 15 minutes. Let cool on the sheets for 3 minutes. Transfer to wire racks and let cool completely. (The cookies can be stored at room temperature in an airtight container for up to 5 days.)

# Berry Mini-Cheesecake Cups

If there is a better summer dessert for a patriotic holiday meal, I don't know what it would be. These bite-sized cheesecake cups are red, white, and blue and almost make me want to sing "The Star-Spangled Banner." When you taste them, you certainly will feel a song coming on. They are best chilled, so make room in the fridge for storage. You will need 24 miniature muffin cups measuring about 1¾ inches in diameter and 1 inch deep and mini paper liners to fit.

Makes 24 cups

### CRUST

⅔ cup graham cracker crumbs
  (from about 6 whole crackers)

1½ tablespoons sugar

3 tablespoons unsalted butter, melted

### FILLING

8 ounces cream cheese, at soft room
  temperature (see Patti's Pointers)

⅓ cup plain low-fat Greek yogurt
  (not nonfat)

⅔ cup sugar

1 large egg, beaten to blend,
  at room temperature

Finely grated zest of ½ lemon

1 teaspoon cornstarch

½ teaspoon vanilla extract

½ cup red raspberry preserves
  or red currant jelly

1 tablespoon water

About 6 ounces (1⅓ cups) fresh
  raspberries and/or blueberries

1. Position a rack in the center of the oven and preheat the oven to 350°F. Line two 12-cup mini-muffin tins with paper liners (see Patti's Pointers).

2. **To make the crust:** Mix the cracker crumbs, sugar, and melted butter in a small bowl. Divide the mixture among the cups, using about 2 teaspoons for each. Firmly press the mixture into the bottoms of the cups. Bake until the crusts are set and smell fragrant, about 8 minutes. Remove from the oven.

3. **To make the filling:** Using an electric mixer at low speed, mix the cream cheese, yogurt, sugar, egg, lemon zest, cornstarch, and vanilla in a medium bowl just until smooth. Do not overmix. Divide the cream cheese mixture among the warm cups; they will be filled to the brims.

4. Bake until the filling is puffed and feels set when a cup is gently pressed on top, about 20 minutes. Do not let the filling brown. Let cool completely in the pans.

5. Bring the preserves and water to a boil over medium heat, stirring often. Reduce the heat to medium-low and cook to reduce very slightly, about 2 minutes. Strain the

preserves through a fine-mesh wire sieve set over a bowl to remove the seeds (no need to stain the jelly).

6. Arrange the berries as desired on top of each cup. Drizzle some of the warm glaze over the berries. Refrigerate to set the glaze. (The cups can be refrigerated, uncovered, for up to 1 day.) Serve chilled, as is, or with the papers peeled off.

**Patti's Pointers:** *The cups can also be made in buttered mini-muffin tins, but they are much easier to remove if they are baked in paper liners.*

*The cream cheese should be well softened before making the cheesecake, so let it stand at room temperature for at least 2 hours. You can speed this up by putting the wrapped cheese (out of its box) on a baking sheet or in a metal (not cast-iron) skillet. Strange science...but it works! It's a good trick for defrosting other items, too, especially meats.*

# The Very Best Lemon Bars

This wonderful recipe shows that you can take a so-called familiar recipe and keep tweaking and tweaking it to make it even better than when you started. These bars have a tender and buttery crust topped with a thicker-than-usual layer of tangier-than-usual lemon topping. It took me a few tries to get them just right, but now they are truly perfect and I am sharing the fruits of my labor (pun intended) with you. Because the lemon topping is extra-sticky, line the entire pan with parchment paper so the pastry comes out easily.

Makes 9 bars

Softened butter and flour, for the pan

### CRUST

1 cup unbleached all-purpose flour

¼ cup confectioners' sugar

⅛ teaspoon salt

½ cup (1 stick) unsalted butter, thinly sliced, at room temperature

### FILLING

1½ cups granulated sugar

4 large eggs

Finely grated zest of 1 large lemon (about 1 tablespoon)

½ cup fresh lemon juice

⅓ cup unbleached all-purpose flour

Confectioners' sugar, for sifting

1. Position a rack in the center of the oven and preheat the oven to 350°F. Lightly butter an 8-inch square nonstick baking pan. Fold a 14-inch-long strip of aluminum foil (preferably nonstick) or parchment paper lengthwise to fit into the bottom and up two sides of the pan. Repeat on the opposite sides of the pan. Let the excess foil hang over the sides as "handles." Butter the foil in the pan, too. Coat the inside of the pan with flour and tap out the excess flour.

2. **To make the crust:** Whisk the flour, confectioners' sugar, and salt together in a large bowl. Add the butter and stir to coat with the flour mixture. Using your knuckles, knead and work the ingredients in the bowl until they make a smooth dough. Crumble the dough into the prepared pan and press it into an even layer with your fingertips. Freeze for 15 minutes. Bake until the crust is golden brown, about 15 minutes. Remove from the oven.

3. **To make the filling:** Whisk the granulated sugar, eggs, lemon zest and juice, and flour together until smooth in a medium bowl. Pour over the hot crust. Return to the oven. Bake until the filling is lightly browned and moves as a unit when the pan is gently shaken, 20 to 25 minutes.

*Continued*

4. Run a small sharp knife around the inside of the pan to loosen the pastry from the pan. Let the pastry cool in the pan on a wire rack for about 30 minutes. Lift up on the foil handles to remove the pastry in one piece. Return to the rack. Let cool completely.

5. Using a long, sharp knife, cut the pastry into 9 equal bars, peeling away and discarding the foil. Just before serving, sift confectioners' sugar over the bars.

# Millionaire's Shortbread

A bedtime story for dessert fans (you know who you are): There once was a millionaire who loved sweets. Shortbread was his favorite cookie, but it just wasn't sweet enough for his taste. So his cook invented these yummy bites, with a cookie bottom, a thick caramel filling, and a chocolate topping. One of the nicest attributes of the cookies is their richness—cut them on the small side, and you will get a lot of servings out of a single pan. The recipe may look long, but it is not hard to make—I just gave detailed instructions in case the words *caramel* and *candy thermometer* scare you, like they do a lot of people.

Makes 18 cookies

Softened butter and flour, for the pan

**CRUST**

1 cup all-purpose flour

¼ cup packed light brown sugar

¼ teaspoon salt

½ cup (1 stick) unsalted butter, thinly sliced, at room temperature

**FILLING**

One 14-ounce can condensed milk

½ cup packed light brown sugar

6 tablespoons (¾ stick) unsalted butter, thinly sliced

2 tablespoons light corn syrup

1 teaspoon vanilla extract

⅛ teaspoon salt

**TOPPING**

1 cup (6 ounces) semisweet chocolate morsels

2 teaspoons vegetable shortening or coconut oil

1. Position a rack in the center of the oven and preheat the oven to 350°F. Lightly butter an 8-inch square nonstick baking pan. Fold a 14-inch-long strip of aluminum foil (preferably nonstick) lengthwise to fit into the bottom and up two sides of the pan, letting the excess foil hang over the sides as "handles." Butter the foil in the pan, too. Dust the inside of the pan with flour and tap out the excess flour.

2. **To make the crust:** Combine the flour, brown sugar, and salt in a medium bowl, crumbling the brown sugar well with your fingers. Add the butter and stir to coat with the flour mixture. Using your knuckles, knead and work the ingredients in the bowl until they make a smooth dough. Crumble the dough into the prepared pan and press it into an even layer with your fingertips. Freeze for 15 minutes. Bake until the crust is crisp and nicely browned, 15 to 20 minutes. Transfer to a wire rack and let cool completely.

*Continued on page 105*

3. **To make the filling:** Combine the condensed milk, brown sugar, butter, and corn syrup in a heavy medium saucepan. Stirring constantly to keep the mixture from scorching, bring to a boil over medium heat. Reduce the heat to medium-low and continue cooking at a moderate boil, stirring constantly, until the filling is thickened, about 5 minutes. This timing usually does the trick, but here is another test for doneness: When a wooden spoon is pulled through the filling in the saucepan, you will be able to see the pan bottom for a brief second. One more test: Drop about 1 teaspoon of the filling into a glass of ice water. If you can gather up the filling into a soft, squishy ball (234°F on a candy thermometer), it is done. Remove from the heat and stir in the vanilla and salt. Pour over the crust, spreading in an even layer. Refrigerate, uncovered, until the filling is chilled and firm, about 2 hours.

4. **To make the topping:** Heat the chocolate and shortening together, stirring occasionally, in the top part of a double boiler set over very hot but not simmering water on low heat, until melted and smooth. Remove from the heat. Let the topping cool for 5 minutes, stirring occasionally.

5. Run a small sharp knife around the inside of the pan to release the pastry. Pull up on the foil handles to remove the pastry from the pan in a single piece. Place the pastry on a baking sheet. Pour the chocolate topping over the caramel filling. Preferably using a small offset metal spatula or the back of a spoon, evenly spread the topping to the edges of the filling. Refrigerate the pastry until the chocolate is firm, about 30 minutes.

6. Using a large sharp knife, cut the pastry into 18 equal bars. Serve chilled or at room temperature. (The cookies can be refrigerated in an airtight container, the layers separated by parchment paper or waxed paper, for up to 5 days.)

# Caramel and Pecan Turtle Brownies

Now, you may think you never met a brownie you didn't like, but these are brownies to *LOVE*. These chunky bars are the perfect combination of cakey and fudgy, and have a topping of caramel, pecans, and chocolate chips to remind you of gooey turtle candies. This is another recipe to have on file when you need a treat that you can whip up in no time but still have everyone oohing and aahing over your baking skills.

Makes 9 brownies

Softened butter and flour, for the pan

½ cup (1 stick) unsalted butter, cut into tablespoons

1½ cups semisweet chocolate chips, divided

½ cup packed light brown sugar

2 large eggs, at room temperature

1 teaspoon vanilla extract

1 cup unbleached all-purpose flour

¼ teaspoon baking soda

¼ teaspoon salt

8 caramel candies, coarsely chopped

1 tablespoon heavy cream

⅔ cup coarsely chopped pecans

1. Position a rack in the center of the oven and preheat the oven to 350°F. Lightly butter the bottom and sides of an 8-inch square baking pan. Fold a 14-inch-long strip of aluminum foil (preferably nonstick) lengthwise to fit into the bottom and up two sides of the pan, letting the excess foil hang over the sides as "handles." Dust the exposed sides of the pan with flour and tap out the excess.

2. Melt the butter in a medium saucepan over medium heat. Remove from the heat and add 1 cup of the chocolate chips. Let stand until the chips soften, about 3 minutes. Whisk until the chocolate is melted and the mixture is smooth. Add the brown sugar and whisk well. One at a time, whisk in the eggs, followed by the vanilla. Add the flour, baking soda, and salt and stir until smooth. Scrape into the pan and smooth the top.

3. Bake until a wooden toothpick inserted into the center of the pastry comes out with a few clinging crumbs, 25 to 30 minutes. Transfer to a wire rack and let cool for about 10 minutes.

4. Heat the caramels and heavy cream in a small heavy saucepan over low heat, stirring often, until the caramels melt and the mixture is smooth, about 4 minutes. Drizzle the caramel mixture over the pastry. Sprinkle with the pecans and the remaining chips. Let the pastry cool completely in the pan.

5. Run a small sharp knife around the inside of the pan to release the pastry from the sides of the pan. Lift up on the foil handles to remove the pastry. Cut into 9 bars. (The bars can be stored at room temperature in an airtight container for up to 3 days.)

# Graceful Stir-It-Up Lace Cookies

Truly the easiest cookies on the planet…just stir 'em up and bake 'em. These are very buttery and crisp, and a good way to balance the selection on a holiday cookie tray that has heavier offerings. Because you can bake only a few cookies at a time per sheet, you might want to have extra pans to speed up the process (as the sheets must cool between batches).

Makes about 2 dozen cookies

Softened butter and flour, for the pans

½ cup (1 stick) unsalted butter

2 tablespoons light cream or half-and-half

¾ cup old-fashioned (rolled) oatmeal

½ cup sugar

¼ cup unbleached all-purpose flour

¼ teaspoon salt

1. Position racks in the top third and center of the oven and preheat the oven to 350°F. Butter and flour two large rimmed baking sheets. (Or line the sheets with parchment paper or silicone baking mats.)

2. Melt the butter in a medium saucepan over medium heat. Stir in the cream. Add the oatmeal, sugar, flour, and salt and bring just to a boil, stirring often. Remove from the heat and let cool for about 3 minutes. Stir well again.

3. Using a rounded measuring teaspoon for each cookie, drop the batter about 4 inches apart onto the prepared baking sheets. These cookies will spread a lot (see Patti's Pointers). Bake until the cookies are lacy and evenly golden brown, switching the sheets from top to bottom and rotating front to back halfway through baking, 10 to 12 minutes. Remove from the oven. Let the cookies cool and crisp on the sheets, about 5 minutes. Using a thin metal spatula, carefully transfer the delicate cookies to a platter. Repeat with the remaining dough, using completely cooled and freshly greased and floured sheets for each batch. (The cookies can be cooled and stored in an airtight container, with folded paper towels between the layers to protect the cookies from breaking, for up to 5 days.)

**Patti's Pointers:** *It's a good idea to bake a test batch to judge how many finished cookies will fit on your sheets. Half-sheet pans, measuring about 18 by 13 inches, will hold 6 cookies. Smaller pans won't hold as many.*

*This recipe is a good argument for using parchment paper or silicone baking mats so you don't have to wash the sheets between batches.*

# Oatmeal and Chocolate Chip Blondies

I love chocolate chip cookies as much as the next person, but sometimes I don't feel like dealing with dropping the cookie dough on a baking sheet. That's when I make these bars, which taste like your favorite oatmeal-chip cookie and are guaranteed to be chewy and moist. If you want to increase the butterscotch-like flavor, go for the optional icing.

Makes 12 blondies

Softened butter and flour, for the pan

1 cup old-fashioned (rolled) oatmeal, divided

2½ cups unbleached all-purpose flour

1 teaspoon baking powder

½ teaspoon salt

¼ teaspoon baking soda

1 cup (2 sticks) unsalted butter, at room temperature

1⅔ cups packed light brown sugar

2 large eggs, at room temperature

2 teaspoons vanilla extract

1 cup (6 ounces) semisweet chocolate chips

1 cup (4 ounces) coarsely chopped pecans

1 cup (6 ounces) butterscotch chips, for icing (optional)

1. Position a rack in the center of the oven and preheat the oven to 350°F. Lightly butter an 11 by 8½-inch baking pan. Line the pan with a 16-inch length of aluminum foil, preferably nonstick, folding the foil lengthwise to fit into the bottom and up the two short sides of the pan. Fold the foil hanging over the two ends to make "handles." Butter the foil and flour the inside of the pan, tapping out the excess flour.

2. Process ½ cup of the oatmeal in a blender or food processor until finely ground into flour. Transfer to a medium bowl and add the remaining oatmeal. Sift the flour, baking powder, salt, and baking soda together through a sieve into the bowl.

3. Beat the butter with a handheld electric mixer on high speed in a large bowl until smooth, about 1 minute. Gradually beat in the brown sugar and beat until the mixture is light in color and texture, scraping down the bowl often, about 2 minutes. One at a time, beat in the eggs, followed by the vanilla. Stir in the flour mixture, just until combined. Mix in the chocolate chips and pecans. Spread the dough evenly in the pan.

4. Bake until the top is golden brown and a wooden toothpick inserted into the center comes out clean, about 35 minutes. Transfer to a wire cake rack. If desired, sprinkle the butterscotch chips over the top of the warm pastry and let them soften and melt for 5 minutes. Using an offset metal spatula, spread the melted chips into a thin layer. Let the blondies cool completely.

5. Lift up on the foil handles to remove the blondies in one piece. Peel off and discard the foil. Cut into 12 bars. (The blondies can be stored in an airtight container at room temperature for up to 3 days.)

# Sprinkledoodles

Snickerdoodles are very easy cookies—make balls of dough, roll in sugar, and bake. They are usually flavored with cinnamon, but I love my spices, so I also add some nutmeg and cloves. The only problem with them is that they look a little plain. So to jazz them up, I roll them in colored sprinkles. Hence, *sprinkle*doodles. It's a simple trick, and you can change the colors for various holidays—red and green for Christmas is a no-brainer.

Makes about 3½ dozen cookies

2¾ cups unbleached all-purpose flour

2 teaspoons cream of tartar
  (see Patti's Pointers)

1 teaspoon baking soda

1½ teaspoons ground cinnamon

½ teaspoon freshly grated nutmeg

½ teaspoon salt

¼ teaspoon ground cloves

1 cup (2 sticks) unsalted butter,
  at room temperature

1½ cups sugar

2 large eggs, at room temperature

1 teaspoon vanilla extract

About ⅔ cup multicolored sprinkles
  (jimmies), for decorating

1.  Sift the flour, cream of tartar, baking soda, cinnamon, nutmeg, salt, and cloves together. Cream the butter and sugar together in a medium bowl with an electric mixer set on high speed. One at a time, beat in the eggs and then the vanilla. Gradually stir in the flour mixture. Cover and refrigerate until the dough is chilled, at least 1 hour or up to 2 hours.

2.  Position racks in the top third and center of the oven and preheat the oven to 350°F. Have two large ungreased rimmed baking sheets ready.

3.  Using a tablespoon for each cookie (a 1-tablespoon portion scoop works best), shape the dough into 1-inch balls. Transfer the balls to a baking sheet and freeze until chilled, 10 to 15 minutes. (This trick keeps the cookies from spreading too much during baking.)

4.  One at a time, press one side of a dough ball into the sprinkles, being sure they adhere. Reshape the dough into a ball. Place, sprinkle-side up, on a baking sheet. Repeat, spacing the balls about 2 inches apart on the two sheets. Bake, switching the position of the baking sheets from top to bottom and rotating front to back halfway through baking, until the edges of the cookies are barely browned, 15 to 18 minutes. Cool on the baking sheets for 5 minutes. Transfer to wire cake racks and cool completely.

**Patti's Pointers:** *This is an old cookie recipe, and before folks could buy baking powder easily in stores, they used a combination of cream of tartar and baking soda as leavening. If you don't have cream of tartar (and not everyone has it in their pantry), substitute 1 tablespoon baking powder for the cream of tartar and baking soda mixture.*

# 5 ) *Love Me Tender Pies, Cobblers, and More*

A culinary match made in heaven, sweet and tender fruit and rich pastry have had a long-standing romance. This beloved group of desserts plays a special role in my memories of my family's cooking. Instead of the popular biscuit-style cobbler (not that there is anything wrong with that), my relatives love the triple-layer version made with apples and peaches with *extra* pastry. And when I see a raspberry pie, its juices bubbling up through its lattice crust, it brings me right back to my aunt Hattie Mae and the pie that made her famous for miles around. I always make the most of fruit in season, and when I am in the Bahamas, I can't resist baking up a pineapple pie. I've extended the fruit and pastry theme a bit to one of my own personal specialties, sweet potato pie, and a recipe that I have been tweaking ever since Chubby—that's what everybody called my mother— taught me how to make her divine version. Be sure to read the tips and techniques for pies and cobblers on pages 242–245.

# Slab Apple Pie

Just thinking about a plump, round apple pie is enough to give most people hunger pangs. However, for a party, a big oblong pie that you can cut into rectangles (large or small, depending on what other desserts are being served) is the way to go. This one has a bunch of details that make it extra-special—some butter in the dough, cornflakes on the bottom crust to protect that area from the apples' juices, and a nice shiny glaze.

Makes 12 servings

**SLAB PIE DOUGH**

3 cups unbleached all-purpose flour

¾ teaspoon salt

¾ cup chilled vegetable shortening, cut into ½-inch cubes

½ cup (1 stick) unsalted butter, cut into ½-inch cubes

1 large egg, separated

About ⅔ cup whole milk, as needed

2½ cups cornflakes, crushed

1½ pounds Golden Delicious apples, peeled, cored, and thinly sliced

1½ pounds Granny Smith apples, peeled, cored, and thinly sliced

½ cup granulated sugar

½ teaspoon ground cinnamon

2 tablespoons unsalted butter, thinly sliced

**THIN SUGAR GLAZE**

1 cup confectioners' sugar

½ teaspoon vanilla extract

1 tablespoon boiling water, as needed

1. **To make the dough:** Whisk the flour and salt to combine in a large bowl. Using a pastry blender or two knives, cut in the vegetable shortening and cubed butter until the mixture resembles coarse cornmeal. Mix the egg yolk and enough milk to make ¾ cup liquid. Gradually stir the milk into the flour to make a dough that clumps together (you may not need all of the milk). Gather up the dough and divide it into two portions, one slightly larger than the other. Shape each portion of dough into a thick rectangle and wrap in plastic wrap. Refrigerate until chilled, about 1 hour. (The dough can be made up to 2 days ahead. Let stand at room temperature for about 10 minutes before rolling out.)

2. Position a rack in the center of the oven and preheat the oven to 375°F.

3. On a lightly floured surface, roll out the larger dough portion into a thin 17 by 12-inch rectangle. Transfer to a 15 by 10 by 1-inch jelly roll pan, letting the excess hang over the edges. If the dough cracks, just press it back together. Distribute the cornflakes evenly over the dough. Arrange the two kinds of apples, mixing them up in a layer over the cornflakes. Sprinkle with the granulated sugar and cinnamon, then dot with the sliced butter. Roll out the smaller dough portion into a thin 16 by 11-inch rectangle and place over the apples. Again, don't worry if the dough cracks; just patch it up. Pinch the edges of the dough together to seal. Cut a few slits in the top of the dough. Beat the egg white until foamy and brush it lightly over the top crust.

4. Bake until the crust is golden brown and the apples feel tender when pierced through the slits in the crust with the tip of a small knife, about 45 minutes. Cool completely on a wire rack.

5. **When the pie is cool, make the glaze:** Sift the confectioners' sugar into a small bowl. Add the vanilla. Stir in enough boiling water to make a glaze about the consistency of heavy cream. Drizzle the glaze over the pie, and then brush it into a thin layer with a pastry brush. Let the glaze set, about 30 minutes. To serve, cut the pie into large rectangles.

# Cherry Crumble Pie

Who doesn't love a great cherry pie? This contender has a streusel topping to differentiate it from the standard double-crust model. Hold out for sour cherries, not the sweet Bings that are so good to eat out of the bag. Sour cherries (sometimes called pie cherries) are not easy to find fresh, but the good news is that the canned ones are excellent and can be found at most supermarkets.

Makes 8 servings

Flour, for rolling the dough

Patti's Favorite Pie Dough (page 151)

**CRUMBLE TOPPING**

1¼ cups unbleached all-purpose flour

2 tablespoons light brown sugar

2 tablespoons granulated sugar

½ teaspoon ground cinnamon

6 tablespoons (¾ stick) unsalted butter, melted

**FILLING**

Three 15-ounce cans sour cherries (see Patti's Pointers) in water or juice (not syrup)

3 tablespoons cornstarch

⅓ cup granulated sugar

½ teaspoon vanilla extract

¼ teaspoon almond extract

1 tablespoon cold unsalted butter, cut into small cubes

1. On a lightly floured work surface, roll out the dough to a 12-inch round about ⅛ inch thick. Fit into a 9-inch pie pan. Fold the edge of the dough under so the fold meets the edge of the pan. Flute the dough. Freeze the lined pie pan to chill well while making the topping and filling. You don't have to cover the crust.

2. **To make the topping:** Mix the flour, brown and granulated sugars, and cinnamon in a medium bowl. Add the melted butter and stir until well combined. Press into a mass. Set the topping aside.

3. **To make the filling:** Drain the cherries well over a medium bowl, reserving the liquid. Transfer ½ cup of the liquid to a medium saucepan. Sprinkle in the cornstarch and whisk to dissolve. Whisk in the granulated sugar. Bring to a simmer over medium heat, whisking almost constantly, until the mixture is thick and boiling. Remove from the heat. Stir in the drained cherries—this will cool the liquid mixture down. Stir in the vanilla and almond extracts. Cool completely.

4. Position a rack in the bottom third of the oven and preheat the oven to 375°F. Line a large rimmed baking sheet with aluminum foil (this will help catch any filling overflow).

*Continued*

5. Pour the filling into the chilled piecrust. Dot with the cubed butter. Crumble the topping evenly over the filling. Place the pan on the baking sheet.

6. Bake for 15 minutes. Reduce the oven temperature to 350°F. Continue baking until the topping is golden brown and the filling is bubbling up through the crust near the center, about 1¼ hours more. (Thick fruit pies like this one always take a long time to cook through, so hang in there.) If the topping is getting too brown, tent the pie with aluminum foil.

7. Let the pie cool completely on a wire rack. Be patient—this usually takes at least 4 hours. Cut into slices and serve.

**Patti's Pointers:** *If you find fresh sour cherries during their short early summer season, substitute 5 cups pitted sour cherries for the canned or bottled ones. Increase the sugar to 1 cup and just mix all of the filling ingredients together, eliminating the step of boiling the canning liquid with the cornstarch.*

# Orange Chiffon Pie in Chocolate Crust

In food, the word *chiffon* has come to mean anything delicate in texture—there are chiffon cakes, like the one on page 50, and this typically light-as-a-feather chilled pie. The combination of orange and chocolate is very refreshing. If you wish, for a fancier citrus flavor, substitute 1 tablespoon orange liqueur (such as Grand Marnier or triple sec) for an equal amount of the orange juice and eliminate the optional orange extract.

Makes 8 servings

**CHOCOLATE GRAHAM CRUST**

1¼ cups crushed chocolate graham crackers (from 9 whole crackers)

¼ cup (½ stick) unsalted butter, melted

3 tablespoons granulated sugar

**FILLING**

2 navel oranges

1½ teaspoons unflavored gelatin powder

4 large eggs, separated, at room temperature

¾ cup granulated sugar, divided

1 tablespoon fresh lemon juice

½ teaspoon orange extract or 1 teaspoon orange oil (optional)

**TOPPING**

1 cup heavy cream

2 tablespoons confectioners' sugar

½ teaspoon vanilla extract

Chocolate curls or additional grated orange zest, for garnish

1. Position a rack in the center of the oven and preheat the oven to 350°F.

2. **To make the crust:** Combine the cracker crumbs, melted butter, and granulated sugar in a medium bowl. Press firmly and evenly onto the bottom and up the sides of a 9-inch pie pan.

3. Place the pan on a rimmed baking sheet. Bake until the crust smells fragrant and looks set, 10 to 12 minutes. Transfer to a wire rack and cool completely.

4. **To make the filling:** Finely grate the zest from one of the oranges and set aside. Juice the oranges; you should have ¾ cup of juice.

5. Sprinkle the gelatin over ¼ cup of the orange juice in a small ramekin or custard cup. Let stand until the gelatin softens, about 5 minutes.

6. Meanwhile, place a wire sieve over a medium bowl near the stove. Whisk the 4 yolks, ½ cup of the granulated sugar, the lemon juice, and the remaining ½ cup orange juice together in a small heavy saucepan. Cook over medium-low heat, whisking constantly, until the sugar dissolves. Change from the whisk to a heatproof spatula. Continue to cook, stirring constantly and being sure to reach the corners and sides of the saucepan,

until the curd is steaming and your finger can cut a swath through the mixture on the spatula, 1 to 2 minutes. (The curd will read 190°F on an instant-read thermometer.) Do not let the curd come to a simmer. Remove from the heat. Immediately add the softened gelatin and stir until it is completely dissolved. Strain through the sieve to remove any bits of cooked egg. Stir in the orange zest. Stir in the orange extract, if using. Place the bowl in a larger bowl of iced water. Let the curd stand, stirring occasionally, until cool and thickened but not set, 5 to 10 minutes.

7. Whip the egg whites in a medium bowl with an electric mixer set on high speed until soft peaks form. Gradually beat in the remaining ¼ cup granulated sugar and whip until the whites form stiff, shiny peaks. Stir one quarter of the whites into the orange mixture and then fold in the remaining whites. Spread in the cooled crust. Cover with plastic wrap and refrigerate until set, at least 1 hour or up to 2 days.

8. **To make the topping:** Whip the heavy cream, confectioners' sugar, and vanilla in a chilled medium bowl with an electric mixer set on high speed until stiff. Spread over the filling. Garnish with chocolate curls, slice, and serve chilled.

# Aunt Hattie Mae's Raspberry Pie

My aunt Hattie Mae was a magician in the kitchen. Her dishes were famous all over Georgia, where for decades she ran the kitchens—and the households—of what she affectionately called "my rich white folk families." Because Aunt Hattie Mae genuinely loved her employers, I'm not going to reveal the lengths to which they would go to secure her culinary services. (Suffice it to say that on more than one occasion, guns were involved.) I will, however, say this: Aunt Hattie Mae's cooking turned rational, levelheaded, normally sensible people into lunatics.

You wouldn't believe the bribes her cooking inspired: Six months' salary to cater a daughter's wedding. (The father of the bride wanted to offer a full year.) The car of her choice for a summer of Sunday suppers. (Luxury brands—Mercedes and Cadillac included—were actively encouraged.) My favorite bribe came from the young newlywed who offered Aunt Hattie Mae an all-expense-paid trip anywhere she wanted to go, *anywhere in the world*, for a few cooking lessons. (The young bride wanted to know how to make the fried chicken she swore made her husband see Jesus.)

Among Aunt Hattie Mae's friends and neighbors, however, it was a sweet dish that sent folks over the edge: her raspberry pie. It was so delectable, so off-the-chain delicious, it caused the most upstanding men and women of the community to lie without shame, guilt, or remorse. If, for example, word leaked that Aunt Hattie Mae was baking her raspberry pie for her church's sick and shut-ins, half the deacons suddenly came down with a bad case of the flu. Or if Aunt Hattie was baking it for a deceased neighbor's funeral reception, at least half a dozen people, people who never even met the dearly departed, showed up at the funeral. I kid you not.

It pains me a little to say this, but, in the interest of total honesty, I must: You'll have to buy your raspberries at their freshest and sweetest or your pie won't turn out like Aunt Hattie Mae's. At least not exactly. (See Patti's Pointers on page 124.) Aunt Hattie grew her own raspberries, and her skill at picking them at the exact right moment, the moment they would yield pure pie perfection, was legendary. Looking back, I believe it was downright telepathic. Aunt Hattie was the raspberry whisperer.

When I was writing this cookbook, her daughter, Penny, reminded me that Aunt Hattie Mae could just look at a bunch of raspberries and tell you exactly, precisely, how many days they needed to ripen. We always joke that if the Beatles had ever tasted Aunt Hattie Mae's raspberry pie, the Fab Four would have been singing "Raspberry Fields Forever."

Now, I know many, many people who don't possess Aunt Hattie's raspberry genius but who make her famous pie every summer nonetheless. I also know why. Because if you follow Aunt Hattie's recipe, the pie will always be delicious; it will never disappoint. Even better, each time you bake it, you'll get a little closer to developing that raspberry genius gene Aunt Hattie was born with.

# Aunt Hattie Mae's Raspberry Pie

When I watch my cooking competition shows, I have to wonder why those people use so many ingredients! More isn't always better. (Unless, of course, we're talking about shoes!) Aunt Hattie Mae could turn a handful of groceries into something incredible. I admit…it takes practice. So get to baking and bring this gorgeous pie, dripping with sweet red juices, to your table.

Makes 8 servings

1 cup sugar

⅓ cup cornstarch

Four 6-ounce containers (5 cups) fresh raspberries

2 tablespoons unsalted butter, cut into small cubes

Double-Crust Pie Dough (variation of Patti's Favorite Pie Dough, page 151)

Flour, for rolling out the dough

Whipped Cream (page 132) or vanilla ice cream, for serving

1. Position a rack in the center of the oven and preheat the oven to 400°F. Line a large rimmed baking sheet with aluminum foil (this will help catch any filling overflow) and place it in the oven.

2. Whisk the sugar and cornstarch together well in a bowl. Add the raspberries and stir gently but thoroughly. Stir in the butter.

3. Roll out the larger portion of dough on a lightly floured surface into a round about 13 inches in diameter and ⅛ inch thick. Fit the dough into a 9-inch pie pan. Trim the overhanging dough to a ½-inch overhang. Spread the filling in the pie shell.

4. Roll out the second portion of dough into a round about 9 inches in diameter and ⅛ inch thick. Using a pizza wheel or a sharp knife and a ruler, cut the dough into ¾-inch-wide strips. Crisscross the strips on the filling into a lattice. Fold the bottom crust over so the edge of the fold is flush with the edge of the pan and the ends of the strips are covered. Flute the dough edge.

5. Place the pie on the hot baking sheet in the oven. Bake for 15 minutes. Reduce the heat to 375°F and continue baking until the filling is bubbling in the center and the pie is golden brown, about 1¼ hours. (This kind of thick fruit pie takes a long time to bake through, so be patient.) If the piecrust is browning too quickly, tent it with aluminum foil. Transfer the pie to a wire rack and let cool completely. Slice and serve with the whipped cream.

**Patti's Pointers:** *Every baker covets the ideal of a perfect slice of pie with firm but juicy filling. The truth is that the juiciness and the acidity of the fruit change throughout the season, and these two factors affect how the thickener sets. So if your filling is a little loose, don't blame yourself—blame Mother Nature.*

# Patti's Perfect Pineapple Custard Pie

If you've never had a fresh pineapple pie, you're in for a treat. Fresh pineapple on its own is fab-u-lous. But in a pie, it's pure deliciousness. The delicious-on-its-own part was brought home to me when I was picking up lunch one afternoon at my favorite spot. Or I should say my favorite spot for fresh fish: the dock near my beach house in the Bahamas. And when I say fresh, I mean *fresh*. The local fishermen bring in their catches a few times a day; so a few hours before my lunch is on my plate, it's still swimming in the sea.

One afternoon, as I was waiting for the boats to come in, I started chatting with one of the locals about the best place to get conch salad, an island specialty I'd been craving since I arrived. (She knew where to get conch chili!) One thing led to another, and, before I knew it, Girlfriend was inviting me to go with her to "the island's best pick-your-own pineapple place."

Now, I know she was just being friendly. That, and showing some completely justified hometown pride: Pineapples are to the island of Eleuthera what cheesesteaks are to Philly. Even so, it took me all of two seconds to decline. Pineapple-picking? In the island sun? *Puhleeeeze.* Either my thoughts showed all over my face, or I accidentally said them out loud, because when I said, "Thanks, but no thanks," Girlfriend looked so crushed I felt the need to explain.

It wasn't personal, I told her. In fact, I thought she was sweet as pie (pun intended). But in my world, doing *anything* in the blazing-hot sun is a serious no-no. Lest Girlfriend think I was blowing smoke up her sundress to spare her feelings,

I pointed to my *wiiiiiiiiiide*-brimmed hat. (That thing has a 24-inch circumference, I kid you not.) She wasn't moved. "But ma'am," she said, looking equal parts confused and crushed, "the sun fills every corner of this island, which you *said* you love. The sun and the sea, they're our *identity*." What can I say? Girlfriend had a point. Plus, she was so young and so sweet, I really wanted to give her a fuller explanation, even if it was going to be a little complicated. So before the boats came in with my lunch, I dove in.

I started with the basics: How things aren't always as they seem—how I might be standing on the docks in the hot sun, but I was leaving in an air-conditioned car heading back to my air-conditioned kitchen—and wound up with the not-so-basics: How different people fall in love for different reasons. (Lord, how I wish I knew *that* at her age.) Yes, I said, most people *do* come to the island for the turquoise water and pink-sandy beaches. But that's not what hooked me. I fell in love with the peace and quiet (no cruise ships, no condos, no crowds), the food (hence me standing here on the dock in the sun with her), and the weather (average high temps are in the mid-70s to mid-80s, and ever since menopause hit, I can't handle anything higher).

When I finished, Girlfriend *said* she understood. But it was clear she didn't. Not really. By then, however, we could see the boats heading in, so we made a mutual, if unspoken, pact to change the subject. As we waited for the ships to dock, we chatted about everything *but* pineapples: Lenny Kravitz (Boyfriend has a recording studio on the island and she was seriously crushing on him), Martha Stewart (she'd heard that she was going to be visiting), and if she knew where I could find fresh arugula to pair with my fish (same place as the pineapples, natch).

Why did I go there? Under the quit-while-you're-behind theory, I paid for my grouper, pulled my hat over my eyes, and headed home to my air-conditioned kitchen. That's my story and I'm sticking to it, I don't care how many people say they saw me picking/buying pineapples at the Island Farm. Maybe I was, and maybe I wasn't. Maybe it's shore lore and maybe it's the gospel truth. I'm not saying. I will, however, say this: That evening, I had the most amazing arugula salad with my grouper…and the sweetest pineapple I've ever tasted for dessert. And oh yeah,

the next morning I made the first version of this fabulous pie.

When you can get your hands on fresh pineapple (store-bought is just fine), give this recipe a try. I'm betting it will make you feel all breezy days / beachy nights. Especially if you rock out to some Lenny Kravitz while making it.

Hey Martha, the next time you're in Eleuthera, give me a shout. I know a bunch of stuff about the island few non-natives do. Like where the locals go for the most amazing conch chili you will ever put in your mouth. And the best place to catch a Lenny Kravitz jam session / beach sighting. Shirtless if you're lucky! I may be 73, but I still like to party like a rock star.

# Patti's Perfect Pineapple Pudding Pie

This is a great recipe to use if you have a pineapple that is thinking about becoming too ripe…as often happens to me when I'm vacationing in the Bahamas. It takes only a few ingredients and bakes into a creamy custard with bits of sweet-tart pineapple running through it. It turns out so delicious, in fact, the next time I'm on the island, I'm going to invite Lenny Kravitz over for a slice!

Makes 8 servings

1 ripe pineapple, peeled, cored, and eyes removed

½ cup sugar

¼ cup cornstarch

4 large eggs

2 tablespoons fresh lemon juice

1 teaspoon vanilla extract

2 tablespoons chilled unsalted butter, cut into ½-inch cubes

Flour, for rolling out the dough

Double-Crust Pie Dough (variation of Patti's Favorite Pie Dough, page 151)

1.  Position a rack in the center of the oven and preheat the oven to 450°F.

2.  Finely chop enough of the pineapple to make 3 cups; reserve the remaining pineapple for another use. Transfer the pineapple and its juice to a bowl.

3.  Whisk the sugar and cornstarch together in a large bowl until well combined. Add the eggs, lemon juice, and vanilla and whisk well. Stir in the butter. Add the pineapple and mix.

4.  On a lightly floured work surface, roll out the larger portion of dough into a 13-inch round about ⅛ inch thick. Fit into a 9-inch pie dish. Pour in the filling. Roll out the smaller portion of dough into a 9-inch round and center over the pie. Pinch together and flute the edges. Cut a ½-inch hole into the middle of the top crust to allow the steam to escape. Place the pie dish on a rimmed baking sheet.

5.  Bake for 10 minutes. Reduce the oven temperature to 350°F. Continue baking until the filling in the center hole looks completely set and custard-like, about 1 hour.

6.  Let the pie cool completely on a wire rack. (Warning: This will take at least 3 hours, and you may want to refrigerate it after it cools for an hour or so to help it along.) Slice and serve.

# *The* Sweet Potato Pie (with compliments and gratitude to Chubby)

✳

*I*t was Christmas come early at the Vogue offices—Patti LaBelle's nearly sold-out sweet potato pie arrived, and the excitement was palpable.

That's what the editors of *Vogue* posted on the magazine's website when, the Walmart craziness (see page viii) notwithstanding, they somehow managed to get their hands on one. I knew their connections were serious. But until they procured one of my sweet potato pies when not even *I* could get/find/buy one, I didn't know *how* serious. *Respect*, ladies, respect.

I'm told that the moment of truth—the much-anticipated taste test—had a YouTube-James-Wright-Chanel-sweet-potato-pie-review kind of feel: Someone pronounced it "Like, earth-shattering." A few seconds later, "That is pretty damn good for $3.48." As the last few pieces were polished off, "the hype was definitely warranted," everyone agreed.

I'm betting that like the *Vogue* editors, you'll agree that this sweet potato pie recipe is equally hype-worthy...and I've got a seriously good reason for my optimism: Like all of my sweet potato pie recipes (Walmart's included), it's based on the OG: Chubby's. As I said in this book's introduction, Chubby's sweet potato pie was famous all over Philly, and I was knee-high to a piano bench when she started showing me how to make it.

Flash back 60-something years. I was probably five or six when Chubby started teaching me her three (ironclad) rules for sweet potato buying. Rule #1: Choose potatoes that have smooth, unbruised skin. "Cuts and bruises spread fast, Patsy," Chubby said, "and before you can say, 'What's that smell coming from my pantry?' *all* of your potatoes will be rotten." Chubby never put a single sweet potato in our grocery cart until she (a) put on her glasses; and (b) examined it at least three times.

Rule #2: Buy small to medium-sized potatoes. "The big ones are as tough as your daddy's feet," Chubby always said, referring to the ½-inch-thick calluses on my father's heels and toes, courtesy of his love of walking barefoot.

Rule #3 wasn't technically about sweet potato *buying*, but whenever we put away groceries, Chubby emphasized it nonetheless. "Never refrigerate your sweet potatoes, Patsy. The cold air makes them go bad faster than a long-tailed cat scampering out of a room full of rocking chairs." Even as a little kid, I knew that was fast.

I learned so many life lessons from Chubby's sweet potato pie recipe. Lessons I want to pass down to my grandkids. Like: Through our most beloved family recipes, we can discover and stay in touch with our roots, our past, our culture, our history. (See Great-Grandmother Mariah's pound cake on page 59 and Daddy's beloved Strawberry Moon shortcake on page 140.)

And I'll never forget another powerful life lesson Chubby and her sweet potato pie recipe taught me. I learned it when a couple of neigh-

Chubby, the sweet potato sorceress.

bors stopped speaking to Chubby when she didn't give them her recipe. To paraphrase Chubby: *In life we never lose friends. We only learn who the true ones are.* See why I say recipes have so much more than cooking skills to teach us?

Speaking of life lessons, I can't share *this* Chubby-inspired sweet potato pie recipe without sharing a really important one that I learned from the story of the Sankofa. Without getting all academic, here's what you need to know: *Sankofa* is a West African word with a symbol of a mythical bird with its feet planted forward and its head turned backward. Its translation ("It is not taboo to fetch what is at risk of being left behind") represents something I truly believe: The past—and the lessons we can learn from it—should never be forgotten. Lessons of the past can keep us from making mistakes in the future, and these are mistakes whose (sometimes serious) consequences we can avoid just by listening to the wisdom of the people who've already made them.

And nothing is more filled with the wisdom of the past than recipes.

When you can't get to Walmart (or you just feel like baking), give this recipe a try. And when you serve it, let it inspire you to start a conversation with *your* loved ones about *your* family's favorite recipes/traditions/history.

And Chubby, if you're listening, thankyou-thankyouthankyou.

# *The* Sweet Potato Pie

As I said in the introduction, "Sweet Talk from Patti," sweet potato pie is in my blood. Any and every sweet potato pie I make is compared to the OG: Chubby's version, which was also the inspiration behind my dear friend Norma's recipe. (It's in my first cookbook, *LaBelle Cuisine*. If you don't have the book, last time I checked the recipe was also online.) Why I can't leave a good thing alone, I don't know. This is my current rendition, which starts with Chubby's pie and throws in some new tricks, too. If you have been boiling sweet potatoes for your pie, try the microwave method here. It is a lot quicker.

Makes 8 servings

Patti's Favorite Pie Dough (page 151)

Flour, for rolling the dough

**FILLING**

2½ pounds orange-fleshed sweet potatoes (yams), about 5 medium, scrubbed but unpeeled

½ cup (1 stick) unsalted butter, melted

1 cup granulated sugar

½ cup evaporated milk (See Patti's Pointers)

2 large eggs

1 teaspoon freshly grated or ground nutmeg

1 teaspoon ground cinnamon

¼ teaspoon salt

**WHIPPED CREAM**

1 cup heavy cream

2 tablespoons confectioners' sugar

1 teaspoon vanilla extract

1. Unwrap the dough and place it on a lightly floured work surface. Sprinkle some flour over the top of the dough. Roll out the dough into a 12- to 13-inch round about ⅛ inch thick. Fit into a 9-inch pie pan. Trim the excess dough to make a ½-inch overhang around the edge of the pan. Fold the dough over so the edge of the fold is flush with the edge of the pan. Flute the edge of the dough. Pierce the bottom of the dough about a dozen times with a fork. Freeze the dough for 20 to 30 minutes.

2. Position a rack in the bottom third of the oven and preheat the oven to 375°F. Line the inside of the piecrust with aluminum foil. Fill the foil with pie weights, dried beans, or uncooked rice. Place the pan on a rimmed baking sheet.

3. Bake until the exposed dough looks set and is beginning to brown, 12 to 15 minutes. Lift up and remove the foil with the weights. Continue baking the piecrust until it looks dry on the bottom, about 10 minutes more. (If the piecrust puffs, pierce the crust with a fork.) Transfer to a wire cake rack.

4. **Meanwhile, make the filling:** Pierce each sweet potato a few times with the tines of a fork. Place them, in a spoke pattern, on the turntable of a microwave oven. Cook on high (100%), turning the sweet potatoes over after 4 minutes, until they are tender, 8 to 10 minutes total. Let cool for a few minutes.

*Continued on page 134*

5. If necessary, return the oven temperature to 375°F. Using a kitchen towel to protect your hands, split each sweet potato and use a spoon to scrape the flesh into a medium bowl. Mash the sweet potatoes—you should have about 2 cups. Using an electric mixer set on medium speed, beat in the melted butter. Add the sugar, evaporated milk, eggs, nutmeg, cinnamon, and salt and beat on low speed just until the sugar is dissolved. Spread the filling evenly in the pie shell. Place the pie on a baking sheet.

6. Bake for 15 minutes. Reduce the oven temperature to 350°F. Continue baking until the filling is set and doesn't jiggle when the pie is gently shaken, about 30 minutes more. Transfer the pie to the wire rack and let cool completely. (The pie can be covered with plastic wrap and refrigerated for up to 1 day. Let stand at room temperature for 1 hour before serving.)

7. **Whip the cream:** Freeze a medium bowl until it is chilled, about 5 minutes. Add the cream, confectioners' sugar, and vanilla. Whip with an electric mixer on high speed until the cream forms soft peaks. (The cream can be covered and refrigerated for up to 1 day. If it separates, whisk until thickened.)

8. Slice the pie and top each serving with a dollop of whipped cream.

Patti's Pointers: *Why evaporated milk? Even if a farmhouse didn't have a refrigerator, country folks usually had canned evaporated milk in the kitchen cupboard. This ingredient is rich and sweet because the excess water has been removed (evaporated) before canning.*

# Picture-Perfect Strawberry-Rhubarb Cobbler with Cornmeal Biscuits

As easy as they are, the timing of biscuit cobblers can be a little iffy, and it can take luck and prayer to get the topping and filling done at the same time. Well, why not cook them separately and put them together at the last minute? Problem solved! Also, you can cut the dough into decorative shapes like stars, or be lazy and just cut them into squares or rounds. Strawberries and rhubarb, during the time in spring when they are in season together, make one of the best cobblers on this planet. By the way, rhubarb is very tart, so don't reduce the sugar unless you like that puckery taste.

Makes 8 servings

### FILLING

2 pounds fresh strawberries, halved or quartered, depending on size (about 6 cups)

2 pounds fresh rhubarb, cut crosswise into ¼-inch slices

¾ cup granulated sugar

¾ cup packed light or dark brown sugar

3 tablespoons cornstarch

Red food coloring (optional; see Patti's Pointers)

1 tablespoon unsalted butter, at room temperature, for the dish

### CORNMEAL BISCUITS

1½ cups unbleached all-purpose flour, plus more for patting out the dough

½ cup yellow cornmeal, preferably stone-ground

2 tablespoons granulated sugar, plus more for sprinkling

1 tablespoon baking powder

½ teaspoon salt

½ cup (1 stick) cold unsalted butter, cut into tablespoons

¾ cup whole milk, plus more for brushing

Vanilla ice cream or Whipped Cream (page 132), for serving

1. **To make the filling:** Mix the strawberries, rhubarb, granulated and brown sugars, and cornstarch well in a large bowl to absorb the cornstarch. Mix in the food coloring, if using. Let stand to give off some juices while the oven is preheating, about 15 minutes.

2. Position racks in the upper third and center of the oven and preheat the oven to 400°F. Use the butter to generously coat the inside of a 9 by 13-inch baking dish.

3. Pour the filling into the baking dish and place on a large rimmed baking sheet. Bake on the center rack, stirring occasionally, until the filling is bubbling and the rhubarb is tender, about 1 hour.

*Continued on page 137*

4. **After the cobbler has baked for about 20 minutes, make the biscuits:** Whisk the flour, cornmeal, granulated sugar, baking powder, and salt together in a medium bowl. Add the butter and toss to coat the butter. Using a pastry blender or two knives, cut the butter into the flour mixture until the mixture resembles coarse crumbs with some pea-sized pieces of butter. Stir in the milk. Gather up the dough in the bowl and knead a couple of times to smooth it out.

5. Turn out the dough onto a floured work surface. Using floured hands, pat the dough into a rectangle about ¾ inch thick. Using a 2¾-inch-diameter cookie or biscuit cutter, cut out rounds of the dough and transfer to an ungreased rimmed baking sheet. Gather up any scraps and just press them together—don't knead them. Cut out more rounds until the dough is used up. This makes 8 biscuits. (You can use other cookie cutters, but you might get a different yield. Enjoy any leftover biscuits as the baker's treat.) Brush the tops with a little milk and sprinkle lightly with granulated sugar. Bake on the top rack until the biscuits are golden brown and risen, 18 to 20 minutes. It doesn't matter if the biscuits and topping aren't done at exactly the same time.

6. Just before serving, place the biscuits on the filling in the baking dish, pressing them about ½ inch into the juices. Serve warm in bowls with ice cream.

**Patti's Pointers:** *Strawberries and rhubarb both lose their color when cooked and look a little washed-out. A few drops of red food coloring will help this problem. If you use food coloring paste or gel, be very judicious, as they are quite strong. You can certainly leave the coloring out.*

# Daddy's Strawberry Moon Shortcake

✳

In the summer, when Aunt Hattie Mae came to visit us in Philly, my father always told her she couldn't go back home to Georgia until: (a) they hosted a block party that showed off their pig-roasting skills to the neighbors; and (b) Aunt Hattie baked her famous raspberry pie (page 124). Like everybody in the family, Daddy was well aware of Aunt Hattie Mae's rule: Unless she could pick her own raspberries, she didn't bake her raspberry pie. Once in a blue moon, Aunt Hattie would agree to use store-bought raspberries—if, say, a dear friend lost a loved one unexpectedly and wanted to serve it at the post-funeral repast. But short of sudden death, getting Aunt Hattie to break her Raspberry Pie Rule, well, let's just say it wasn't likely.

Anyone who knew Aunt Hattie will tell you that's a *serious* understatement. Aunt Hattie breaking her Raspberry Pie Rule was about as likely as me slathering on suntan lotion, putting on a thong bikini, and lying in the sun at my beach house in the Bahamas (see page 126). Or Mariah Carey (she's my goddaughter) and Nicki Minaj joining together and, in an act of peacemaking, covering the Elton John / Dionne Warwick / Stevie Wonder / Gladys Knight pop-soul hit, "That's What Friends Are For."

There was only one person on the planet to whom Aunt Hattie's Raspberry Pie Rule didn't apply: Daddy. Aunt Hattie Mae would do anything for him. I think it's because when they were just kids, they lost both their parents in less than a year, and that tragedy forged a bond between them that lasted until the day my father died. As I shared in my memoir, *Don't Block the Blessings*, Daddy was just fifteen when he lost his mother, my grandmother Tempie, to leukemia. She was the love of my grandfather's life, and eight months after she died, Granddaddy Henry was gone, too. The doctors said Henry Holte Sr. had a massive stroke. Aunt Hattie Mae said he died from something much more painful: a broken heart.

Not long after Daddy lost his parents, he went to work full-time to help his grandparents take care of his brothers, William and Addison, and, of course, Aunt Hattie and Aunt Josh. For years, Aunt Hattie said, Daddy sent his check home so there would be enough money to take care of all of them, even though he was my aunts' baby brother. When Aunt Hattie got engaged, Daddy even bought her wedding dress. See why she would do *anything* for him? Including throwing her Raspberry Pie Rule to the wind, even if it meant using *frozen* raspberries. And that was like me using Velveeta in a recipe that called for Crottin de Chavignol.

I repeat this story here, in this cookbook, because it illustrates so beautifully what I believe so strongly: Recipes are a special and unique form of genealogy. Like birth and death certificates, they can explain, illuminate, and, most importantly, pass on our family history. And if we take the time to look into their origin, they can unravel a lot of family mysteries, too.

It was, for example, a recipe for strawberry shortcake that made me understand why every single summer my father wanted to go strawberry-picking: It reminded him of some of the best times of his life. The times he always wanted to remember and never wanted to forget. The times he spent on the family farm with his mother, my grandmother Tempie, before he lost her to cancer.

*You have to wait for the full moon, Henry.*

Daddy said that's what Grandmother Tempie always told him when he bugged her about going strawberry-picking. He said that as soon as the weather turned warm, he pestered her about it all the time. Daddy loved all kinds of berries. He could, for example, eat half of Aunt Hattie's raspberry pie in a single sitting, which is why he never let her leave Philly until she made him at least three or four. But in a raspberry/strawberry contest, well, it really isn't even fair to call it a contest. Daddy picked strawberries every time.

It's because of a recipe that I know why: Some of the best moments of my father's life involved strawberries. Actually, strawberry-picking. Which, as I mentioned, Grandmother Tempie told him he should never—not ever—do unless it was after a full moon. The morning after it hung in the June sky, that's when Grandmother Tempie said strawberries were at their sweetest. When the earth and the sun were aligned and the moon was full, Grandmother Tempie told Daddy that the moonbeams did something magical to the strawberries. Something so otherworldly, mere mortals would never understand it. But even if she didn't understand the *how* of it, Grandmother Tempie said she was sure of the *fact* of it.

And it happened every June.

As sure as the gravitational pull of the moon made the tides roll in, Grandmother Tempie told Daddy its silvery light made the strawberries sweet. That's why, if you wanted to be certain you picked your strawberries when they were at their peak sweet, red, and juicy deliciousness, you had to gather them the morning after the full moon. Early, Grandmother Tempie said. When dawn was breaking. Not long after the moon had shown its full face to the earth. And the strawberries. I bet my grandmother never knew just how right she was. According to the *Old*

*Farmer's Almanac*, the Algonquin Native American tribes named the full moon in June the Strawberry Moon because its appearance signaled it was time to go strawberry-picking.

Sometimes—not often but sometimes—the good Lord sent *two* full moons in June, Grandmother Tempie told Daddy. And while it rarely happened—once in a blue moon, Daddy always said, giving me and my sisters a wink whenever he told the story—when it did, he and Grandmother Tempie would rise with the sun and spend hours gathering strawberries. He said she always used the sweetest ones to make him her famous Strawberry Moon cake, and that they never came inside until they'd picked enough strawberries to last until September, when the Harvest Moon signaled it was time to go pumpkin-picking.

The next time you need a truly special dessert, give this big, beautiful strawberry shortcake a try. Even better, the next time we're scheduled for a Strawberry Moon, go strawberry-picking with someone you love as much as Daddy loved Grandmother Tempie. No nearby strawberry fields? No problem. The night of the Strawberry Moon, do the next best thing: Go sky-gazing. Moon-watching. Extra credit if you sing along to "Moondance." (The Al Jarreau/Luba Mason version, 'cuz that was Daddy's kind of groove.)

I can't make any promises about what either activity—the cake-baking or the moon-gazing—may or may not trigger. So I'll just say this: If you sing along to "Moondance" and you pick your own strawberries and your shortcake turns out really, really well—Daddy and Grandmother Tempie might be tempted to send special culinary blessings your way. I know they've sent them to me. That's probably why, each time I make this cake, I feel them smiling down from heaven.

Just like the moonbeams smile on strawberries.

# Daddy's Strawberry Moon Shortcake

It may seem like a long recipe, but Daddy and Grandmother Tempie would think it's worth it. If the length concerns you, just remember that the simple components can be made well ahead of serving, and then it takes just a few minutes to assemble it. If you have made the typical biscuit-style shortcakes before, give this sponge cake upgrade a try.

Makes 12 to 14 servings

**BERRIES AND SAUCE**

4 pounds fresh strawberries

½ cup packed light brown sugar, or more as needed

A few drops red food coloring (optional)

**HOT MILK SPONGE CAKE**

½ cup (1 stick) unsalted butter, plus more for the pans

1 cup whole milk

2 teaspoons vanilla extract

Grated zest of 1 large lemon

2 cups cake flour (not self-rising)

2 teaspoons baking powder

½ teaspoon salt

4 large eggs

2 cups granulated sugar

2 batches Whipped Cream (page 132)

Confectioners' sugar, for sifting

1.  At least 6 hours before serving, prepare the strawberries. Choose 12 of the best-looking strawberries with leaves for the decoration and refrigerate them. Hull and slice the remaining strawberries. Mix the sliced berries and brown sugar in a large bowl. Cover and refrigerate, stirring occasionally, until the berries give off some juices, at least 4 hours or overnight.

2.  **To make the cake:** Position a rack in the center of the oven and preheat the oven to 350°F. Lightly butter the bottom only of two 9 by 1½-inch round cake pans. Line the bottoms of the pans with parchment paper or waxed paper rounds.

3.  Melt the butter in a small saucepan over medium heat. Add the milk and heat until small bubbles form around the edges. Remove from the heat. Stir in the vanilla and lemon zest.

4.  Sift the cake flour, baking powder, and salt together. Crack the eggs into the bowl of a heavy-duty standing mixer or a large bowl. Place the bowl of eggs in a larger bowl of hot tap water and stir occasionally with your finger until the eggs feel warm, about 2 minutes.

5. Beat the eggs with the whisk attachment (or a handheld electric mixer) on high speed, gradually adding the sugar a few tablespoons at a time. Continue beating until the mixture is pale yellow and tripled in volume, about 4 minutes (or 5 to 7 minutes with a hand mixer). It should look like old-fashioned shaving cream and almost form peaks. Reduce the speed to medium-low. Gradually pour in the hot milk mixture. Remove the bowl from the mixer stand. In two additions, sift in the flour mixture, and use a large balloon whisk or rubber spatula to fold in each addition. This is a thin batter. Pour the batter equally among the prepared pans.

6. Bake until the cakes are golden brown, spring back when gently pressed in the center with a fingertip, and are just beginning to shrink away from the pans, 30 to 35 minutes. Let cool in the pans on wire cake racks for 30 minutes. (These delicate layers need a longer cooling period to set in their pans than other cakes.) Run a small sharp knife around the edges of the pans to release the cakes. Invert and unmold onto the racks. Discard the papers. Using a wide spatula, turn the cakes right side up and cool completely. (The cakes can be cooled, individually wrapped in plastic wrap, and stored at room temperature for up to 1 day.)

7. **A few hours before serving, make the sauce:** Drain the sliced strawberries in a colander over a bowl, reserving the juices. Puree 3 cups of the strawberries with ¼ cup of their juices in a blender or food processor to make a smooth sauce. Taste for sweetness and blend in more brown sugar, if needed. If the sauce looks pale, blend in the food coloring, if desired. Transfer the sauce to a bowl, cover, and refrigerate.

8. **Just before serving, assemble the cake:** Using a long serrated knife, cut the cakes in half horizontally to make 4 layers. Place a layer, cut side up, on a serving platter. Top with one-third of the sliced berries and their juices. Using a metal spatula, spread with one-fourth of the whipped cream, going right to the edge of the cake. Repeat with two more cake layers, using one-third of the berries and one-fourth of the cream for each layer. Finish with the fourth cake layer, top with the remaining cream, and swirl the cream with the spatula. Mound the reserved whole berries in the center of the cake. Sift the confectioners' sugar on top. (The cake can stand at room temperature for about 15 minutes.)

9. Slice the cake with a serrated knife, transfer to dessert plates, and serve with the strawberry sauce poured around each portion.

# Zuri and Dodd's Peach-Apple Cobbler

I named this cobbler after two of my sons because of all the desserts I make, it is their favorite. Both have loved it since they were teenagers. Both think I came up with the recipe after months of taste-testing different fruit combinations: peach and pear, peach and plum, peach and apple—you name it—Zuri and Dodd think I tried them all. But I'll let you in on a little secret: Not a single taste test was involved!

I'm not proud of what I'm about to tell you, but here it is: This pie should be called Fake-It-'Til-You-Make-It Peach-Apple Cobbler, because, had I been willing to go to the market for more peaches, this recipe wouldn't exist. Sorry, Zuri and Dodd, but you're old enough to know the

truth now. And the truth is this: One minute there was a bowl of sliced peaches on my kitchen counter, the next minute that bowl of peaches was all over my kitchen floor. (My girlfriend Cassie and I had been Pouilly-Fuissé-ing our way through a lazy summer afternoon, so my memory of how they ended up on the floor is foggy.)

What I do remember clearly is giving Cassie a choice: We could either (a) go to the market and get more peaches; or (b) open another bottle of wine and use the apples I had in the pantry. It took Cassie about half a second to choose the wine-and-apples option, which left me relieved but not surprised. It was, after all, Cassie who mastered the fine art of martini-making because, as she likes to say, "Wine doesn't always do it." Fun fact: Cassie's signature—and most requested—martini features raspberry juice and raspberry vodka. Girlfriend is definitely channeling Aunt Hattie Mae (page 123)!

I toyed with the idea of going to the market, though. Believe me I did. But it was raining and I was chilling and the thought of changing out of my pajamas, well, let's just say I wasn't feeling it. So I refilled Cassie's glass, wiped the peaches up from the floor, added apples instead, and—*voilà!*—Zuri and Dodd's favorite dessert was born.

I think you're going to love it as much as they do.

*Preparing to make Zuri and Dodd's favorite dessert: peach-apple cobbler. Thank God they're old enough to know the truth about the recipe's creation!*

# Zuri and Dodd's Peach-Apple Cobbler with Brown Sugar Crust

In my household, our favorite cobblers don't just have a single layer of pastry on top. They have three: bottom, middle, and top. To keep the layers from getting soggy, their baking is staggered with the fruit filling, just the way Zuri and Dodd like it. *Everybody* in my family says it's not Thanksgiving without this cobbler, whether peaches are in season or not. When it's cold outside, use canned fruit. It will work just fine.

Makes 8 to 10 servings

**COBBLER DOUGH**

4½ cups unbleached all-purpose flour

1½ teaspoons salt

1½ cups chilled butter-flavored
vegetable shortening

1½ cups ice water, as needed

**FILLING**

3 tablespoons unsalted butter

3 pounds firm baking apples, preferably
Fuji, peeled, cored, and cut into ½-inch
wedges

Four 16-ounce cans sliced peaches in pear
juice, drained, with 1 cup pear juice
reserved (see Pattie's Pointers)

¼ cup raw blue agave nectar, preferably
organic, or ¼ cup packed brown sugar

2 teaspoons cornstarch

1 teaspoon ground cinnamon

½ teaspoon almond extract

¼ teaspoon salt

Nonstick cooking oil spray, for the dish

Flour, for rolling the dough

1 large egg yolk, beaten to blend

½ cup packed light brown sugar

Finely grated zest of ½ large orange

Vanilla ice cream, for serving (optional)

1. **To make the cobbler dough:** Whisk the flour and salt into a medium bowl. Add the shortening. Using a pastry blender or two knives (drawing them apart in a crisscross pattern), cut the shortening into the flour until the mixture resembles coarse crumbs with a few pea-sized bits.

2. Stirring with a fork, gradually add enough of the water for the mixture to clump together (you may not need all of the water). When you press the dough together, it should be moist and malleable, without cracking, so add a bit more water if need be. Gather up the dough and press it into a mound. Divide the dough into 3 equal thick rectangles (the dough will be rolled into rectangles to fit the baking dish, so it is easier to start out with that shape than a disk). Wrap each and refrigerate until chilled but not hard, 30 minutes to 1 hour.

*Continued*

3. **To make the filling:** Melt the butter in a very large skillet over medium heat. Add the apples and cook, tossing them occasionally, until lightly browned and crisp-tender, about 10 minutes. Stir in the peaches and their reserved pear juice, the agave, cornstarch, cinnamon, almond extract, and salt and mix well to dissolve the cornstarch. Set aside to cool completely.

*When peaches aren't in season, I use canned. I promise, they'll work fine.*

4. Position a rack in the center of the oven and preheat the oven to 375°F. Lightly spray a 9 by 13-inch baking dish with oil.

5. Lightly flour a work surface. Unwrap one portion of dough, keeping the remaining dough refrigerated, and place on the work surface. Dust the top with flour and roll into a 9 by 13-inch rectangle about ⅛ inch thick, using the bottom of the dish as a template and trimming as needed. Transfer to a baking sheet. Repeat with the remaining dough, separating the layers with waxed paper or parchment paper. Freeze or refrigerate until needed.

6. Transfer one dough portion to the prepared baking dish and pierce a few times with a fork. Bake until the dough in the dish is beginning to brown, about 15 minutes.

7. Remove the dish from the oven, spread one half of the cooled filling over the bottom crust, top with another dough rectangle, and pierce the dough with a fork. Bake until the dough is beginning to brown, 15 to 20 minutes.

8. Remove the dish from the oven. Top with the remaining filling, followed by the last dough rectangle. Lightly brush the dough with some of the beaten yolk. Mix the brown sugar and orange zest and sprinkle evenly over the dough. Return to the oven and continue baking until the edges of the crust are golden brown, about 40 minutes. Let cool for about 10 minutes. Serve warm in individual bowls with ice cream, if desired.

**Pattie's Pointers:** *If you want to use fresh peaches instead of canned, peel, pit, and cut 6 to 8 ripe peaches to get 6 cups, and use 1 cup canned pear or peach juice to replace the juice from the canned fruit.*

*My best friend, Norma, and me showing Gia and her mom, Lona, the perfect way to finish a cobbler while Gia's other glamma, Ro, smiles in agreement!*

# Armstead's Easy-as-Pie Berry Buckle

Okay, let me give you a little background. A few years ago, my sons, Zuri, Stanley, and Dodd, spent months planning a big shindig to celebrate Armstead getting his PhD. I think my nephew, Michael, was in on it, too. The day Zuri told me about the party, he also told me this: He wanted to have it at my house. *Say what?* That's what I was thinking when Zuri told me that wasn't the only contribution he wanted me to make to his father's party. He also wanted me to bake something fabulous. Something his dad would love, Zuri said. Something that said, "Congratulations, I know what a really big deal this is." Partly to get him out of my hair, and partly because I meant it at the time, I told Zuri yes. And then I promptly forgot about it.

What was *I thinking*? I should have known Zuri would hold me to my word, since I always hold him to his. (Don't forget, Z; you promised to move heaven and earth to make sure my hotel suites have kitchens, or at least kitchenettes!) Of course, the weekend the party rolled around, I wasn't feeling it. Truth be told, the thought of my ex-husband and all his friends hanging out at my house for a few hours, never mind the whole day, made me feel like, well, let's just say it made me feel blue. (The word that *really* describes what it made me feel like is four letters, too. All you happily divorced ladies out there know exactly what I'm talking about. Sorry, Armstead; just keeping it real.)

So the night before the party, I called Zuri and dropped a "Your mama's not feeling well so I'll be staying in my bedroom" on him. He didn't

*Three of the masterminds behind Armstead's party celebrating him earning his doctorate degree—son Zuri, nephew Michael, and son Dodd.*

say a word. But I felt the energy between us shift. Every mother on the planet knows where this story's headed: I decided to attend the party because (a) I didn't want to let down my son; and (b) I didn't want him to think I didn't care about breaking my promises. Especially the ones I make to him.

After I called Zuri back to tell him I'd be mixing and mingling, I realized I had a bunch of reasons to hang out at the party that had nothing to do with Armstead: Stanley and Aki were coming up from D.C. and bringing Ellington, so I'd get to meet my first grandchild. (I couldn't believe that he was even cuter than his pictures!) My nephew, Michael, was flying in from Atlanta and I hadn't seen him in a month of Sundays. And, last but not least, I could put this dessert together in a flash, and Zuri would think I spent the whole night in the kitchen making it.

On the serious side, though, there was another reason I needed to show up for Armstead's party. A reason that, if I'm real-talking, was far more important than the gazillion reasons I had for staying in my bedroom: Because, whatever I may think of Armstead's husband skills, his father skills are A+. And he passed them down to my sons, as the moving toasts they made at the party made clear. Each toast had its own flavor (pun intended; this is a cookbook, after all!). But the theme of all three was the same: Because of their father, my sons said they knew the meaning of the saying "Any man can be a father; it takes a special man to be a Dad."

Because Stanley and Dodd didn't come to live with us until they were teenagers, when they lost their mom, our much-loved neighbor, far too soon, I think Zuri benefited the most from Armstead's dad skills. Not just his deep dedication to the role, but his discernment, his devotion, his direction. I know, for example, that it's because of Armstead that Zuri got to see Gia being born. Zuri can't stand the sight of blood, and throughout Lona's pregnancy he made it clear he wouldn't be going anywhere near the delivery room. Four decades earlier, Armstead had said "No thanks" when I asked him if he wanted to come into the delivery room with me, and I'm pretty sure he wishes he'd been there when Zuri took his first breath. I *know* he told Zuri to think long and hard about missing his own child's birth; that a moment like this comes but once in a lifetime.

I'm also pretty sure of this: Zuri decided he could handle it because his father *told* him that he could. And Zuri knew Armstead would never lie to him. Hmmmmm. I think I'm going to have to add the Winstons' soul classic, "Color Him Father," to my brunch playlist (see my brunch tip #2 on page 212). For the record, Zuri drew the line at cutting the umbilical cord; Lona's mother, Ro, handled that.

Me? I drew the line at staying at Armstead's party the whole afternoon; about an hour after it started, I told Zuri I had to jet. But everyone said my cakey berry buckle was divine. I think you'll love it as much as Armstead's guests did.

*It's a family affair! Aki (holding Ellington), Stanley, Armstead, me, Zuri, and Lona (holding Gia) at Armstead's graduation party.*

Love Me Tender Pies, Cobblers, and More  147

# Armstead's Easy-as-Pie Berry Buckle

An example of the cake type of cobbler, this wonderful dessert is almost a big muffin. And what is wrong with that? It is probably called a *buckle* because of the bumpy look of the fruit in the batter. It's especially easy because you mix up the dough with a mixer all at once—no separated eggs, no creaming of the butter and sugar, and no sifting. And you can leave off the streusel if you prefer. Another time, substitute two ripe peaches (peeled or not), cut into ½-inch wedges, for the berries.

Makes 6 to 8 servings

Softened butter, for the pan

**STREUSEL**

¼ cup unbleached all-purpose flour

2 tablespoons light brown sugar

¼ teaspoon ground cinnamon

2 tablespoons unsalted butter, at room temperature

**BUCKLE DOUGH**

1½ cups unbleached all-purpose flour

¾ cup granulated sugar

2 teaspoons baking powder

½ teaspoon salt

½ cup whole milk

2 large eggs, at room temperature

¼ cup (½ stick) unsalted butter, cut into tablespoons, at room temperature

1 teaspoon vanilla extract

2 cups blackberries, blueberries, or raspberries (or a combination)

Whipped Cream (page 132), for serving

1. Position a rack in the center of the oven and preheat the oven to 400°F. Lightly butter the inside of an 11 by 8½-inch baking dish.

2. **To make the streusel:** Mix the flour, brown sugar, and cinnamon in a small bowl, being sure the brown sugar is well crumbled. Add the butter and work the mixture with your knuckles and fingertips until it is uniform. Set aside.

3. **To make the buckle dough:** Whisk the flour, granulated sugar, baking powder, and salt in a large bowl. Add the milk, eggs, butter, and vanilla. Mix with an electric mixer set on low speed for 30 seconds (set a timer). Increase the speed to high and mix for 2 minutes (set a timer), scraping down the sides of the bowl as needed. Spread in the prepared pan. Arrange the berries in a single layer on the batter. Crumble the streusel on top.

4. Bake until the buckle is golden brown and a toothpick inserted into the center comes out clean, 30 to 35 minutes. Let cool on a wire rack for about 20 minutes. Serve warm or cooled to room temperature, with the whipped cream.

# Pear and Cranberry Crisp with Oat-Walnut Topping

This is what to make when it's autumn and pears are really in season and cranberries are everywhere. The tart berries are a kind of counter-point to the sweet pears. Use juicy pears (such as Comice, Anjou, or Bartlett) and steer away from the drier Bosc variety. Because the crumbly browned topping is such an important part of this kind of dish, I provide lots of it.

Makes 8 servings

Softened butter, for the dish

**FILLING**

8 ripe pears (about 3½ pounds), peeled, cored, and cut into ½-inch wedges

One 12-ounce bag fresh cranberries

1¼ cups packed light brown sugar

¼ cup cornstarch

1 teaspoon ground cinnamon

½ teaspoon ground ginger

½ teaspoon ground nutmeg

Pinch of salt

**TOPPING**

2 cups old-fashioned (rolled) oats

1 cup packed light brown sugar

½ cup all-purpose flour

1 teaspoon ground cinnamon

½ teaspoon ground ginger

¼ teaspoon ground nutmeg

¼ teaspoon salt

1 cup (2 sticks) unsalted butter, at room temperature

1 teaspoon vanilla

1 cup coarsely chopped walnuts

1. Position a rack in the center of the oven and preheat the oven to 350°F. Lightly butter a 9 by 13-inch baking dish.

2. **To make the filling:** Toss all of the filling ingredients together in a large bowl. Let stand for a few minutes to dissolve the cornstarch. Pour into the prepared dish.

3. **To make the topping:** Combine the oats, sugar, flour, cinnamon, ginger, nutmeg, and salt in a large bowl. Add the butter and vanilla. Squish the mixture between your hands until it looks homogeneous. Add the walnuts and work them into the mixture. Crumble the topping in an even layer over the filling.

4. Bake until the filling is bubbling in the center and the topping is browned, about 1 hour. If the topping is browning too quickly, tent it with aluminum foil. Let the crisp stand for 5 minutes. Serve warm.

# Patti's Favorite Pie Dough

Some cooks make their dough with butter because they like the flavor, but it bakes into a more crumbly crust. For the flakiest piecrust, you need to use vegetable shortening (or lard, but that's another story because good slow-rendered lard is not that easy to find outside of farm country). In my family, flaky is the name of the game. My solution: Use butter-flavored Crisco. It never lets me down.

Makes one 9-inch piecrust

1½ cups unbleached all-purpose flour

½ teaspoon salt

½ cup chilled (see Patti's Pointers)
  butter-flavored vegetable shortening

½ cup ice water, as needed

1.  Sift the flour and salt into a medium bowl. Add the shortening. Using a pastry blender or two knives (drawing them apart in a crisscross pattern), cut the shortening into the flour until the mixture resembles coarse crumbs with a few pea-sized bits.

2.  Stirring with a fork, gradually add enough of the water for the mixture to clump together (you may not need all of the water). When you press the dough together, it should be moist and malleable, without cracking, so add a bit more water if need be. Gather up the dough and press it into a thick disk. Wrap in plastic wrap or waxed paper and refrigerate for 30 minutes to 1 hour. The dough is easiest to roll out if it is chilled but not hard. (The dough can be refrigerated for up to 1 day. If the dough is chilled until it is very firm, let it stand at room temperature for about 10 minutes to soften slightly before rolling it out.)

**Double-Crust Pie Dough:** *Following the instructions above, use 2 cups all-purpose flour, ¾ teaspoon salt, ⅔ cup butter-flavored vegetable shortening, and about ⅔ cup ice water. Divide the dough into 2 thick disks, one slightly larger than the other. Wrap each and refrigerate for 30 minutes to 1 hour.*

**Patti's Pointers:** *If you forgot to chill the shortening beforehand, do not panic. Just put the shortening, cut up into tablespoon-sized chunks, on a plate or piece of aluminum foil, and stick it in the freezer. It will be properly chilled in about 15 minutes. (I know some pie-making fanatics who keep their shortening in the refrigerator so it's always cold and ready for making pie dough, but I'm not sure that's a good idea. Sometimes, the shortening will absorb moisture from the refrigerator's humidity, and it's hard to gauge how much water to add to the dough.)*

# 6 ) Dish-It-Up Puddings and Custards

Certain desserts take me right back to my childhood, simpler times when the blues could often be soothed away by dipping my spoon into a cup of nutmeg-dusted custard or a serving of rice pudding. These soft and comforting sweets were easy to make from ingredients that were always in the house—if you had eggs, sugar, and milk, then you could make custard. And very often, they used up leftovers like rice and stale bread, too. Custards and puddings sometimes take a little extra care because they are baked in a water bath, but then they sit waiting in the fridge for when you have a craving for something cool and creamy. I can report that the new generation of my family loves these treats as much as I do, as my little granddaughter Gia's favorite dessert is the sweet potato flan on page 184. For picture-perfect puddings, be sure to check out my tips and techniques on pages 245–247.

# Double-Decker
# Butterscotch Pudding

Butterscotch pudding is something that many of us know from our child-hoods, and it was always made from a boxed mix. For a knock-your-socks-off, from-scratch version, this is the one. Not one to leave a good thing alone, I've added some chocolate to the pudding so the two can be layered for a dessert that will make both chocolate and butterscotch lovers happy.

Makes 6 servings

**PUDDING**

3 tablespoons cornstarch

3 cups whole milk

1 cup packed dark brown sugar
(or use 1 cup packed light brown
sugar and 1 tablespoon molasses)

½ teaspoon salt

1 large egg plus 2 large egg yolks

5 tablespoons (½ stick plus 1 tablespoon)
unsalted butter, cut into 1½-inch cubes

1 teaspoon vanilla extract

1½ ounces unsweetened chocolate,
finely chopped

**WHIPPED CREAM**

½ cup heavy cream

2 teaspoons confectioners' sugar

½ teaspoon vanilla extract

1. **To make the pudding:** Place the cornstarch in a medium bowl. Gradually whisk in ½ cup of the milk to dissolve the cornstarch. Pour the dissolved mixture into the remaining milk and mix well.

2. Combine the brown sugar and salt in a medium heavy-bottomed saucepan. Gradually whisk in the milk mixture, being sure to include any cornstarch on the bottom of the bowl. Cook over medium heat, whisking often, until the mixture is bubbling. Remove from the heat.

3. Whisk the egg and the yolks together in a small bowl. Gradually whisk in about half of the hot milk mixture, then return the egg mixture to the saucepan. Return to a boil over medium-low heat and cook, whisking constantly, for about 1 minute. (The mixture must be fully cooked or the pudding will thin out when chilled.) Remove from the heat. Add the butter and vanilla and whisk until the butter melts into the pudding. Strain the pudding through a medium-mesh sieve into a clean medium bowl to remove any bits of cooked egg white.

4. Transfer about one-third of the butterscotch pudding to a small bowl and add the chocolate. Let stand for 1 minute to soften the chocolate. Whisk until the chocolate melts into the pudding. Divide the chocolate pudding evenly among 6 custard cups,

small wine glasses, or parfait glasses. Top each with equal amounts of the butter-scotch pudding. Cover the tops with plastic wrap or waxed paper pressed directly onto the pudding surface to keep a skin from forming. Poke a few holes in the plastic with the tip of a knife to let the steam escape. Refrigerate until chilled and set, at least 4 hours or overnight.

5. **To whip the cream:** Whip the cream, confectioners' sugar, and vanilla together in a chilled small bowl until stiff.

6. Just before serving, discard the plastic wrap and drop a dollop of the whipped cream on top of each pudding. Serve chilled.

# Chocolate Flan Cake

Here is a crazy-good Mexican dessert that looks like a zillion dollars—
a classic chocolate Bundt cake topped with a thick layer of custard flan.
(And for that reason, we put the recipe in the puddings, not cake, chapter.)
For such a showstopper, you won't believe how easy it is to make. Some
versions use cake mix, but this from-scratch one is so simple you won't
need the boxed kind. Allow at least 6 hours for the cake to chill so it is
easy to unmold.

Makes 12 servings

Softened butter, for the pan

½ cup caramel ice cream syrup, plus
more as needed for serving

**CAKE LAYER**

2 cups unbleached all-purpose flour

1¼ cups sugar

⅓ cup plus 1 tablespoon natural
unsweetened cocoa powder, such
as Hershey's

2 teaspoons baking soda

½ teaspoon salt

1 cup mayonnaise (not low-fat or light)

1 cup cold brewed coffee
(see Patti's Pointers) or water

1 teaspoon vanilla extract

**FLAN LAYER**

4 large eggs

One 14-ounce can condensed milk

One 12-ounce can evaporated milk

1 teaspoon vanilla extract

1. Position a rack in the center of the oven and preheat the oven to 350°F. Butter a
   10-inch nonstick Bundt (fluted tube) pan. Pour ½ cup (no more) of the caramel sauce
   into the bottom (not the sides) of the pan.

2. **To make the cake layer:** Sift the flour, sugar, cocoa, baking soda, and salt into a large
   bowl. Add the mayonnaise, cold coffee, and vanilla and whisk until smooth. Scrape
   the batter into the prepared pan and smooth the top.

3. **To make the flan layer:** Whisk the eggs well in a medium bowl. Gradually whisk in the
   condensed and evaporated milks and mix until well combined. Whisk in the vanilla.
   Gently pour the flan mixture into the pan, taking care not to disturb the cake layer.
   (During baking, the flan will sink to the bottom.) Cover the pan with an oiled piece of
   aluminum foil, oiled side down.

4. Place the cake pan in a roasting pan. Add enough hot tap water to come about ½ inch
   up the outside of the pan. Place the roasting pan setup in the oven. Pour in enough hot
   tap water to raise the water level by another ¼ inch. Bake for 1 hour and 15 minutes.
   Remove the foil and continue baking until a wooden toothpick inserted about 1 inch

from the inner tube comes out clean and the cake has barely begun to shrink from the sides of the pan, about 15 minutes more.

5.  Remove the pan from the water and let it cool to tepid, about 1 hour. Cover the pan with plastic wrap and refrigerate until chilled, at least 6 hours or overnight.

6.  To unmold, slip a thin, sharp knife down the sides and inner tube to release the cake. Place the pan in a large bowl. Add enough hot water to come about halfway up the sides of the pan. Let the pan stand for about 30 seconds. Remove the pan and wipe the outside dry with a kitchen towel. Place a large platter over the pan. Holding the pan and the platter together, flip them over. Give them a good shake to unmold the cake onto the platter. The flan will be on top, which is as it should be. (The cake can be loosely covered and refrigerated for up to 1 day.)

7.  Drizzle some more caramel syrup on top to give it an ooey-gooey look. Slice and serve chilled.

**Patti's Pointers:** *Be sure to use light-roast or medium-roast coffee (of, for example, Colombian or "breakfast blend" beans) and let it cool completely before using it. Dark roast can make the cake too bitter.*

# Chocolate-Banana Pudding with Raspberries

You are having a big family party and you need a big ol' dessert to feed a crowd. Look no further. It is a variation on the Southern banana pudding theme, but mashed up with homemade chocolate pudding and graham crackers. Top with some fresh red berries for their bright color.

Makes 12 servings

1 cup granulated sugar

¼ cup cornstarch

3 tablespoons natural or Dutch-processed cocoa powder

½ cup heavy cream

3½ cups whole milk

4 large eggs, beaten

2 ounces unsweetened chocolate, finely chopped

3 tablespoons unsalted butter, cut up

1 teaspoon vanilla extract

Pinch of salt

About 21 whole graham crackers

4 ripe bananas, cut into ⅛-inch rounds

Whipped Cream (page 132), for serving

One 6-ounce container fresh raspberries, or 2 cups sliced strawberries, for serving

Chocolate syrup, for serving (optional)

1.  **To make the pudding:** Whisk the granulated sugar, cornstarch, and cocoa in a heavy medium saucepan. Gradually whisk in the cream to make a paste, followed by the milk. Whisking constantly, and being sure to reach the corners of the saucepan, cook over medium heat until the mixture comes to a boil. Remove from the heat.

2.  Whisk the eggs in a medium bowl. Whisk in about 1 cup of the hot milk mixture, then whisk this mixture into the saucepan. Return to medium heat and whisk until the mixture comes to a full boil. Reduce the heat and let it bubble for about 30 seconds. Remove from the heat. Add the chocolate, butter, vanilla, and salt and let stand for about 1 minute to soften the chocolate. Whisk well until combined. Strain the pudding through a medium-mesh wire sieve into a bowl to remove any bits of cooked egg. Cover with plastic wrap pressed directly onto the surface to keep a skin from forming. Poke a few holes in the wrap to let the steam escape. Let cool until tepid, about 1 hour.

3.  Line the bottom of a 9 by 13-inch baking dish with enough graham crackers to cover the bottom (there can be some small gaps). Spread with half of the pudding and top with one third of the bananas. Make two more layers, then finish with the bananas.

4.  Spread the whipped cream over the pudding. Cover and refrigerate until well chilled, at least 6 hours or overnight.

5.  To serve, spoon the pudding into dessert dishes and top with a scattering of berries. Drizzle with chocolate syrup, if desired. Serve chilled.

# No-Bake Double-Chocolate Éclair Cake

Step away from the stove! God bless this no-oven-required recipe for chocolate éclair cake. It takes almost no effort, yet tastes like you spent all day in the kitchen making it. (Who doesn't want to be the grandmother who bakes everything from scratch, the one everyone believes has never bought a box cake in her life, never mind seen the inside of a tub of Cool Whip!)

If I didn't think it would scare off the under-forty set, I would have named it "What-to-Make-When-Menopause-Hits Chocolate Éclair Cake" because that's when I started "baking" it. As anyone who knows me well can tell you, "the change of life" didn't glide gently or gradually into my world. *Oh, no, no, no, no, no.* Menopause hit me *hard*. Like a brick. No, make that a boulder.

I've heard it said that some women go through menopause without ever breaking a sweat. (Pun intended. To paraphrase one of my favorite Peggy Lee songs: *It gave me fever in the morning, fever all through the night. When menopause wrapped its arms around me, I got a fever that was so hard to bear.*)

I've heard, too, that some women actually sail through menopause with such ease, they have only the vaguest recollection of going through it at all because they had none of the problems, issues, or symptoms typically associated with it. Who *are* these women? What planet are they from? I had every single problem, every single issue, and every single symptom that's ever been associated with menopause since a French doctor coined the term for it back in the 1800s. (*La*

*menepausie*, Dr. Charles Pierre Louis de Gardanne called it, but don't ask me to pronounce either the French term or the doc's name.)

True story: Back then, some doctors prescribed opium and cannabis to their menopausal patients suffering from intense hot flashes. How, exactly, did *that* conversation go? *Having severe hot flashes, ma'am? Smoke a joint and call me in the morning.*

I wanted/needed to take *something* that would relieve my symptoms. Maybe not the eighteenth-century opium-weed prescription, but something every bit as—how can I put this?—*effective*; because I had every menopausal symptom you've ever heard of...and probably some you haven't.

Exhaustion? Check. (I was tired every day.)

Insomnia? Uh-huh. (I woke up three and four times a night.)

Carb cravings? Yep. (Bread and chocolate cake; they were my top two obsessions.)

And don't even get me started on the fuzzy-thinking thing—"menopause brain," as a girlfriend who had it almost as bad as I did recently started calling it. I'd open the fridge to pull out some butter or eggs and promptly forget what the heck I was looking for. Add the hot flashes and the mood swings, and I honestly thought menopause might make me lose my natural mind.

If you talk to some of my family members, they will tell you that I did. I'm not going to say they're right; but I can't say they're wrong. The first few years I was going through the so-called change of life just the *thought* of opening the drapes and letting in the sun's rays, never mind turning on my oven, put me in the bed. Of course, I would have happily stayed there 24/7 had the night sweats not forced me to get up and change my (completely soaked) sheets.

After more years than I care to count, I'm happy to say the symptoms have eased. To this day, however, a hot flash will hit me out of the blue, and, depending on (a) how strong it is; (b) how long it lasts; and (c) where I am when it hits me, I might strip down to, well, let's just say you'd probably be able to see the color of my La Perla lingerie.

If, like me, you can't deal with the menopause monster, I have just two things to say:

(1) I feel your pain; and (2) this cake is for you. Trust me; you can pull it together without breaking a sweat. (You can add some white chocolate shavings if you're feeling Gwyneth-y.) If you won't be facing the menopause monster for many, many years, consider this a cheat sheet for the perfect cake to "bake" in the dog days of summer when it's 90 degrees in the shade and you have to take dessert to a family dinner / school bake sale / party at the office.

You can thank me when you hit your forties.

# No-Bake Double-Chocolate Éclair Cake

Éclairs, oblong cream puffs filled with vanilla pastry cream and topped with chocolate icing, are something that you may crave...but probably not make at home. This is a down-and-dirty "back of the box" recipe that uses convenience products for a quick version that resembles the from-scratch chocolate, banana, and raspberry pudding on page 160. This comes together in no time, but remember to thaw the whipped topping before mixing it into the pudding, and refrigerate the "cake" for at least 3 hours before serving.

Makes 12 servings

Two 3.9-ounce packages instant chocolate pudding (not "Cook & Serve" or sugar-free)

2 cups whole milk

1 cup half-and-half

Two 8-ounce containers thawed frozen whipped topping, such as Cool Whip

36 squares graham cracker cookies (about 2 sleeves)

One 16-ounce container chocolate frosting, stirred well

1. Whisk the pudding mix, milk, and half-and-half together in a large bowl and let stand for 2 minutes to thicken. Fold in the whipped topping.

2. Line the bottom of a 9 by 13-inch baking dish with 12 graham cracker squares (the crackers don't have to be touching). Spread with half of the pudding mixture. Top with 12 more squares and the remaining pudding mixture. Finish with the remaining 12 squares. Using an offset metal spatula, spread the frosting over the top of the cake. Cover loosely with plastic wrap and refrigerate for at least 3 hours and up to 1 day.

3. Cut the cake into rectangles and serve chilled.

**Classic Éclair Cake:** *Substitute vanilla for the chocolate pudding.*

# Child, That's Good Chocolate Bread Pudding

*Whoa, Ms. LaBelle. This is the shizzle.*

That's what a friend of Zuri's said to me the other day when he tasted my chocolate bread pudding. For reasons he could not possibly know, those seven little words made my whole day. Actually, they made my entire week. That's because that off-the-cuff compliment made me think of my dear friend, the late, great Luther Vandross, and all the good times we shared.

Back in the '80s, the two of us headlined shows together at Six Flags and Kings Dominion. During those sweet summer days, we spent countless hours bonding over our mutual love for music, food—and each other. (Back in the day, we had to be singing for love because it sure wasn't for money. During the summer of 1987, for example, when we played the hotter-than-July outdoor amphitheater at Kings Dominion, ticket prices started at three bucks and maxed out at six!)

I loved Luther for another reason, too: He started my very first fan club. I've told this story a thousand times and it never fails to take me back to the days when both of us were thin, neither of us was diabetic, and Luther was still here. So if you've heard it before, please indulge me. As a fresh-faced teenager, Luther used to cut school to catch our show at Harlem's famed Apollo Theater. He even told the Apollo's public relations director that he was doing a school report on the Bluebelles so he could get backstage to meet Sarah, Nona, and me when we were known as the Sweethearts of the Apollo. (Hey, Luther, if you're listening, that was a seriously smooth move! I got nothing but love for you, baby.)

I was running an errand at the time, but Luther was so convincing, he scored his "interview" with Sarah and Nona. Shortly afterward, he and his friend choreographer Bruce Wallace founded the Patti LaBelle and the Bluebelles Fan Club. Bruce was the first president, with Luther serving as his vice president. I know everyone gets jazzed about our being the first black vocal group to land the cover of *Rolling Stone*. But as proud as that makes me, you know what makes me even prouder? That Luther loved us so much he wanted to turn all his friends on to our sound. And that for the far-too-brief time we had him on this earth, he was one of my dearest friends. Yep, *that's* what makes me smile.

That's a long way of telling you why that compliment made my whole week. When Zuri's friend told me my chocolate bread pudding was "the shizzle," all those wonderful memories came rushing back. Because that's pretty much what Luther used to say about it. Of all the desserts I used to make for him, it was one of his favorites. There's one more reason I wanted to tell my Luther story in this book. Because it illustrates so clearly what I tried to explain in the introduction, "Sweet Talk from Patti": the amazing power that recipes have to bring loved ones back to us—if not literally, then certainly emotionally, psychologically, sometimes mystically.

Baking bread pudding, for example, brings my beloved father back to me, too. When Daddy opened one of his two restaurants, Baby Henry's Place, back home in Georgia, it was the most popular dessert on the menu. He said the regulars ordered it every single day. "I couldn't stop making it if I wanted to," Daddy used to tell me whenever he baked his famous bread pudding for me. "My customers wouldn't give Baby Henry—the restaurant or me—a moment's peace until I put it back on the menu."

There are spirits in my kitchen. Yes, really.

*Me with my dad, who baked the first bread pudding I loved!*

# Child, That's Good Chocolate Bread Pudding

If bread pudding is mostly bread, it makes sense that the better your bread, the better the pudding. I usually make my bread pudding with challah, the way Luther liked it best. For this book, I decided to mix things up a little. This recipe uses raisin-cinnamon bread for that hint of spice I love. The big secret, as with all bread pudding, is to use stale bread; otherwise, it will disintegrate in the custard.

Makes 8 servings

1 quart half-and-half

1 cup granulated sugar

1½ cups semisweet chocolate chips, divided

8 large eggs

2 teaspoons vanilla extract

One 1-pound loaf sliced raisin-cinnamon bread, stale or baked, cut into 1-inch pieces (see Patti's Pointers)

Softened butter, for the dish

Confectioners' sugar, for serving

Whipped Cream (page 132) or vanilla ice cream, for serving

1. Heat the half-and-half and granulated sugar in a medium saucepan over medium heat, stirring often to dissolve the sugar, until the mixture comes to a simmer. Remove from the heat. Add 1 cup of the chocolate chips and let stand until the chips soften, about 3 minutes. Whisk well to melt the chocolate.

2. Whisk the eggs and vanilla well in a very large bowl. Gradually whisk in the warm chocolate mixture. Add the bread pieces and let stand, stirring occasionally, until the bread has absorbed some of the chocolate mixture, 15 to 20 minutes.

3. Meanwhile, position a rack in the center of the oven and preheat the oven to 325°F. Butter a 9 by 13-inch baking dish.

4. Spread the bread mixture evenly in the prepared dish. Sprinkle the remaining ½ cup chocolate chips on top. Place the dish in a larger pan. Pour hot tap water into the larger pan to come about ½ inch up the sides of the dish. Place in the oven and bake until the pudding is evenly puffed, about 40 minutes.

5. Remove the dish from the pan and let cool for 10 to 15 minutes. Sift confectioners' sugar on top. Serve in bowls, topped with the whipped cream.

**Patti's Pointers:** *For best results, the bread should be firm and dry. If you have soft bread, you have a couple of options. The day before baking, arrange fresh slices on a large baking sheet (they can overlap) and let them stand, uncovered, at room temperature, turning the slices occasionally, for at least overnight or up to 1 day. Or bake the slices, spread out on two large baking sheets, in a preheated 350°F oven until the bread is dry but not toasted, about 15 minutes. Let cool completely before cutting up the bread.*

# Chocolate Mousse for All Seasons

Some desserts go in and out of fashion. But there is no reason for chocolate mousse to have gone the way of platform shoes, because it is really good. It is also perfect for parties because you must make it ahead of time. Because you will really taste the chocolate, this is a time to spring for one of the more expensive brands. This is a basic recipe that lets you get creative. Swap in other liqueurs or liquids for the rum to change flavors. Garnish it with fresh berries or chocolate shavings. But just make it and watch your guests' eyes light up like the Eiffel Tower at Christmas.

Makes 6 to 8 servings

8 ounces semisweet or bittersweet chocolate, coarsely chopped

1¾ cups heavy cream, divided

3 tablespoons sugar

3 large egg yolks

2 tablespoons dark rum, brandy, orange liqueur, orange juice, or brewed coffee

1 teaspoon vanilla extract

Whipped Cream (page 132), for serving

1. Melt the chocolate in the top part of a double boiler over barely simmering water, stirring occasionally. Remove from the heat. Place a wire sieve over the bowl of chocolate.

2. Heat ½ cup of the heavy cream with the sugar in a small saucepan over medium-low heat, stirring often to dissolve the sugar, until the mixture is simmering. Whisk the egg yolks in a small bowl, then whisk in the hot cream mixture. Return to the saucepan and cook over medium-low heat, stirring constantly with a heatproof spatula, until the mixture has thickened to the consistency of eggnog, 1 to 2 minutes. Strain the custard through the sieve into the chocolate to remove any bits of cooked egg white. Add the rum and vanilla and whisk until smooth.

3. Place the bowl with the chocolate mixture in a larger bowl of iced water. Let stand, whisking occasionally, until the mixture is cool but not set, 5 to 10 minutes. Remove the bowl from the iced water.

4. Whip the remaining 1¼ cups heavy cream in a chilled medium bowl until it forms stiff peaks. Stir about one-fourth of the whipped cream into the chocolate mixture to lighten it and then fold in the remaining cream. Divide the mousse among 6 to 8 ramekins, custard cups, or serving bowls. Cover each with plastic wrap and refrigerate until chilled and set, at least 2 hours or up to 2 days.

5. Just before serving, top each mousse with a dollop of the whipped cream and serve chilled.

# Mrs. Chapman's Make-You-Wanna-Dance Sweet Corn Pudding

*Cleanliness is next to godliness.*

That's what my favorite choir director, Mrs. Harriett Chapman, used to say every Sunday morning before passing out the freshly cleaned and pressed robes we donned before entering the chapel of Philly's Beulah Baptist Church. There, with Mrs. Chapman playing the organ, we sang for her, the congregation, and God. But not before we got Mrs. Chapman's blessing. And not for the way we sounded; for the way we looked.

Her daughter, Zara, was in the choir, too, and when I was writing this book, she reminded me what a stickler her mother was about clean choir robes. Actually, Mrs. Chapman was a stickler about clean everything. Mrs. Chapman was so serious about the cleanliness-is-next-to-godliness thing, for example, she didn't even let us sit in the pews unless we passed her inspection. And she didn't play that "come as you are"

*Zara Bradley and her mother, Mrs. Harriett Chapman— my church choir director who gave me my first church solo.*

stuff: Girls who wanted to sing at Sunday morning service had to wear a dress or skirt; boys needed a suit and tie.

There was only one thing Mrs. Chapman believed in more than the importance of being clean: the importance of being prepared. For a dedicated choir director (and Christian) like her, that meant knowing "the proper way," as Mrs. Chapman called it, to sing God's praises. And not just some of God's praises; Mrs. Chapman believed you should be prepared to sing all of God's praises. Or at least all of the ones she could teach us on Tuesday night.

Back in the '60s, that's when the Young Adults Choir held practice. It was the one night of the week Mrs. Chapman could get 50 teenagers (my sisters and Armstead were in the choir, too) all together in a church chapel and teach us everything we needed to know about the hymn we'd be singing on Sunday for the Beulah Baptist faithful and, as Mrs. Chapman always reminded us, for the Lord. According to Mrs. Chapman, what we needed to know about the selected hymn was, well, everything...or at the very least every single verse. If she found out you knew only the first one or two, heaven help you. She wouldn't call you out publicly, but you could forget about singing on Sunday. "Ladies and gentlemen," Mrs. Chapman would announce before sitting down at the organ, "anybody can sing the first and second stanzas. Serious choirs know the whole hymn."

Thanks to Mrs. Chapman's insistence on proper preparation, a serious choir is exactly what we became. Not only did we know every verse of every hymn; we knew every melody and harmony, too. We may have looked like a bunch of average teenagers from the West Side of Philly, but on Sunday morning, we sounded like a bunch of musical prodigies from the gilded halls of Juilliard. People came from all over Philly to hear us sing. How I loved those Sunday mornings singing solo in Mrs. Chapman's choir.

There was only one other church event that could draw a second-Sunday-of-the-month kind of crowd: the Beulah Baptist bake sales. I don't know how or why, but it seemed like all the sisters who attended Beulah were serious bakers. I'd bet good money that every one of them could bake the apron off the best French pastry chef in Paris without breaking a sweat.

The desserts the women of Beulah Baptist brought to those bake sales were nothing short of a-ma-zing. Some were so gorgeous, they looked like they belonged in a magazine. All were so fly-you-to-the-moon delicious, even double cobblers and four-tier cakes didn't last the week. Sometimes they didn't make it through the day! You wouldn't believe the things I saw churchgoing people do to get their hands on those desserts. Without going into detail, suffice it to say that when cakes and cobblers got low, some very un-Christian-like competitions went down in the vestibule.

There was one church member, however, whose baking skills were—how can I put this gently?—less than fabulous: Mrs. Chapman. I'm not telling tales out of school (or is it church?).

If she were here, Mrs. Chapman would be the first to tell you that dessert-baking wasn't her thing. Of course, in the same breath, she'd also tell you that her kitchen was so spotless, you could eat whatever dessert *you* were baking right off of her floor.

When I asked Zara for her mom's corn pudding recipe to include in this book, she told me two things about it I never knew: (1) The only reason the recipe became so famous in the church (and the neighborhood) was because Mrs. Chapman spent hours perfecting it so that Zara would have something to take to the bake sales; and (2) Mrs. Chapman made it sweet so it could pass for dessert. "Mom knew her cakes and pies weren't going to win any prizes," Zara told me. "So she worked on her corn pudding recipe until she knew every single time she took it out of the oven, she'd have a pan of sweet perfection."

See what I mean about how recipes can teach us so much about the people we love? I always thought Mrs. Chapman's corn pudding was the only dish Zara ever brought to the bake sales because it was so delicious. And it *is* delicious. It's so good, in fact, that every time I bake it, it makes me think of something I heard the award-winning chef and restaurateur Edward Lee—"one part Southern soul, one part Asian spice, one part Brooklyn attitude," as PBS describes him—say: "Dessert is like a feel-good song, and the best ones make you dance."

Mrs. Chapman made every single hymn she taught me a feel-good song. And her sweet corn pudding will make you dance.

# Mrs. Chapman's Make-You-Wanna-Dance Sweet Corn Pudding

Dead simple, this is the kind of dish that you can make in a few minutes to feed a hungry group of teenagers, as Mrs. Chapman sometimes did if we had a really good rehearsal. You could cut the sugar back to 2 tablespoons, but then it wouldn't be Mrs. Chapman's.

Makes 8 servings

Softened butter, for the baking dish

½ cup sugar

3 tablespoons cornstarch

Two 14.75-ounce cans creamed corn

One 12-ounce can evaporated milk

2 large eggs, beaten to blend

3 tablespoons unsalted butter
(2 tablespoons melted, 1 tablespoon
cut into small pieces)

1. Position a rack in the center of the oven and preheat the oven to 350°F. Lightly butter a 2-quart round baking dish.

2. Whisk the sugar and cornstarch together. Add the creamed corn. Gradually whisk in the evaporated milk, followed by the eggs and the melted butter. Mix until thoroughly combined. Pour into the prepared dish. Dot with the butter pieces. Put the dish into a larger pan. Pour enough hot water into the pan from a kettle to come about ½ inch up the sides of the dish.

3. Bake until the pudding is golden brown and barely set (a knife inserted near the center of the pudding will come out mostly clean), about 1 hour. Remove the dish from the water. Let stand for 5 minutes and serve.

# Make-It-Your-Way Egg Custards

There is a reason baked custard cups were so popular back in the day: The lady of the household (and in my house, Dad was a cook, too) could get them ready in a few minutes with a handful of ingredients that were already in the kitchen. Also, you can enjoy them warm or chilled. And they are creamy, sweet, and delicious. With the eggs and milk, Chubby knew they were nutritious, too (folks didn't worry about sugar much back then). Here is the classic version, with plenty of tips to be sure that yours turn out perfectly…too many people overbake custard, causing it to curdle. I've also given some variations, although the plain vanilla version is one of the all-time classic desserts.

Makes 6 servings

3 cups whole milk

4 large eggs

½ cup sugar

1 teaspoon vanilla extract

Freshly grated or ground nutmeg
    or ground cinnamon, for topping

1. Position a rack in the center of the oven and preheat the oven to 325°F. (A low oven temperature is one of the secrets of smooth and creamy custard.)

2. Heat the milk in a large saucepan over medium heat until tiny bubbles form around the edges. Remove from the heat. (Warm milk in the custard mixture will help it bake more quickly.)

3. Whisk the eggs, sugar, and vanilla together in a large bowl until combined. Gradually whisk in the hot milk. Strain the mixture through a medium-mesh sieve into a 1-quart liquid measuring cup or a pitcher to remove the egg chalazae (cords on the yolks).

4. Place six ¾-cup ramekins or custard cups in a large roasting pan. Fill the ramekins with the liquid custard. (Pouring the custard into the ramekins is much neater and easier than using a ladle.) Sprinkle a little nutmeg over each custard. Carefully slide the pan with the ramekins into the oven. Quickly pour enough hot water from a kettle into the pan to come ¼ inch or so up the sides of the ramekins. (The water doesn't

have to come very far up the ramekin sides—just enough to insulate the ramekins and keep them from getting too hot in the oven, which could overcook the custards.)

5. Bake until the custards are set and jiggle as a unit when a ramekin is gently shaken, 30 to 35 minutes. If you insert a small knife into the custard about an inch from the sides, the blade will come out clean. (The very center—about the size of a dime—may seem unset, but it will firm up when cooled.)

6. Carefully remove the custards from the pan. Let them cool for 15 minutes. Serve warm, if desired. Or let cool completely, cover each with plastic wrap, and refrigerate until chilled, at least 2 hours. (The custards can be refrigerated for up to 3 days.)

**Coffee Custards:** *If you like coffee, you'll love these custards. Add 3 tablespoons coarsely chopped coffee beans to the milk and bring to a simmer. Let stand for 15 minutes. Strain the milk mixture into a 1-quart liquid measuring cup or pitcher to remove the coffee beans. Whisk the hot flavored milk into the egg mixture. Strain again to remove the chalazae.*

**Earl Grey Custards:** *You can add just about any tea that you prefer here, even a fruit-flavored one, but Earl Grey has a nice citrus perfume to it. Add 1½ table-spoons loose-leaf Earl Grey tea to the milk and bring to a simmer. Let stand for 15 minutes. Strain the milk mixture into a 1-quart liquid measuring cup or pitcher to remove the tea. Whisk the hot flavored milk into the egg mixture. Strain again to remove the chalazae.*

**Vanilla Bean Custards:** *While vanilla extract is just fine, fresh vanilla will add a touch of elegance to this dessert. Omit the vanilla extract. Cut a vanilla bean in half crosswise; save one half for another use. Split the remaining bean lengthwise. Add the split bean to the milk and bring to a simmer. Let stand for 15 minutes. Remove the bean and set it aside. Whisk the hot infused milk into the egg mixture. Strain to remove the chalazae. Using the tip of a small knife, scrape the seeds from the bean halves into the custard liquid and discard the bean halves.*

**Chai Custards:** *Add 2 teaspoons loose-leaf black tea, ½ of a 3-inch cinnamon stick, about 10 cardamom seeds (if you have them), 2 whole cloves, and a few gratings of fresh nutmeg (or a pinch of ground nutmeg) to the milk and bring to a simmer. Let stand for 15 minutes. Strain the milk mixture into a 1-quart liquid measuring cup or pitcher to remove the tea and spices. Whisk the hot flavored milk into the egg mixture. Strain again to remove the chalazae.*

**Citrus Custards:** *Using a swivel-blade vegetable peeler, remove the zest from ½ large orange or 1 lemon (or use a combination of ½ orange and ½ lemon) in strips. Add the zest strips to the milk and bring to a simmer. Let stand for 15 minutes. Strain the milk mixture into a 1-quart liquid measuring cup or pitcher to remove the zests. Whisk the hot flavored milk into the egg mixture. Strain again to remove the chalazae.*

# Lemon Mousse with Blackberries

This sweet but puckery pudding is another make-it-and-forget-it dessert. It is cool, creamy, and refreshing—just the ticket for a summertime treat. Other berries are good, too, but the purple blackberries against the yellow lemon mousse are especially pretty.

Makes 4 to 6 servings

2 lemons

5 large egg yolks

¼ cup granulated sugar

½ cup (1 stick) unsalted butter, cut into ½-inch cubes

1 cup heavy cream

1 tablespoon confectioners' sugar

One 6-ounce container (about 1⅓ cups) fresh blackberries

Additional finely grated lemon zest and confectioners' sugar, for garnish (optional)

1. Finely grate the zest from the lemons and set the zest aside. Juice the lemons. Measure ¼ cup lemon juice and save the remainder for another use.

2. Set a wire sieve over a medium bowl near the stove. Whisk the lemon juice, yolks, and granulated sugar together in a small heavy saucepan. Add the butter. Cook over medium-low heat, whisking constantly, until the butter has melted into the mixture. Change from the whisk to a heatproof spatula. Cook, stirring constantly and being sure to reach the corners and sides of the saucepan, until the curd is steaming and looks like commercial lemon pudding and your finger can cut a swath through the curd on the spatula, 1 to 2 minutes. (The curd will read 180°F on an instant-read thermometer.) Do not let the curd come to a simmer. Strain through the sieve to remove any bits of cooked egg white. Stir in the lemon zest.

3. Place the bowl in a larger bowl of iced water. Let the curd stand, stirring occasionally, until cold, about 15 minutes.

4. Whip the cream with the confectioners' sugar in a chilled medium bowl with an electric mixer set at high speed until it forms stiff peaks. Stir one quarter of the cream into the curd to lighten it. Fold in the remaining cream.

5. Divide half of the berries among 4 to 6 dessert bowls or glasses and top with equal amounts of the mousse. Cover each mousse and refrigerate until chilled and set, at least 1 hour or up to 1 day. Top the mousses with the remaining berries and garnish with additional confectioners' sugar and lemon zest, if desired. Serve chilled.

# Cousin Penny's Really, Really Good Rice Pudding

*Cooking well doesn't mean cooking fancy.*

Every time I think about that Julia Child quote, I want to do what the sisters at the Beulah Baptist Church did when I was singing in the choir: Stand up and say, "Amen." Since the Patti Pie Phenomenon (page viii), I've been quoting it on the regular to home cooks across America. Especially the newbie bakers.

When beginner bakers ask me for a "fabulous" dessert recipe, I know they're hoping I'll give them step-by-step instructions for some fancy concoction a French pastry chef would make. A recipe for a complicated, highfalutin confectionery delight is what newbie bakers always expect me to share. They're stunned when I give them this unfussy rice pudding recipe instead. In fact, they usually go slack-jawed before I finish listing the ingredients. "Rice pudding, Ms. LaBelle?" they always ask, not even trying to hide their shock. "Rice pudding, really?"

"Yes, Sugar, really," I always answer. You're probably not going to find it in the window of a Paris bakery, I know. But I also know this: When you make it with tender loving care, like Aunt Hattie did, rice pudding can be every bit as fabulous as, say, that $1,000 "golden opulence sundae" they serve at Serendipity 3, the New York City restaurant on the Upper East Side where celebs are often spotted. You *have* to hear its description:

Five scoops of the richest Tahitian vanilla bean ice cream infused with Madagascar vanilla and covered in 23K edible gold leaf, the sundae is drizzled with the world's most expensive chocolate, Amedei Porcelana, and covered with chunks of rare Chuao chocolate, which is from cocoa beans harvested by the Caribbean Sea on Venezuela's coast. Suffused with exotic candied fruits from Paris, gold dragées, truffles, and Marzipan cherries, the sundae is topped with a tiny glass bowl of Grand Passion caviar, exclusive dessert caviar made of salt-free American Golden Caviar, known for its sparkling golden color. It's sweetened and infused with fresh passion fruit, orange and Armagnac, and served in a Baccarat crystal goblet with an 18k gold spoon.

I just have three questions: (1) Do you get to keep the goblet and the spoon?; (2) are Aunt Buba's tarts still on the menu?—because that's what I'd order; and (3) who in their right mind drops a mortgage payment on ice cream? Aunt Hattie Mae would come back and smack me if I spent a grand on dessert, I don't care how fancy it's prepared.

Which brings me to my cousin Penny and what she told me about her mother's rice pudding, something I never knew: Just as getting bragging rights wasn't the sole reason Aunt Josh wanted to cook breakfast for President Eisenhower (pages 68–69), getting a delicious dessert on her dinner table wasn't the only reason Aunt Hattie served rice pudding to her kids. "It was cheap, Patsy," Penny told me when I was writing this book. "And Mom could buy enough rice to make dessert for all of us, so no one would be left out."

Wow. The things a recipe can teach you. Other than telling you that Aunt Hattie's rice pudding was really, really good, even if it was really, really cheap, there's really nothing else to say. (Calling all French pastry chefs: You may stand up and applaud now.) So I'll end the way I began: with a quote I love...and truly believe.

It's not from Julia, but from the James Beard award–winning chef Thomas Keller. And I'm sharing it not because this rice pudding recipe illustrates it beautifully and perfectly, though it does. I'm sharing it because it's something Aunt Hattie always taught me, something she herself would have said: "A recipe has no soul. You as the cook must bring soul to the recipe."

If you bring *your* soul to this rice pudding recipe, I'm betting it will be every bit as fabulous as that $1,000 sundae. Probably better.

# Cousin Penny's Really, Really Good Rice Pudding

Busy cooks with households full of hungry people have to keep a repertoire of surefire easy recipes on hand to whip up in no time. Aunt Hattie Mae could stretch a grocery dollar into the middle of the next week, and she knew rice pudding was one of those classics. Just take leftover rice, stir it into custard, then bake it up. These days, it doesn't have to be white rice, so use brown rice, wild rice, or even quinoa if you wish. You can serve it with whipped cream on top, but it is just as good plain. Everyone should know how to make this dish.

Makes 4 to 6 servings

Softened butter, for the baking dish

4 large eggs

½ cup sugar

1 teaspoon vanilla extract

2 cups whole milk

1 cup cooked white rice

½ cup seedless raisins

Ground cinnamon or freshly grated nutmeg, for sprinkling

1. Position a rack in the center of the oven and preheat the oven to 325°F. Lightly butter an 8-inch square baking dish.

2. Whisk the eggs, sugar, and vanilla in a medium bowl. Gradually whisk in the milk. Mix in the cooked rice and raisins. Pour the mixture into the prepared dish, being sure the rice and raisins are distributed evenly. Sprinkle with a light dusting of cinnamon.

3. Place the dish in a larger pan. Pour water into the larger pan to come about ½ inch up the sides of the dish. Place in the oven and bake until the pudding jiggles as a unit when the dish is lightly shaken, about 55 minutes. Remove from the oven. Remove the dish from the pan and let cool for 30 minutes. Serve warm or cover and refrigerate until chilled. (The pudding can be refrigerated for up to 2 days.)

# Gia's Over-the-Rainbow Sweet Potato Flan

I was standing in my kitchen when it happened. (How many times have I said *that*?) Gia was fussing and fidgeting, but when I tried to lift her out of her high chair, Girlfriend had the nerve to push me away...and then start pointing to the sweet potatoes I'd just taken out of the oven. Dr. Diabetes, take note: I wasn't making sweet potato pie; I was baking them as part of a healthy lunch. But I digress. At the time, Gia wasn't even a year old. So I thought she couldn't possibly be trying to get out of her high chair so she could get over to those sweet potatoes. But that's *exactly* what she was doing. Gia got fussier and fidgetier (trust me; when you've got a toddler under your charge, that's a real word) until I let her taste the tiniest piece.

Now, I would have bet good money that she was going to spit that sweet potato right out, since when Zuri was that age, he was such a picky eater. Long before Whole Foods was even a thought in anybody's head, I used to buy that kid fresh fruits and vegetables and make his baby food from scratch. And what thanks did I get? Let's just say, with few exceptions, Zuri acted like I was trying to feed him some expired canned peas. So you can see why I was so surprised when Gia went absolutely nuts over that half a bite of sweet potato.

I wish you could have seen her. The way she was smiling and clapping, you would have thought I'd given her a pony or a puppy, not a piece of potato. Or, even better, a pair of those darling little Armani baby shoes. Okay, fine... those are more for me than for Gia. And don't think I didn't seriously consider buying them. But when I mentioned it to Lona and Zuri, they gave me the side eye so I took the hint. (Note to my daughter-in-law: I know you will teach Gia the really important stuff, but I plan to be her go-to person in the shoe shopping department. Ditto the cooking and baking areas.)

Looking back, I really don't know why I was so surprised—either that Gia would be so crazy about the taste of sweet potato or that she was ready to eat solid food at six months old. For one thing, Gia has always been advanced. I know *every* grandmother makes that claim, but she

*My darling Gia loves whipping up goodies in her kitchen almost as much as I love whipping up goodies in mine.*

was holding her own bottle when she was *four days old*. And yes, I have the photo to prove it. For another, ever since that you-had-to-see-it-to-believe-it run at Walmart on my sweet potato pies, I've gone from wondering *if* I have some kind of mystical/spiritual/ancestral connection to sweet potatoes to being convinced that I do. There's just no other way to explain it.

So you'll understand why I'm so convinced of the connection, I need to tell you about the Patti Pie Phenomenon, as it came to be known. As I said in the introduction, it happened a few years ago when a fan purchased one of my sweet potato pies and then put a musical review on YouTube. (Shout-out to James Wright Chanel for that memorable performance!) *Twenty million* views later, everyone was rushing to Walmart to get their hands on one. In a single weekend, every one of my sweet potato pies sold out… *at every single Walmart store*. You couldn't get your hands on one for love or money. I was in London playing Wembley Stadium at the time, but the corporate "suits" told Zuri that Walmart sold one pie *per second* for 72 hours straight.

And the craziness didn't stop there. When word leaked that no one at Walmart knew when the pies would be restocked, the would-be pie scalpers started cropping up here and there, eager to create a thriving resale market. Before it was all over, my sweet potato pies—which cost less than four bucks—were selling on eBay for $45. I knew something serious was happening when people started auctioning them off with bid prices ranging from $50 to $12,000. Things got downright insane when someone actually offered to pay the high bid. See why I believe I have a cosmic connection with sweet potatoes?

A quick word to the gentleman who offered $12,000 for my $3.48 pie: While I'm flattered beyond words, there are so many people who go to bed hungry, so many families who wonder where they'll get their next meal, I'd much rather you give that money to a local food bank or some other organization you respect and admire that's dedicated to helping those in need. Should you decide to do *that* with your twelve grand, I'll personally bake you a *dozen* of my sweet potato pies.

*Zuri, Gia, Lona, and THE pie.*

A long time ago, I *did* bake a bunch of sweet potato pies for someone else who really loved them: my sister Barbara. They were for the reception I hosted after her wedding. Two years later, I baked them again. This time, they were for the repast I hosted after Barbara's funeral. Both times, two of my dear friends, women from the old neighborhood, stayed up all night with me helping cook Barbara's favorite dishes. They knew how badly I wanted/needed to do it, but that it would be too much for me to handle alone. Maudie Hurd and Llona Gullette both are gone now. But because of those all-night cooking/baking sessions, I'm pretty sure Barbara had *something* to do with the Patti Pie Phenomenon.

I think my grandmother Tempie had something to do with it, too. She died of leukemia when she was only 33, so I never got to meet her. But my father told me her sweet potato biscuits were *epic*. All her homemade breads were. He said Grandmother Tempie never even measured the flour; she just knew when the dough "felt right." I'm still looking for her sweet potato biscuit recipe, but until I find it, give the mile-high biscuits on page 203 a try. I promise; they're so good, they'd make Grandmother Tempie proud. (But you should measure the flour!)

I *know* my aunts and my mother had something to do with the Patti Pie Phenomenon. I wouldn't be surprised if they orchestrated the whole thing. Aunt Hattie, Aunt Josh, and Chubby were sweet potato sorceresses, and they passed their recipes down to me. (I based my Walmart sweet potato pie on Chubby's recipe, and *The* Sweet Potato Pie [page 132] is based on it, too.) Aunt Hattie's sweet tater bread is almost as legendary. She and Aunt Josh made certain it was on the menu when they cooked breakfast for President Eisenhower (pages 68–69). A little secret from me to you: While I have *never* tasted

any sweet potato bread as good as Aunt Hattie's, there's a little bakery right outside of Philly, Sweet Jazmines, that makes a sweet potato muffin she would have been proud to put on her table.

Which brings me back to why I shouldn't have been surprised when Gia went nuts the first time she tasted sweet potato. Girlfriend couldn't help herself; sweet potatoes are in her DNA. I also should have known that my (Chubby-inspired) sweet potato pies would fly off of Walmart's shelves faster than the speed of light. Given my family history with sweet potatoes, I don't think any other outcome was possible. I definitely don't think it was a coincidence. As I'm always telling Zuri, coincidence is just God's way of staying invisible.

Today, as I sit feeding this over-the-rainbow sweet potato flan to the great-granddaughter that Bertha "Chubby" Holte and Anna Edwards would never get to meet, and the grandniece that Vivian and Barbara and Jackie would never get to hold, and the grand-grandniece that Aunt Hattie and Aunt Josh would never get to see, I'm reminded of something I heard on *The Wonder Years* a long time ago, long before Gia was even a twinkle in Lona's and Zuri's eyes: *Memory is a way of holding on to the things you love. The things you are. The things you never want to lose.*

So are recipes.

# Gia's Over-the-Rainbow Sweet Potato Flan

Flan is an unmolded custard baked right in its own caramel sauce. Do not let making the caramel scare you, and just think of how many people make flan every day around the world! The main thing is not to freak out when you see a little smoke coming off of the caramel, as that is a sign that it is done.

Makes 8 servings

**CARAMEL SYRUP**

1 cup granulated sugar

3 tablespoons water

**CUSTARD**

1¼ pounds orange-fleshed sweet potatoes (yams), scrubbed but unpeeled

1½ cups whole milk, divided

4 large eggs plus 1 large egg yolk

⅔ cup packed light brown sugar

1 teaspoon ground cinnamon

1 teaspoon vanilla extract

½ cup heavy cream

1. Position a rack in the center of the oven and preheat the oven to 325°F.

2. **To make the caramel syrup:** Combine the granulated sugar and water together in a medium saucepan. Cook over medium-high heat, stirring constantly, until the mixture comes to a simmer. Continue cooking without stirring, occasionally washing down any sugar crystals that form on the sides of the saucepan with a bristle brush dipped into cold water, and gently swirling the saucepan by the handle, until the syrup is the color of an old penny (you will see wisps of smoke), about 5 minutes. Immediately pour the hot syrup into an ungreased 9-inch round metal cake pan. Using pot holders, quickly tilt the pan to coat the bottom and partway up the sides of the pan. Don't worry if the caramel cracks as it cools in the pan.

3. **To make the custard:** Pierce each sweet potato a few times with a fork. Microwave the sweet potatoes on high (100%) power, turning them over halfway through cooking, until tender, about 6 minutes. (The timing will vary according to the exact size and shape of the sweet potatoes and the wattage of the oven.) Let stand until cool enough to handle. Scoop the flesh into a bowl, discard the skins, and mash the flesh with a fork. Measure 1 cup sweet potato flesh. Discard the remainder or save for another use. Puree the sweet potato flesh and 1 cup of the milk in a blender until the mixture is smooth.

*Continued on page 186*

4.  Whisk the eggs and the egg yolk with the brown sugar, cinnamon, and vanilla in a medium bowl to dissolve the sugar. Add the sweet potato mixture, the cream, and the remaining ½ cup milk and whisk until combined. Pour into the prepared cake pan. Put the custard-filled cake pan in a larger roasting pan.

5.  Slide the roasting pan with the cake pan into the oven. Carefully pour enough hot water into the roasting pan to come about one-fourth of the way up the sides of the cake pan. Bake until the custard jiggles as a unit when the pan is shaken and a small knife inserted near the center comes out clean, 50 to 60 minutes. Carefully remove the cake pan from the roasting pan. Let the flan cool on a wire rack until tepid, about 2 hours.

6.  Cover the flan with plastic wrap and refrigerate until well chilled, at least 8 hours or overnight. (A long chilling time is important as it lets the hardened caramel dissolve back into a fluid sauce.)

7.  To serve, place the flan, still in the pan, in a larger pan and pour in enough warm tap water to come about ½ inch up the sides of the cake pan. Let stand for 3 to 5 minutes. Remove the cake pan and dry the outside of the pan with a towel. Using your thumb, gently pull the sides of the flan away from the cake pan. Using the heel of your hand, firmly rap all around the side of the pan to further loosen the flan. (You can also run a knife around the inside edge of the pan, but this can cut into the flan.) Place a round serving platter with a lip over the flan. Hold the pan and invert the pan and platter together. Give them a good shake to unmold the flan onto the platter. Pour any remaining syrup over the flan. Cut into wedges and serve chilled, spooning caramel syrup over each serving.

# Coconut Tapioca Pudding with Mango Sauce

Now, I know there are some of you who don't care for the look or texture of tapioca, but to everyone else, there is *nothing* like a cool, comforting bite of creamy tapioca pudding. This one is a bit more exotic than other recipes, with a simple mango sauce to give it a splash of bright color, similar to the flashy necklace that you might wear to set off a plain outfit. You can substitute other fruit for the mango for a different color and flavor combination—raspberries and papaya are both good swaps. This looks especially good in tall parfait glasses so you can see the layers. By the way, the coconut flavor is fairly mild, so if you want it to be stronger, use the optional coconut extract.

Makes 6 servings

### PUDDING

⅓ cup plus 1 tablespoon sugar

¼ cup instant tapioca

One 13.5-ounce can coconut milk, well shaken

1¼ cups whole milk

3 large egg yolks

1 teaspoon vanilla extract

½ teaspoon coconut extract (optional)

### MANGO SAUCE

1 large ripe mango (about 1 pound), peeled, pitted, and coarsely chopped (see Patti's Pointers)

2 tablespoons sugar

1 tablespoon fresh lime juice

⅓ cup sweetened coconut flakes

½ batch Whipped Cream (page 132) (optional)

1. **To make the pudding:** Whisk the sugar and tapioca together in a medium heavy saucepan. Add the coconut milk and whole milk and let stand for 5 minutes. Stirring constantly, and being sure the spoon reaches the pudding in the corners of the saucepan, bring to a boil over medium heat. Remove from the heat.

2. Whisk the yolks in a small bowl. Whisk in about a third of the hot tapioca mixture. Stir this mixture back into the saucepan. Return to medium heat and stir constantly until the pudding thickens and comes to a full boil. Remove from the heat and stir in the vanilla and the coconut extract, if using. Transfer to a medium bowl. Cover with plastic wrap pressed directly onto the pudding surface. Poke a few holes in the plastic wrap with the tip of a knife to let the steam escape. Let cool to room temperature.

3. **To make the sauce:** Puree the mango in a blender or food processor and measure; you should have 1 cup. Return to the blender and process with the sugar and lime juice until smooth. Cover and refrigerate the sauce.

*Continued on page 189*

4. Heat a small skillet over medium heat. Add the coconut and cook, stirring almost constantly, until toasted, about 1 minute. Transfer to a bowl and let cool completely.

5. To serve, divide the pudding and sauce in layers (about three layers of sauce, alternating with two layers of tapioca) among 6 tall parfait glasses. (The puddings can be covered and refrigerated for up to 1 day.) Top each with a dollop of whipped cream, if desired, and a sprinkle of toasted coconut. Serve chilled.

**Patti's Pointers:** *Mangoes are a little confusing to prep if you aren't familiar with the process. Place the fruit on the work surface where it will balance itself; the pit runs horizontally through the center of the fruit. Don't cut vertically into the mango or you'll run into the pit. Use a sharp knife to cut off the side of the fruit, around the pit. Turn the mango around and cut off the other side of the fruit. Using a large metal spoon, scoop the mango flesh from each portion in one piece. Pare the pit portion with a small knife and trim off any clinging fruit.*

# 7 ) *Breakfast Time*

If you have a family full of lazybones, you might have to develop ways to entice them out of bed on weekend mornings. There is no more surefire method than baking a tempting breakfast treat and filling the house with the enticing aromas of sugar and cinnamon. Fry up some bacon at the same time, and you will have the household in the kitchen in no time. I use the same basic sweet yeast dough in a few of these recipes: If you wish, the dough can rise in the refrigerator overnight to be baked first thing in the morning. I also give recipes for the very best pancakes and waffles around, as well as another way to make biscuits. And if you haven't ever had popovers, get ready to find a new breakfast favorite for slathering with butter and jam.

# Breakfast Time Yeast Dough

The three recipes that follow, Cinnamon Buns with Cream Cheese Icing (page 195), Philadelphia Extra-Sticky Buns (page 196), and Claudette's Magnificent Monkey Bread (page 201), use this dough. For no-fuss, freshly baked breakfast goodies, make it the night before baking and let it rise slowly in the refrigerator. You certainly can make it the morning of baking (it doesn't take very long to rise), but a slow rise does improve the dough's flavor a bit as the ingredients "get to know each other." This sweet dough is rich with milk, sugar, eggs, and butter. These ingredients will make the dough feel a little tacky, even when the correct amount of flour has been used.

Makes about 2¼ pounds

One ¼-ounce package (2¼ teaspoons) quick-rising yeast (also called instant or bread-machine yeast)

2 tablespoons warm water (see Patti's Pointers)

1 cup whole milk

½ cup (1 stick) unsalted butter, melted

½ cup granulated sugar

2 large eggs

1¼ teaspoons salt

4¾ cups unbleached all-purpose flour, as needed

Softened butter, for the bowl

1. Sprinkle the yeast over the warm water in a ramekin or custard cup. Let stand until the yeast softens and is gently bubbling, about 10 minutes. Stir to dissolve the yeast.

2. **To make the dough in a mixer:** Combine the milk, melted butter, and sugar in the bowl of a heavy-duty standing mixer. Add the dissolved yeast, eggs, and salt. Attach the mixer to the stand and fit with the paddle. With the mixer on low speed, gradually beat in enough of the flour to make a soft, sticky dough that cleans the sides of the bowl. Change to the dough hook and knead at medium speed until the dough is smooth and supple but still feels tacky, about 8 minutes. Turn out the dough onto a lightly floured work surface, knead briefly, and shape into a ball.

   **To make the dough by hand:** Whisk the milk, melted butter, and sugar together in a large bowl. Add the dissolved yeast, eggs, and salt and mix again. Gradually stir in flour until the dough cannot be stirred. Scrape the dough out onto a well-floured work surface. Knead, adding more flour as necessary, until the dough is smooth and supple but still feels tacky, about 8 minutes. Shape the dough into a ball.

   In either case, do not add too much flour. The dough will feel tacky, but as long as it only lightly sticks to the work surface, it is fine. It will also firm up during rising.

3. Butter a large bowl. Add the ball to the bowl and turn to coat with butter. Cover tightly with plastic wrap and let stand in a warm place until doubled in volume, about 1½ hours. (Or refrigerate for up to 16 hours. Do not extend the refrigeration time or the dough may develop a sour flavor.)

**Monkey Bread Dough:** *Follow the instructions above, using 1 package (2¼ teaspoons) instant yeast; ¼ cup warm water; ½ cup whole milk; 4 tablespoons (½ stick) unsalted butter, melted; 3 tablespoons sugar; 1 large egg; ½ teaspoon salt; and 2⅔ cups unbleached all-purpose flour, as needed. If you wish, let the dough rise in the refrigerator in the covered bowl for 8 to 12 hours.*

**Patti's Pointers:** *If you don't consider yourself a baker, no worries. This dough is made with instant yeast (also called bread-machine or quick-rising yeast), which, unlike active dry yeast, does not need to be dissolved in water at a specific temperature. The dough is easiest to prepare in a heavy-duty mixer, although it can also be kneaded by hand.*

*Don't worry about the exact temperature of the water. It should be the approximate temperature of bathwater. With old-fashioned active dry or fresh yeast, the water must be at an exact temperature, but the contemporary instant yeast is a lot more forgiving (as long as the temperature isn't above 140°F, which will feel uncomfortably hot). But for this kind of rich sweet dough, it is still a good idea to dissolve the yeast first.*

*Some people don't like to bake breakfast goodies because of the various rising times—you have to get up pretty early to have cinnamon buns on the table by a reasonable hour. The beauty of this dough is that after its initial rise of about 1½ hours, the buns can be shaped, put in the baking dish, covered, and then refrigerated for up to 16 hours. The next morning, just let the buns stand at room temperature for about 2 hours to lose their chill before baking. You don't save much actual time this way, but it does cut down on cleanup on a weekend morning.*

# Cinnamon Buns with Cream Cheese Icing

Here is a bakery classic that you really can make at home. The recipe makes big but not enormous rolls that kids of all ages love to tear into. The great thing about these home-baked rolls is that you can control the amount of cinnamon and icing to fit your taste—and they are almost ridiculously tasty.

Makes 12 buns

Softened butter, for the pan

⅓ cup packed light brown sugar

1 tablespoon ground cinnamon

Flour, for the dough

Breakfast Time Yeast Dough (page 192)

6 tablespoons (¾ stick) unsalted butter, well softened (not just at room temperature)

ICING

2 ounces cream cheese, at room temperature

1 teaspoon vanilla extract

1½ cups confectioners' sugar

3 tablespoons whole milk, as needed

1. Lightly butter a 10 by 15-inch baking dish. Mix the brown sugar and cinnamon together in a small bowl.

2. On a lightly floured work surface, pat and stretch the dough into a 14 by 12-inch rectangle, with a long side facing you. (This soft dough is very easy to work with, so you probably won't need to use a rolling pin.) "Square off" the corners. Using your fingers or an offset metal spatula, spread the softened butter over the dough, leaving a 1-inch border at the top. Brush a little water along the exposed dough border. Evenly sprinkle the brown sugar mixture over the butter. Starting at the long side nearest you, roll up the dough and pinch the long seam shut.

3. Using a sharp knife, cut the rolled dough crosswise into 12 equal pieces. Arrange the buns, flat side down, in the baking dish in 3 rows of 4 buns, shaping the soft dough in the pan into neat rolls. Cover the dish tightly with plastic wrap. Refrigerate for at least 8 hours or up to 16 hours, no longer. (Or place the dish in a warm place and let stand until the rolls look nicely puffed but not doubled, about 45 minutes.)

4. Position a rack in the center of the oven and preheat the oven to 350°F. Uncover the dish and bake until the rolls are golden brown and the crevices between the rolls look dry, about 30 minutes. Let the rolls cool in the pan on a wire cake rack for 15 minutes.

5. **Meanwhile, make the icing:** Beat the cream cheese and vanilla in a medium bowl with a handheld electric mixer at high speed until smooth. With the mixer set on low speed, gradually add the confectioners' sugar and mix until crumbly. Gradually beat in enough of the milk to make a smooth, spreadable icing.

6. Spread the icing over the rolls. Let stand for 5 minutes. Serve warm.

# Philadelphia Extra-Sticky Buns

Philadelphia is the birthplace of the American sticky bun, and every bakery has their own way of making these rolled-up pastries. Some fill the buns with raisins; others use walnuts or pecans or even a combination of all three. That's all good, but what really matters is the gooey caramel sauce that separates great rolls from others, and this recipe has more of the good stuff. The recipe is designed for preparing the rolls the night before and then baking them the next morning just before serving.

Makes 12 buns

**CARAMEL SAUCE**

1 cup heavy cream

1 cup packed light brown sugar

2 tablespoons light corn syrup

2 tablespoons unsalted butter, plus
   softened butter for the dish

Pinch of salt

1 cup coarsely chopped pecans

**FILLING**

½ cup packed light brown sugar

½ cup finely chopped pecans

1 teaspoon ground cinnamon


Flour, for the dough

Breakfast Time Yeast Dough
   (page 192)

2 tablespoons unsalted butter,
   well softened

2 tablespoons unsalted butter,
   melted, for brushing

1. **To make the sauce:** Bring the cream, brown sugar, corn syrup, butter, and salt to a boil in a medium saucepan over medium-high heat, whisking often. Remove from the heat; let the sauce cool.

2. Lightly butter a 10 by 15-inch baking dish. Sprinkle the coarsely chopped pecans evenly in the bottom of the dish. Pour in the caramel sauce (see Patti's Pointers). Set aside.

3. **To prepare the filling:** Mix the brown sugar, finely chopped pecans, and cinnamon in a medium bowl.

4. Lightly flour a work surface. Pat and stretch the dough into a 14 by 12-inch rectangle, with a long side facing you. (This soft dough is very easy to work with, so you probably won't need to use a rolling pin.) "Square off" the corners. Using your fingers or an offset metal spatula, spread the softened butter over the dough, leaving a 1-inch

border at the top. Brush a little water along the exposed dough border. Evenly sprinkle the filling over the butter. Starting at the long side nearest you, roll up the dough and pinch the long seam shut.

5. Using a very sharp knife, cut the rolled dough crosswise into 12 equal pieces. Arrange the buns, flat side down, in the baking dish in 3 rows of 4 buns, shaping the soft dough in the pan into neat rolls. Cover the dish tightly with plastic wrap. Refrigerate for at least 8 hours or up to 16 hours, no longer. (Or place the dish in a warm place and let stand until the rolls look nicely puffed but not doubled, about 45 minutes.)

6. Position a rack in the center of the oven and preheat the oven to 350°F. Uncover the dish and bake until the buns are golden brown and the crevices between the buns look dry, about 30 minutes.

7. Brush the tops of the buns with the melted butter. Place a large rimmed baking sheet (preferably a half-sheet pan) over the dish. Using pot holders and holding them together, flip the dish and baking sheet over to unmold the buns onto the sheet. Let the buns cool for 10 to 15 minutes. Separate the buns and serve warm.

**Patti's Pointers:** *While these buns are extra gooey, don't add more caramel sauce than the recipe calls for, or it will bubble over in the oven, which is an awful mess. (Take my word for it and don't ask how I know...) So if you want more sauce, simply boil up a double batch, pour 1¼ cups in the pan for baking, and reserve the remainder. When ready to serve, just warm the reserved sauce, whisking it well, and pour some over each roll before serving.*

# Claudette's Magnificent Monkey Bread

I'm smiling as I write this. That's because just *thinking* about baking monkey bread takes me back. *Waaaaay* back. Back to the '60s when my sisters and I spent countless hours in my mother's kitchen cooking (we threw down on Sundays!), drinking wine (raise your hand if you remember Manischewitz), and dancing to the radio (we were, as Grace Jones sang years later, slaves to the rhythm). If my closest friend, Claudette, was hanging with us—and she usually was—monkey bread was always in the mix.

You've heard the saying "Life is short, eat dessert first"? Well, that was Claudette's mantra. Claudette Henderson Grant could consume her body weight in fat and sugar and never gain an ounce. She loved all things sweet, but my monkey bread was her favorite. I once watched her polish off an entire pan of it and, a few hours later, change into her skinniest pair of jeans. Had I tried that, well, suffice it to say I would have been making a very different wardrobe choice. (Think: elastic-waist pants…not that I'm bitter.)

All kidding aside, Claudette's magic metabolism wasn't the only special thing about her. For one thing, she was beautiful. Fall-down-on-the-floor-and-weep gorgeous. But unlike a lot of strikingly beautiful people I've known, Claudette seemed oblivious to the effect her supermodel looks had on us mere mortals. Which, of course, only made everyone love her more.

Neither her beauty nor her humility, however, explains why I loved Claudette. At least not entirely. I loved Claudette because she was a shaman. Or I should say a shawoman. From the day my baby sister, Jackie, introduced us, I could tell Claudette was born an old soul. She was

perceptive, clued-up, wise beyond her years. She understood the way women love ("All the unconditional love in the world isn't going to change him from who he is to who you want him to be"), the way men think (trust me; that's a whole different book), and how to maximize all the resources the good Lord gave you.

The sharpest thing about Claudette wasn't her looks; it was her mind. She knew so much about life in general…and me in particular. Don't ask me how, but Claudette had a knack for saying exactly what I needed to hear at the exact moment I needed to hear it. Her counsel ran the gamut from the practical ("Don't wear that shade of green, Patsy. It makes your face look ashy") to the profound ("I don't care who doesn't want you to go through with your pregnancy. It's your body, your baby, your decision"). See why I asked her to be Zuri's godmother?

Claudette's gone now; she was only 38 when we lost her to breast cancer. But in her all-too-brief time on this earth, she taught me so much; so many priceless life lessons. Like: Friends are the family we choose. (I feel so blessed we chose each other.) And what looks good from afar is often far from good. (I'm talking to you, Mr. Player.) And my personal favorite, although I admit this particular lesson took me years to learn: Love is demonstration, not declaration. (Need I say more?)

These days, when I want to demonstrate my love, I often head for the kitchen and bake. Nothing says "I love you" like perfectly frosted cinnamon buns (page 195) or hummingbird cake made from scratch (page 27).

Except, of course, Claudette's magnificent monkey bread.

# Claudette's Magnificent Monkey Bread

This bread with the strange name is more fun than a barrel of monkeys to make because it allows you to play with your food. And with its cinnamon-sugar aroma, it will make your kitchen smell like the best bakery in town. Speaking of which, not many bakeries even make monkey bread anymore, so this is one of those desserts that if you want it, you are probably going to have to make it yourself, just like I always made it for Claudette. Give yourself a head start and make the Monkey Bread Dough on page 192 ahead of time and allow it to rise. It can even be made and refrigerated the night before.

Makes 8 servings

¼ cup granulated sugar

1 teaspoon ground cinnamon

Softened butter, for the pan

Monkey Bread Dough (variation of
   Breakfast Time Yeast Dough, page 192)

½ cup (1 stick) unsalted butter

½ cup packed light brown sugar

1. Mix the granulated sugar and cinnamon together well in a small bowl.

2. Generously butter a 10-cup nonstick Bundt (fluted tube) pan. Turn out the dough onto an unfloured work surface. Cut the dough into 24 equal pieces. One at a time, roll the balls under your cupped palm to shape them into balls. Roll each ball in the sugar mixture and arrange the balls in the prepared pan in a double layer, making the depth as even as possible. Cover with plastic wrap and let stand in a warm place until the balls look gently puffed, about 30 minutes. (If the dough is chilled, allow about 1¼ hours.)

3. Melt the butter in a small saucepan over medium heat. Add the brown sugar and bring to a simmer, whisking constantly. Let the sauce cool, whisking often, until lukewarm, about 15 minutes.

4. Meanwhile, position a rack in the center of the oven and preheat the oven to 350°F.

5. Uncover the pan. Evenly pour the sauce over the dough balls in the pan. Bake, uncovered, until the balls are golden brown and any cracks between them look dry, 30 to 35 minutes. (A surefire way to test the monkey bread is with an instant-read thermometer, which should read about 200°F when inserted into the center of the dough.)

6. Place a large platter over the pan. Holding the pan and the platter together, flip them over to unmold the monkey bread onto the serving platter. Let cool for 15 to 30 minutes. Serve warm.

# Mile-High Biscuits

These are a cross between a biscuit and a dinner roll, with a bit of yeast to contribute fluffiness and flakiness. An advantage is that the dough does not require kneading and can be mixed a couple of days ahead of baking, which is great if you want to jump out of bed and bake some biscuits without any work at all. For those of you who like round biscuits, you can re-roll the scraps without their toughening.

Makes about 9 biscuits

2½ cups unbleached all-purpose flour, plus more for rolling

2 tablespoons sugar

1½ teaspoons baking powder

½ teaspoon baking soda

½ teaspoon instant yeast (also called quick-acting or bread-machine yeast)

¾ teaspoon salt

½ cup chilled vegetable shortening, cut into ½-inch chunks

1 cup buttermilk

1. Whisk the flour, sugar, baking powder, baking soda, yeast, and salt together in a large bowl. Add the shortening and cut it into the flour mixture with a pastry blender or two forks until the mixture resembles coarse crumbs. Stir in the buttermilk to make a shaggy dough. Turn out the dough onto a lightly floured work surface and pat into a 1-inch-thick rectangle (the size isn't that important).

2. Slip the dough into a 1-gallon zip-tight plastic bag, press out the air, and seal the bag. Refrigerate the dough for at least 6 hours or up to 2 days. If refrigerated for longer than 6 hours, punch down the dough whenever it occurs to you, but no less than twice every 24 hours.

3. Position a rack in the center of the oven and preheat the oven to 400°F. Turn out the dough onto a lightly floured surface and knead briefly. On a lightly floured surface, pat out the dough with lightly floured hands (or dust the top of the dough with flour and roll out to ¾- to 1-inch thickness). Using a 2½-inch round biscuit or cookie cutter, cut out biscuits and place them 1 inch apart on an ungreased large rimmed baking sheet. Gather up the dough scraps and knead briefly to combine, and cut out more biscuits until the dough is used up. For the final biscuit, you might even simply press the dough into the cutter.

4. Bake until the biscuits are golden brown, 20 to 25 minutes. Let cool a few minutes, then serve warm.

# Patti's Popovers

For those mornings when you just need something special and simple to start the day off right, make popovers. These treats used to appear on breakfast tables a lot more often than they do now, and they deserve a comeback—just stir up some batter, pour it into a hot muffin tin (don't forget to preheat the pan), and bake for about 30 minutes to get crusty, golden brown pastries with moist, custardy insides. They aren't sweet, so serve with plenty of your favorite jam and, of course, butter.

Makes 9 popovers

1 cup unbleached all-purpose flour

1 teaspoon sugar

½ teaspoon salt

1 cup whole milk, at room temperature
   (see Patti's Pointers)

2 large eggs, at room temperature

1 tablespoon unsalted butter, melted

Softened butter, for the muffin cups

1. Position a rack in the center of the oven and preheat the oven to 425°F.

2. Whisk the flour, sugar, and salt in a medium bowl. Add the milk, eggs, and butter and whisk until combined (the batter can be a little lumpy). Set the batter aside.

3. Butter 9 cups of a muffin pan (see Patti's Pointers). Place the pan in the oven and heat the pan until it is very hot, about 3 minutes. (The butter in the cups can be brown but should not be burned.) Remove the pan from the oven and pour equal amounts of the batter into the greased cups. Return to the oven. Bake, without opening the oven door, until the popovers are deep golden brown, 25 to 30 minutes. Remove from the oven again and quickly pierce the side of each popover with the tip of a small, sharp knife to release some steam. Return to the oven one final time to bake the popovers for about 3 minutes to help dry out the insides a bit. Remove the popovers from the pan and serve warm.

**Patti's Pointers:** *To bring the milk to room temperature, microwave for about 20 seconds on high (100%). You just need to take the chill off the milk, not actually warm it.*

*Popover pans are sold at many kitchenware stores and online. The problem with them is that you can really only use them for making (wait for it) popovers. Just use a muffin pan.*

# Cinnamon Crumb Cake

Cinnamon crumb cake, with a very thick layer of streusel on a buttery cake, can be found in about every corner delicatessen and neighborhood bakery in New York City. But making it at home is a thousand times better than buying one of those plastic-wrapped hockey pucks. Give it a try. I bet you'll be hooked. If you wish, stir ½ cup chocolate chips into the cake batter.

Makes 8 servings

**CAKE**

Softened butter and flour, for the pan

1¼ cups unbleached all-purpose flour

2 teaspoons baking powder

⅛ teaspoon salt

¼ cup (½ stick) unsalted butter, at room temperature

¾ cup granulated sugar

1 large egg, at room temperature

½ teaspoon vanilla extract

½ cup whole milk

**STREUSEL TOPPING**

1½ cups unbleached all-purpose flour

¾ cup (1½ sticks) unsalted butter, at room temperature

½ cup packed light brown sugar

¼ cup granulated sugar

2 teaspoons ground cinnamon

1. **To make the cake:** Position a rack in the center of the oven and preheat the oven to 350°F. Lightly butter and flour a 9-inch springform pan and tap out the excess flour.

2. Sift the flour, baking powder, and salt into a large bowl. Beat the butter and granulated sugar in a medium bowl with an electric mixer at high speed until the mixture is pale yellow (it will be gritty), about 3 minutes. Beat in the egg, beating until it is completely absorbed. Beat in the vanilla. Reduce the mixer speed to low. In thirds, add the flour mixture, alternating with two equal additions of the milk, beating after each addition until the batter is smooth. Scrape into the pan and smooth the top.

3. **To make the crumb topping:** Combine the flour, butter, brown and granulated sugars, and cinnamon in a medium bowl. Using your hands, squeeze the ingredients together until they form a soft dough. Crumble the dough in pea-sized chunks evenly over the batter.

4. Bake until the topping is firm and a wooden toothpick inserted into the center of the cake comes out clean, about 40 minutes.

5. Cool the cake in the pan on a wire cake rack. Remove the sides of the pan and slice into wedges to serve.

# Pancakes with Blueberry Maple Syrup

Pancakes, flapjacks, or griddle cakes—no matter what you call them—are always a crowd-pleaser. The typical way to make blueberry pancakes is to stir berries into the batter. But using my way, with the berries simmered in maple syrup, you'll end up with a luscious homemade topping that is miles beyond anything that you can buy. And the same goes for from-scratch batter versus the kind from the box. But be forewarned: Once you make them, it won't be breakfast at your house unless they're on the menu and the table.

Makes 12 to 14 pancakes; 4 to 6 servings

**BLUEBERRY MAPLE SYRUP**

1 cup maple syrup, preferably pure, or use pancake syrup (see Patti's Pointers)

1 cup fresh blueberries

**PANCAKES**

2¼ cups unbleached all-purpose flour

2 tablespoons sugar

1 tablespoon baking powder

½ teaspoon salt

2 cups whole milk

3 large eggs, separated, at room temperature

¼ cup (½ stick) unsalted butter, melted

Vegetable oil, for the griddle

Warm melted butter, for serving

1. **To make the syrup:** Heat the syrup and blueberries in a small saucepan over medium heat until simmering. Remove from the heat and crush about one quarter of the blueberries into the syrup with a fork. Set aside.

2. Position a rack in the center of the oven and preheat the oven to 200°F.

3. Heat a griddle over high heat until a flick of water from your fingertips immediately forms skittering balls. Reduce the heat to medium-low.

4. **Meanwhile, to make the pancake batter:** Whisk the flour, sugar, baking powder, and salt in a large bowl. Make a well in the center. Add the milk, egg yolks, and melted butter to the well and stir together just until combined—there can be a few lumps.

5. Whip the egg whites with an electric hand mixer on high speed until they form soft peaks. Fold the whites into the batter.

6. Lightly oil the griddle. Using a heaping ⅓ cup for each pancake, spoon the batter onto the griddle. Cook until bubbles appear all over the top of each pancake and the undersides are golden brown, about 1½ minutes. Flip the pancakes over and brown on the other side, about 1 minute more. Place the pancakes directly on the oven rack to keep warm while making the remaining pancakes.

7. Transfer the blueberry syrup to a pitcher with a ladle. Serve the pancakes with the syrup and melted butter.

**Patti's Pointers:** *Sure, you can use supermarket pancake syrup, but if you are making from-scratch flapjacks, why not go for the good stuff and get pure natural maple syrup? Maple syrup is now graded by color: golden, amber, dark, and very dark. The darker the color, the stronger the maple flavor.*

*It's a good idea to make a single pancake as a test run. The first pancake is usually too dark, and you can adjust the heat as needed.*

*Keep the pancakes warm by putting them directly on the oven rack—don't put them on a baking sheet, where they will get soggy. You want the warm air to circulate around them.*

# The-Spirit's-in-It Chicken and Cornmeal Waffles with Spicy Maple Syrup

✳

Every dietitian I know says the same thing about breakfast: It's the most important meal of the day. My own doctor has been on the breakfast bandwagon for years. In fact, he thinks it's such an important part of a healthy lifestyle that he talks about it at every single one of my appointments. But first he brings up the only thing he loves talking about more than breakfast: my sugar levels. Our conversations usually go like this:

> Dr. Diabetes: Tell me, Ms. LaBelle, how are you doing with your diet and fitness program?
>
> Me: Well, Doc, I'm not sipping kale juice and SoulCycle-ing twice a day, but I know what my blood sugar levels are supposed to be and I keep them within those limits...most of the time.

I always let a couple of seconds pass before I hit him with the truth, the whole truth, and nothing but the truth: "But I'm human, Doc. And every now and then I cheat."

He always looks at me as if I'd said I'd eaten an entire box of Krispy Kreme doughnuts for lunch. (Don't think I haven't thought about it.) But, to Dr. Diabetes's credit, he usually says nothing; just shoots me a have-you-not-listened-to-anything-I've-told-you? look and moves on to the why-you-should-never-skip-breakfast part of the lecture. I've heard it so many times, I can recite the top three reasons in my sleep: (1) It provides you with the energy and nutrients that lead to increased concentration; (2) it staves off that hungry-before-lunch sensation; and (3) it helps maintain a healthy overall body weight.

(For the record, Doc, reason #3 got me on the breakfast bandwagon years ago, so how about we dispense with this portion of the lecture at future appointments?)

Hunger management, healthy body weight: You'd think either would have turned me into a die-hard breakfast fan, but, truth be told, I'm not a devotee. I mean, let's be honest here: Breakfast can be so *boring*. (Four words: Oatmeal and boiled eggs.) Which is why my heart belongs to brunch. I love brunch for so many reasons. For starters, it's so Zen...spending the afternoon lazing and grazing is an excellent way to nourish the stomach *and* the soul. And it's the opposite of boring. There's something so badass about brunch. It's like, "I don't care if it isn't even noon yet. I'm having wine and fried chicken in the middle of the day, and depending on what else is on the menu, I may indulge in a few other goodies."

Speaking of menus, they're another reason I'm such a big brunch fan. Even the basic ones feature dishes both savory (shrimp and grits!) and sweet (pillowy pancakes and perfect pies). And brunch menus have no rules. Or I should say they have only *one* rule: They must include the three Bs: bacon, biscuits, and Bloody Marys. At the brunch parties my sisters and I hosted back in the day, the menu had two additional requirements: (1) fried chicken and waffles; and (2) a well-stocked bar. What honey is to bees, that's what this dynamic duo—or is it a trio?—was to our brunch guests. Those we invited and those who just showed up. People flocked to our brunches from all over Philly. Next to our backyard crab feasts, they were summer's hottest ticket.

If I *had* to choose the bigger draw—the chicken and waffles or the super-stocked bar—my money would be on the chicken and waffles. Dismiss me if you like, but my mother's fried chicken wasn't just good; it was out of this world. And I don't use that phrase lightly. I witnessed more than a few brunch guests bite into Chubby's fried chicken…and then start speaking in tongues.

I know it was Chubby's cooking skill that made people flip out over her chicken. Or I should say I know it *logically*. But part of me has always wondered if it was because of what her close friend, my adopted aunt Naomi, always said. Aunt Naomi said Chubby's chicken was so good because Ernest Evans stuck his foot in it. All through my childhood, Chubby took me to Henry Colt's Ninth Street Market in South Philly to buy our chickens. She said Henry had the best chickens in town. He definitely had the best chicken plucker—pudgy little Ernest Evans used to sing and dance and do impressions for us before he went in the back and cleaned our chickens. Today, the world knows Ernest Evans as Chubby Checker, the internationally famous recording artist who had me—and every other teenager in 1960s America—dancing to his number one smash hit, "The Twist." How I loved those days hanging out with Chubby and Chubby.

It's the memory of those days that calls me back. Sometimes it comes in the intoxicating smell of chicken frying on the stove. Sometimes it comes in the low, soothing hum of a mixer blending the perfect batter. Lately, it's been coming in childhood memories of neighbors I also called friends: George Peters, who, on the second Sunday of every month, played hooky from his family church so he could come to Beulah Baptist to hear me sing. Harriett Chapman, the church organist and Young Adults Choir director, who

told me my voice was pure magic long before I thought there was anything special about it… or me. Llona Gullette and Maudie Hurd, who stayed up all night helping me cook my sister Barbara's favorite dishes for her wedding…and her funeral.

If I could hop in a DeLorean and go back in time, brunch at Chubby's house would be one of my very first stops. Who knows? Maybe one day I'll be able to do just that. Don't laugh; a whole lot of people a whole lot smarter than me say the "Back to the Future" thing isn't as crazy as it sounds. That time travel, like travel to Mars, will someday be a reality. Until it is, however, do what I do: Clear your calendar and throw an old-fashioned brunch party. Pull out the cast-iron skillets and stock the bar. Invite all your favorite people…those still with you and the spirits of those who aren't. Fair warning: If you call their names out loud, you just may feel their presence in your kitchen. *Hey sister, soul sister, soul sister, soul sister.*

If it's been awhile since you hosted a brunch, no worries. Successful brunch-giving is all about the food and the mood, both of which you can master with a few insider tips. Follow them carefully, and you'll be ending the afternoon telling your guests the same thing I do: "Of course you'll be invited to my next party, Sugar. I wouldn't dream of not including you."

Tip #1: Be choosy at the market. Whether you're ordering from the deli or buying chicken to fry at home, fresh is always—*always*—better. Repeat after me: Fresh. Delicious. Simple. These are words to cook by. Speaking of simple, that's exactly how you should keep the menu. At least until you get the whole cooking/baking thing down pat. Serve your favorite frittata, these to-die-for chicken and waffles, and, of course, the three Bs. Add the pass-it-on party cake (page 41) and the peach-apple cobbler (page 143) and—*voilà!*—you'll have a menu that would make my sisters proud.

Tip #2: Pay attention to ambience; it should scream "Relax!" The best at-home brunches have a peaceful, serene, enter-here-and-lay-your-troubles-down vibe. To achieve it, you need the right music and the right dress code. Get them right and people will be talking about that voodoo that you do and you'll have to *kick* your guests out. Especially if you hook up the music. Music has the power to penetrate the soul. It amplifies, clarifies, glorifies, sanctifies. Which is why I put my playlist together in advance. While it changes with my mood, it always includes some jazz (a little Miles, a little Monk), some Motown (that bass hook in "My Girl" never fails to get folks from eight to eighty to bust out their best Temptations-inspired choreography), and some Buffett (I have to hand it to Jimmy; nothing says *chill out* like his signature hit "Margaritaville"). Side note to Jimmy: I'll make you some chicken and waffles if you sing it at my next brunch!

While we're on the subject of Margaritaville, your guests should dress as if that's where they'll be spending the afternoon. To that end, put the word out early that the dress code is kick-back chic, aka comfy-cozy. At my sisters' brunches, where I'd describe the vibe as Caribbean chill crossed with a West Philly edge, they took it a step further: They told everyone to come dressed to lounge, loaf, and laze. Vivian, the fashion plate, used to stroll around the house in silk pajamas passing out Harvey Wallbangers and removing Sunday morning ties.

In their honor—and to keep the vibe from ever veering uptight—I have been known to post the following instructions on a visible-to-all wall. Especially when I invite certain people, and you know who you are, Armstead and Dr. Diabetes.

**Brunch Rules**

Eat

Drink

Mingle

Doze

Repeat

I know it's old-school, this idea that you spend hours eating and drinking and lounging and lazing and emerge a calmer, more chilled-out, more in-touch-with-your-loved-ones you. But you do. You really do. But don't take my word for it. Host your own brunch for friends and family and see for yourself.

My sisters would like that. And so would I.

# The-Spirit's-in-It Chicken and Cornmeal Waffles with Spicy Maple Syrup

No one is sure who invented the hearty combination of chicken and waffles, and a lot of places, from the South to Chicago to Harlem, have laid claim. This top-notch version has cornmeal in the batter and uses Chubby's recipe for fried chicken, along with a sweet-spicy syrup that is downright addictive. The recipe is all about timing, so I give a lot of pointers below.

Makes 4 to 6 servings

### CORNMEAL WAFFLES

1⅓ cups unbleached all-purpose flour

⅔ cup yellow cornmeal, preferably stone-ground

2 tablespoons sugar

1 tablespoon baking powder

1 teaspoon baking soda

¼ teaspoon salt

2½ cups buttermilk

3 large eggs, separated, at room temperature

3 tablespoons unsalted butter, melted

### CHICKEN

2 skinless, boneless chicken breast halves, 8 to 10 ounces each

1 large egg

½ cup unbleached all-purpose flour

½ teaspoon salt

½ teaspoon freshly ground black pepper

Vegetable oil, for frying

### SPICY MAPLE SYRUP

2 cups maple syrup, preferably pure, or use pancake syrup (see Patti's Pointers, page 209)

2 teaspoons hot pepper sauce, such as Patti's Good Life Hot Flash

Warm, melted unsalted butter, for serving

1. Position a rack in the center of the oven and preheat the oven to 200°F. Preheat a waffle iron according to the manufacturer's directions.

2. **To make the waffles:** Sift the flour, cornmeal, sugar, baking powder, baking soda, and salt through a wire sieve into a large bowl. Add any cornmeal left in the sieve. Whisk the buttermilk, egg yolks, and melted butter together in another bowl. Whip the egg whites in a medium bowl with an electric mixer set at high speed until they form soft peaks. Add the buttermilk mixture to the dry ingredients and whisk until almost smooth. Add the whipped whites and use the whisk to fold them into the batter. The batter can be slightly lumpy.

*Continued*

3. In batches, add the batter to the waffle iron and cook according to the manufacturer's directions until golden brown. Transfer the waffles directly to the oven rack to keep warm. Makes about 16 waffles.

4. **To make the chicken:** Line a baking sheet with waxed paper. One at a time, pound a chicken breast half between two sheets of plastic wrap with a flat meat pounder or rolling pin until the chicken is about ½ inch thick. Beat the egg in a wide, shallow bowl. Mix the flour, salt, and pepper in a second bowl. Dip each chicken breast into the egg, followed by the flour mixture, to coat. Transfer to the baking sheet. Let the chicken stand for a few minutes to set the coating.

5. Line a plate with paper towels. Heat a very large skillet, preferably cast iron, over high heat. Pour in enough oil to come ¼ inch up the sides of the skillet and heat until the oil shimmers. Add the chicken to the oil and reduce the heat to medium. Fry the chicken, turning halfway through cooking, until golden brown on both sides, about 6 minutes. (The chicken is too thin to check doneness with a thermometer. If you wish, transfer the chicken to a plate and cut into the center with a small, sharp knife—the meat should be white with no sign of pink.) Transfer the chicken to the paper towels and let drain and cool for 3 minutes.

6. Meanwhile, heat the syrup and hot sauce together in a small saucepan over medium-low heat just until warm, about 2 minutes. Transfer to a small pitcher for serving.

7. Transfer the chicken to a cutting board. Cut the chicken crosswise into 4 to 6 equal portions. For each serving, place 2 or 3 waffle squares on a plate with a portion of chicken. Serve immediately with the warm syrup and melted butter.

**Patti's Pointers:** *Timing is everything with chicken and waffles so that all the components are good and hot when served. It helps if one cook tends to the waffles and another to frying the chicken. Also, heat the syrup and serve warm melted butter to help with temperature control.*

*The batter makes about 16 standard 4-inch-square waffles. Your yield may vary depending on your waffle iron model. If you have leftover waffles, just cool, wrap, and freeze for up to 2 months. To serve, cook the unfrozen waffles in the toaster until heated through.*

You can keep the cooked waffles warm in a 200°F oven. Put the waffles directly on the oven rack. If they are placed on a baking sheet, they can get soggy.

Definitely use boneless chicken for this recipe because it cooks quickly and is easier to cut. This is a very filling dish, so it is best to serve smaller portions of chicken. I use medium-sized chicken breast halves (about 8 ounces each), pounded to an even thickness so they cook at the same rate, and then cut into halves crosswise to make two smaller portions. You can always make extra and serve seconds, if you wish.

Instead of making individual servings, you can serve the different components and let people make their own. In that case, cut the fried chicken crosswise, across the grain, into ½-inch-thick slices, and transfer to a platter. Heap all of the waffles on another platter. Serve the chicken and waffles with pitchers of the syrup and melted butter.

# 8 ) New Attitude Desserts

There is a fact of life that I have to face every day: I have diabetes. And, like many African Americans, so do many members of my family. I have rethought my attitude about eating, especially desserts, and especially now that I'm a glammother. (I plan to be around to sing at Gia's wedding!) I rely on nutritional charts to help me count the numbers to come in under my daily allowance of calories, carbohydrates, and sugars. If I know I am going to treat myself to dessert that day, I cut back on the other carbs that I might otherwise eat. In my life, it's all about portion control! Read those two words again and let them sink in: *portion control*. You can make the "healthiest" dessert in the world, but that doesn't mean you can sit down and eat the entire batch! Here is a group of low-sugar, reduced-fat sweets that I enjoy every bit as much as my old-school treats. But please keep in mind that I am not a doctor, and I am only sharing what works for me.

# New Attitude Desserts

When making diabetes-friendly desserts, there are many tips that you can use in your everyday baking:

- Learn about the various sugar substitutes (see below), and choose the ones that you like the best. I will sometimes use small quantities of standard sugar.

- Experiment with various substitutes for saturated fats in baking (such as the applesauce in the chocolate cake on page 229). But remember, applesauce and other fruits popular in reduced-fat baking (such as prune puree and mashed bananas) are carbohydrates and still must be counted.

- Enjoy fruit, but again...count the carbs. Fresh, frozen, and canned fruit in juice (not syrup) are good ways to get a naturally sweet flavor in desserts along with their benefits of vitamins and fiber.

- Be informed about the glycemic index (GI), a system that judges how a food affects your blood glucose level during digestion. Most carbs, especially those made from processed or refined foods (such as white flour, white bread, and sugar) are high on the GI scale.

- Take advantage of some convenience products when making these desserts because the nutrition information on the label will make it easier to keep track of your carb and sugar counts.

## Sugar Substitutes

There is more to living the good life with diabetes than reducing or eliminating (good luck with that!) sugar. Keep in mind that sugar plays so many roles in a recipe. Of course, sugar is a sweetener, but it also helps baked goods brown through caramelization. Also, it provides bulk in batters and doughs. Therefore, if you substitute a few teaspoons of stevia for a cup of sugar, the bulk difference is going to wreak havoc on the recipe, and the browning is not going to be the same. But you can still make some great desserts—think about what you can do instead of what you *cannot* do!

There are four main categories of sweeteners:

- **Natural sweeteners** include agave, honey, maple syrup, and blackstrap molasses. Keep in mind that these sweeteners do pack calories, even if some of them may be lower on the glycemic index.

- **Artificial sweeteners** pass through the body undigested. Because the body doesn't burn any of their calories, they are sometimes called no-calorie sweeteners. You'll recognize some name brands in this category—Splenda (sucralose), NutraSweet and Equal (aspartame), and Sweet'N Low (saccharin). Only sucralose is recommended for baking, but if you are making a batter or dough that will be heated, be sure to buy the version that is labeled "for baking." The other sweeteners can be used in chilled desserts.

- **Stevia** is a leaf that can be used as a sweetener. It is sold only in a refined form and is designated as a dietary supplement, and not a food, by the USDA. You'll see it in supermarkets under brand names like Truvia and SweetLeaf.

- **Sugar alcohols** are considered natural because they are plant-derived. The body does not digest them like other foods, so they can be either low- or no-calorie. You can tell these by their names, which always end in *-ol*. Erythritol and xylitol are the most commonly available sugar alcohols, but that doesn't mean they are actually easy to find.

I use a variety of sugar substitutes instead of a one-size-fits-all approach. You will make your own decisions as you experiment. Here are my favorite sugar substitutes, based on what I can easily get at my supermarket and my personal preferences for taste:

- **Agave nectar:** This brown syrupy liquid is harvested from the agave plant, the same succulent used to make tequila. It comes in a variety of colors from light to dark (indicating flavor strength) and can be purchased raw or slightly cooked. I prefer raw agave from the blue agave, named for the plant's blue-gray leaves. Agave has a rich flavor that might remind you of maple syrup. I use it to sweeten hot beverages and for desserts where bulk isn't an issue. It is approximately twice as sweet as sugar so you don't use as much.

- **Stevia:** Native to South America, it has been used for centuries by the locals as a sweetener, but it wasn't until the 1970s that it was developed in laboratories as a "natural" alternative to saccharin and other artificial sweeteners. Stevia is often sold refined into a white powder called *stevia extract* and packaged in small packets. There are a few different brand names. Powdered stevia extract is 200 to 300 times sweeter than sugar. In the case of stevia, extract does not refer to a liquid. (Some of the product in the packets is a bulking agent in addition to the minuscule amount of actual stevia.) Like agave, stevia extract works best in recipes where you need the sweetness but not the volume of sugar.

- **Sucralose:** When sucralose hit the grocery store shelves in the late 1990s, many cooks were happy because, finally, here was an artificial sweetener that acted more like sugar than the competition. Most sugar alternatives can't be used in baking because of their poor interaction with heat, but sucralose works pretty well (it still doesn't brown perfectly). The big advantage with sucralose is that it is available granulated (actually mixed with dextrose for bulk), so it can be measured in the exact same volume as standard sugar. In other words, ½ cup of granulated sucralose can be swapped in for ½ cup of sugar. This kind of sucralose is sometimes labeled "no-calorie sweetener for baking." Keep in mind that you can also buy packets of pulverized, intensely sweet sucralose to use in small amounts to flavor liquids, and I use them in some recipes. Splenda is a well-known brand of sucralose.

# Almost No-Bake Pumpkin Cheesecake

Here's a reduced-fat and lower-sugar Thanksgiving dessert that everyone in the family can enjoy. During the holidays, there can be a lot of desserts crowding the oven, but this recipe is virtually no-bake; only the crust needs a quick bake. This is a cool, creamy, and light end to a big meal.

Makes 12 servings

**CRUST**

Nonstick cooking oil spray, for the pan

½ cup graham cracker crumbs

¼ cup very finely chopped pecans (a food processor works best)

1 tablespoon unsalted butter, melted

**FILLING**

¾ cup skim milk

1 packet (2½ teaspoons) unflavored gelatin powder

Two 12-ounce containers light cream cheese, at room temperature

⅔ cup granulated no-calorie sweetener for baking, such as Splenda

One 15-ounce can solid-pack pumpkin

1 tablespoon fresh lemon juice

1½ teaspoons pumpkin pie spice (or ½ teaspoon each ground ginger, ground cinnamon, and ground allspice, plus a pinch of ground cloves)

1. **To make the crust:** Position a rack in the center of the oven and preheat the oven to 350°F. Lightly spray a 9 by 3-inch springform pan with oil.

2. Mix the graham cracker crumbs, pecans, and melted butter in a small bowl (or pulse in a food processor) until combined. Press the mixture firmly and evenly onto the bottom of the pan. Bake until the crust smells fragrant and is barely beginning to brown around the edges, about 10 minutes. Cool completely on a wire rack.

3. **To make the filling:** Pour the milk into a microwave-safe liquid measuring cup. Sprinkle the gelatin evenly on top. Let stand until the gelatin softens, about 5 minutes. Microwave the gelatin mixture on high power (100%) in 10-second intervals, stirring well after each, until the mixture is warm and the gelatin dissolves. Do not let the mixture boil. (Or place the cup in a small skillet of barely simmering water. Stir constantly until the mixture is warm and the gelatin dissolves completely, about 2 minutes.)

4. Beat the cream cheese and the no-calorie sweetener in a large bowl with an electric mixer on high speed until smooth. Add the pumpkin, lemon juice, and pumpkin pie spice and mix until smooth. With the mixer on low speed, beat in the gelatin mixture until thoroughly combined. Spread the pumpkin mixture in the cooled crust.

5. Cover loosely with plastic wrap and refrigerate until set, at least 3 hours or up to 2 days. To serve, run a thin knife around the inside of the pan. Remove the sides of the pan. Slice and serve chilled.

**Per serving: 200 calories; 12g fat (7g saturated fat); 30mg cholesterol; 210mg sodium; 10g protein; 11g carbohydrates; 7g sugar; 2g fiber; 0.5mg iron; 108mg calcium.**

# Fresh Strawberry Pie

Big, bold, and beautiful, this scrumptious fruit pie is bursting with fresh berries. Stevia is the sweetener here, and a little goes a long way. The pie is especially good when local strawberries are in season, but it also does wonders with the supermarket variety, too. Frozen pie shells are thinner and less caloric than homemade and are a good option when counting your nutritional numbers.

Makes 10 servings

One 9-inch frozen pie shell

1 teaspoon unflavored gelatin powder

2 tablespoons water

2 pounds fresh strawberries, preferably small ones, hulled, about 6 cups

2 teaspoons fresh lemon juice

2 teaspoons (6 packets) powdered stevia extract

10 tablespoons thawed frozen light whipped topping, for serving

1. Bake the pie shell according to the package directions. Let the shell cool completely.

2. Sprinkle the gelatin over the water in a small heatproof ramekin. Let stand until the gelatin softens, about 5 minutes.

3. Meanwhile, slice the strawberries into halves or quarters, depending on their size. Process enough of the strawberries (about 1½ cups) in a blender or food processor to make 1 cup puree. Transfer the puree to a bowl. Whisk in the lemon juice and stevia. Set the remaining sliced berries aside.

4. Place the ramekin in a small skillet of simmering water (the water should come about halfway up the sides of the ramekin) and stir the gelatin mixture constantly until it is completely dissolved, about 2 minutes. (Or microwave the mixture on high power in 10-second intervals, stirring after each period until the mixture is completely dissolved, about 30 seconds total. Do not let the mixture boil.) Stir a few tablespoons of the puree into the dissolved gelatin. Whisk the gelatin mixture into the puree.

5. Fold the remaining strawberries and the puree together in a large bowl. Heap the mixture in the baked pie shell. Refrigerate, uncovered, until the filling is chilled and set, at least 1 hour. (The pie can be refrigerated for up to 8 hours.) Slice and serve, topping each piece with a tablespoon of the whipped topping.

**Per serving: 120 calories; 5g fat (2g saturated fat); 0mg cholesterol; 75mg sodium; 2g protein; 17g carbohydrates; 6g sugar; 2g fiber; 1mg iron; 18mg calcium.**

# Free-Form Apple Tart

A rustic-looking dessert bursting with apples is a fine way to celebrate autumn. The free-form construction means you won't need a tart pan—and the uneven shape is part of the dessert's charm. The tart dough has less butter than most, but a little low-fat sour cream helps keep it tender. Give the apples a quick sauté to parcook them so the filling is done at the same time as the crust.

Makes 10 servings

**REDUCED-FAT PASTRY DOUGH**

1⅓ cups unbleached all-purpose flour, plus more for rolling out the dough

¼ teaspoon salt

3 tablespoons ice water, as needed

2 tablespoons light sour cream

5 tablespoons chilled unsalted butter, cut into ½-inch cubes

**FILLING**

3 teaspoons unsalted butter, divided

2 Golden Delicious, Fuji, or other baking apples, peeled, cored, and cut into ¼-inch wedges

2 tablespoons very finely chopped pecans or walnuts (a food processor works best)

1 tablespoon granulated no-calorie sweetener for baking, such as Splenda

Frozen vanilla low-fat yogurt, for serving (optional)

1. **To make the dough:** Whisk the flour and salt together in a medium bowl. Whisk the 3 tablespoons water and the sour cream together in a small bowl. Add the butter to the flour mixture and cut it in with a pastry blender or two knives until the mixture is crumbly. Gradually stir in the sour cream mixture and stir until it clumps together. Press the crumbs together in your hand and check the consistency—it should be moist, pliable, and not cracking. If it is too dry, stir in more water, a teaspoon at a time. Shape the dough into a flat disk. Wrap in plastic and refrigerate for 30 minutes to 1 hour.

2. **To make the filling:** Melt 1 teaspoon of the butter in a large nonstick skillet over medium heat. Add the apples and cook, stirring occasionally, until they begin to soften, about 5 minutes. Remove from the heat and let cool completely.

3. Position a rack in the center of the oven and preheat the oven to 400°F.

4. On a lightly floured work surface, roll out the dough into an 11- to 12-inch round about ⅛ inch thick. Leaving a 1-inch border, sprinkle the pecans on the round. Set aside the smallest apple wedges. About 1 inch from the edge, working around the circumference of the round, arrange the remaining apple wedges in a large circle, overlapping as needed. Use the smaller wedges to fill the empty center area of the circle. Sprinkle the apples with the sweetener. Fold up the edges of the dough to partially cover the apples, gently folding the dough. Cut the remaining 2 teaspoons butter into small cubes and use to dot the exposed apples.

5. Slide the tart onto an ungreased rimless baking sheet. Bake until the crust is golden brown and the apples are barely tender, 30 to 35 minutes. Let stand to cool briefly, about 5 minutes. Slice and serve warm, with the frozen yogurt, if desired.

**Per serving: 190 calories; 11g fat (6g saturated fat); 25mg cholesterol; 80mg sodium; 3g protein; 21g carbohydrates; 3g sugar; 1g fiber; 1mg iron; 16mg calcium.**

# Peanut Butter and Jelly Pie

If a dessert can be "fun," this one is it. Peanut butter and jelly is a childhood combination that most of us never get tired of, even as adults. But because jelly, jam, and preserves are essentially concentrated fruit, they also pack a lot of carbs, so I use the minimum amount to get the flavor. (And note that these are fruit-sweetened preserves, and not actually jelly...but you get the idea.)

Makes 10 servings

One 8-ounce package Neufchâtel cheese, at room temperature

½ cup peanut butter (look for a brand with no added oil or fat)

2 teaspoons (6 packets) powdered stevia extract

One 8-ounce container thawed fat-free whipped topping, divided

One 6-ounce granola or graham cracker piecrust

6 teaspoons fruit-sweetened strawberry preserves

1. Beat the Neufchâtel, peanut butter, and stevia together in a medium bowl with an electric mixer set at medium speed until smooth and combined. Fold in half of the whipped topping. Spread the mixture in the piecrust.

2. Top the filling with the remaining whipped topping. Dollop teaspoons of the fruit spread over the whipped topping. Using the tip of a small knife, swirl the fruit spread through the filling to get a marble effect.

3. Refrigerate the pie, uncovered, until chilled, at least 2 hours or up to 4 hours. Slice and serve chilled, with a dollop of the remaining whipped topping on each piece.

**Per serving: 280 calories; 16g fat (6g saturated fat); 15mg cholesterol; 160mg sodium; 6g protein; 19g carbohydrates; 9g sugar; 2g fiber; 0mg iron; 43mg calcium.**

# Creamy Mango Ice Pops

These pops, reminiscent of a Dreamsicle on a tropical vacation, are just a bit on the icy side, but actually that texture makes them even more refreshing. You will need a set of plastic ice pop molds to make them. If you don't already own a set, they are inexpensive and easy to find at supermarkets during the summer, and online regardless of the season (or see Patti's Pointers to DIY with paper cups). This makes about 2½ cups of the mango mixture, enough to fill five ½-cup-capacity molds.

Makes about 5 pops, about ½ cup each

2 very ripe large mangoes, pitted, peeled, and coarsely chopped

1 cup plain low-fat Greek yogurt (see Patti's Pointers)

2 tablespoons granulated no-calorie sweetener for baking, such as Splenda

1 teaspoon vanilla extract

Finely grated zest of 1 lime

1 tablespoon fresh lime juice

Special equipment: 5 or 6 molds for frozen ice pops

1. Puree the mango in a blender or food processor; measure out and return 1 cup to the blender. Add the yogurt, sweetener, vanilla, and lime zest and juice. Process the mixture until smooth.

2. Divide the mango mixture evenly among the molds and cover. Freeze until firm, at least 6 hours or preferably overnight.

3. To serve, half fill a large bowl with warm water. Submerge the pops up to their lids and let stand until the pops barely melt enough around the edges to be unmolded, about 10 seconds. Serve immediately.

**Patti's Pointers:** *To use standard yogurt, drain 1½ cups in a wire sieve lined with paper towels set over a bowl in the fridge until you've collected about ½ cup whey in the bowl (about 2 hours). You can speed up the process by putting a saucer right on the yogurt to weigh it down. Discard the whey and measure 1 cup of the drained yogurt.*

*If you don't have ice mold pops, use small paper cups. Fill the cups with the mango mixture. Cover each cup tightly with plastic wrap, pulling it taut. Insert a wooden craft stick through the plastic into the mango mixture; the taut plastic will hold the stick in place. Freeze as directed. When ready to serve, discard the plastic and cut away the paper.*

**Per serving: 90 calories; 1g fat (0.5g saturated fat); 5mg cholesterol; 10mg sodium; 4g protein; 17g carbohydrates; 15g sugar; 2g fiber; 0mg iron; 41mg calcium.**

# Banana Whole Wheat Bread

Every cook has a time when they have to face a bunch of too-ripe bananas. No problem: Make banana bread. This tasty recipe is especially attractive because it is much lower in sugar and fat than the traditional version, and it has extra nutrition from the whole wheat flour. In fact, you may find yourself buying extra bananas just so they can ripen to make this loaf. I bet this version replaces your sugary recipe—it is that good.

Makes 8 servings

Softened butter and flour, for the pan

¾ cup unbleached all-purpose flour

¾ cup whole wheat flour

1 teaspoon baking powder

½ teaspoon baking soda

¼ teaspoon ground cinnamon

¼ teaspoon salt

1 cup mashed ripe bananas
   (from about 3 bananas)

⅔ cup unsweetened applesauce

⅓ cup granulated no-calorie sweetener
   for baking, such as Splenda

1 large egg, at room temperature

2 tablespoons canola or vegetable oil

1 teaspoon vanilla extract

½ cup coarsely chopped pecans

1. Position a rack in the center of the oven and preheat the oven to 350°F. Lightly butter an 8½ by 4½-inch loaf pan. Line the bottom of the pan with waxed paper or parchment paper. Dust the inside of the pan with flour and tap out the excess.

2. Sift the all-purpose flour, whole wheat flour, baking powder, baking soda, cinnamon, and salt together, adding any bran left in the sieve or sifter to the mixture. Whisk the bananas, applesauce, sweetener, egg, oil, and vanilla together in a medium bowl. Add the flour mixture and stir just until combined. Fold in the pecans. Transfer to the prepared pan and smooth the top.

3. Bake until a wooden toothpick inserted into the center of the bread comes out clean and the bread is beginning to shrink from the sides of the pan, 40 to 50 minutes. Let the bread cool in the pan on a wire cake rack for 10 minutes. Invert and unmold the bread onto the rack and discard the paper. Turn the bread right side up and let cool completely on the rack. Slice and serve.

**Per serving: 200 calories; 8g fat (1g saturated fat); 20mg cholesterol; 180mg sodium; 4g protein; 32g carbohydrates; 13g sugar; 3g fiber; 1mg iron; 47mg calcium.**

# Chocolate Applesauce Cake

When you crave a thick chunk of chocolate cake and a glass of cold milk, give this recipe a try. It will be ready in no time and has less fat and sugar than a standard chocolate cake. The secret is unsweetened applesauce, a baking ingredient that every baker should keep as a staple, as it can be substituted for much of the fat (that is, butter) in many recipes. Some chopped nuts add extra fiber. This is excellent topped with fresh raspberries.

Makes 12 servings

Nonstick cooking oil spray, for the pan

1 cup unbleached all-purpose flour

½ cup unsweetened natural cocoa powder, such as Hershey's

1 teaspoon baking powder

½ teaspoon baking soda

¼ teaspoon salt

⅔ cup unsweetened applesauce

½ cup sugar

¼ cup vegetable oil

1 large egg plus 2 large egg whites

1 teaspoon vanilla extract

½ cup coarsely chopped pecans

1. Position a rack in the center of the oven and preheat the oven to 350°F. Spray an 8-inch square baking pan with oil.

2. Sift the flour, cocoa, baking powder, baking soda, and salt together. Beat the applesauce, sugar, oil, egg, egg whites, and vanilla together in a large bowl with an electric mixer on high speed until well combined, about 1 minute. With the mixer on low speed, gradually mix in the flour mixture and mix just until smooth, scraping down the sides of the bowl as needed. Stir in the pecans. Scrape into the prepared pan and smooth the top.

3. Bake until a wooden toothpick inserted into the center comes out clean, 25 to 30 minutes. Let cool on a wire rack. Cut into 12 equal pieces and serve.

**Per serving: 170 calories; 9g fat (1g saturated fat); 15mg cholesterol; 160mg sodium; 3g protein; 21g carbohydrates; 10g sugar; 2g fiber; 1mg iron; 35mg calcium.**

# Walnut Biscotti

Most cookie recipes use sugar not just as a sweetener, but also to add bulk to the dough. So I use granulated sugar substitute in this recipe. The biscotti are perfect for dipping into coffee or tea. If you have the time, toasted walnuts make them even better. To toast the walnuts, spread them on a baking sheet and bake in a 350°F oven, stirring occasionally, for about 10 minutes. Cool completely before chopping.

Makes about 2½ dozen biscotti

Nonstick cooking oil spray, for the baking sheet

2 cups unbleached all-purpose flour, plus more for forming the logs

1 teaspoon baking powder

1 teaspoon baking soda

⅛ teaspoon salt

1½ cups granulated no-calorie sweetener for baking, such as Splenda

3 large eggs, at room temperature

3 tablespoons skim milk

2 teaspoons vanilla extract

1½ cups toasted, cooled, and coarsely chopped walnuts

1. Position a rack in the center of the oven and preheat the oven to 350°F. Lightly spray a large baking sheet with oil.

2. Sift the flour, baking powder, baking soda, and salt together. Beat the granulated sweetener, eggs, skim milk, and vanilla in a medium bowl with an electric mixer set on high speed until the mixture is pale, about 2 minutes. Stir in the flour mixture, followed by the walnuts.

3. Divide the dough in half. On a lightly floured work surface, shape each portion into a log about 8 inches long and 1 inch thick. Place the logs well apart on the baking sheet. Bake until the logs are golden brown and feel somewhat firm when the tops are pressed in the center with a fingertip, 20 to 25 minutes. Remove from the oven and let cool on the sheet for about 15 minutes.

4. Transfer the logs to a cutting board. Using a serrated knife held at a slight diagonal with a gentle sawing motion, cut the logs into ¼-inch slices. Arrange the slices, flat side down, on the baking sheet. Return to the oven and bake, turning halfway through, until lightly browned on both sides, about 20 minutes. Let the biscotti cool. (The biscotti can be stored in an airtight container at room temperature for up to 2 days.)

**Per cookie: 80 calories; 4.5g fat (0.5g saturated fat); 20mg cholesterol; 75mg sodium; 2g protein; 7g carbohydrates; 0g sugar; 1g fiber; 0mg iron; 21mg calcium.**

# Yogurt "Panna Cotta" with Cherry Compote

*Panna cotta* means "cooked cream" in Italian, which this cool, custardy dessert usually contains. But oops…I forgot to put in the cream! Instead, I use Greek yogurt and skim milk to give the custard its creamy texture. Cherries are low on the glycemic index, and you could swap in other fruits in that category (such as berries, but not melon or pineapple).

Makes 4 servings

**PUDDINGS**

1½ teaspoons unflavored gelatin powder

1 cup skim milk, divided

3 tablespoons granulated no-calorie sweetener for baking, such as Splenda

1 cup plain low-fat Greek yogurt

1 teaspoon vanilla extract

Nonstick cooking oil spray, for the cups

**COMPOTE**

4 ounces fresh cherries, such as Bing or Queen Anne, pitted and coarsely chopped (½ cup after chopping)

1 teaspoon granulated no-calorie sweetener for baking, such as Splenda

1. **To make the puddings:** Sprinkle the gelatin over ½ cup of the milk in a small heatproof bowl. Let stand 5 minutes to soften the gelatin. Stir in the sweetener.

2. Bring about ½ inch of water to a simmer in a small skillet. Reduce the heat to very low to maintain the simmer. Put the bowl with the gelatin mixture into the water and stir constantly until the gelatin dissolves, about 1 minute. Remove the bowl from the water. Add the remaining ½ cup milk and stir to dissolve the sweetener.

3. Whisk the yogurt and vanilla together in a medium bowl. Gradually whisk in the milk mixture. Lightly spray four 6-ounce (¾-cup) custard cups or ramekins with oil. Pour equal amounts of the yogurt mixture into the cups. Refrigerate, uncovered, until the puddings are set, at least 4 hours or overnight.

4. **To make the compote:** Mix the cherries and sweetener in a medium bowl. Cover and refrigerate until the cherries give off some of their juices, at least 1 hour or overnight.

5. To serve, use your thumb to gently pull the edges of each pudding away from the sides of its cup. Place a dessert plate over the cup. Invert the two together and unmold the custard onto the plate. Spoon the compote with some juices over each pudding and serve chilled.

**Per serving: 90 calories; 1g fat (1g saturated fat); 5mg cholesterol; 45mg sodium; 9g protein; 11g carbohydrates; 10g sugar; 1g fiber; 0mg iron; 136mg calcium.**

# 9 ) Baking, Patti-Style: Tips, Tricks, and Techniques

As I have said a few times already in this book, I consider myself a natural baker with solid baking genes passed down through generations. But if you don't think baking is in your DNA, no worries. You can *learn* how to be a good baker! It is invaluable to know *why* you do something a certain way—say, lining the cake pan. (And lining a cake pan is different from lining a baking sheet for cookies.) In this chapter, I've gathered up the tips, organized by the recipe chapters, that I've collected over the years from many bakers—from my aunts and parents to the chefs I've cooked with on television, and more.

# Cakes

## PREPARING CAKE PANS

Round cake pans are used for baking layer cakes. I use the standard 9 by 1½-inch pans, but the ones with 2-inch sides will do. You can use nonstick pans, but sometimes, even with your best efforts, the cake will still stick to the bottom. Also, because these have a dark coating, they tend to absorb the heat in the oven, and the batter bakes more quickly than with uncoated metal pans.

The bottom line is (pun intended)—line your pan bottoms with a round of waxed paper or parchment paper. Waxed paper is okay because the batter will cover it and the wax won't melt. If you bake a lot of cakes, consider buying parchment pan liners already cut to size, easily found at craft stores and online. (For these recipes, you can use either the 8-inch or the 9-inch round papers because the 8-inch rounds still cover most of the surface of a 9-inch bottom and actually fit more easily without trimming.)

Some people like nonstick spray to grease the pans, but there is a problem. These sprays contain lecithin, which will actually stick to nonstick surfaces and eventually build up into a goo that is impossible to remove. It is a safer bet to use butter or shortening for greasing.

First, grease the inside of the pan lightly with the butter or vegetable shortening. A folded paper towel or pastry brush works best, not your fingertips. Put the bottom of the pan on a sheet of waxed paper or parchment paper to use as a template, then mark and cut out the round. Fit the round into the pan—the butter will help it adhere. Now dust the inside of the pan with a tablespoon or two of all-purpose flour, and roll the flour in the pan to coat the sides. Don't worry about buttering or flouring the bottom of the pan, because the paper liner is nonstick. Turn the pan upside down to tap out the excess flour, and you are done.

For Bundt pans or other tube pans, grease the pan thoroughly with butter, being sure to get in the crevices in the design (if there is one). Recipes often call for flour for dusting, but plain dried bread crumbs (not flavored!) work better because they create a barrier between the sides of the pan and the batter. If you want to be sure that your cake unmolds without a hitch, use bread crumbs to coat the tube pan.

## MIXING CAKE BATTER

There are basically two kinds of cake batters. The first is **butter-based,** which starts with butter and sugar creamed together. These cakes have a buttery flavor and somewhat firm texture that holds up to frosting. (If only my hair held up as well in the humidity!) The other is **foam-based,** which relies more on beaten eggs, especially egg whites, for the cake's moisture and lighter flavor. The Lemon–Poppy Seed Chiffon Cake on page 50 is an example of a foam-based cake. (Note that I've included plenty of tips for the Irish Cream Cheesecake on page 54 that are specific to that recipe and not covered here.)

Be sure the oven is preheating and the pans are lined before making either type of batter. Prepare the ingredients—sift the dry ingredients together; be sure the eggs, butter, and dairy products are at room temperature; and have any flavorings ready to go (nuts chopped, zest grated, and so on). You don't want to stop in the middle of mixing the batter to chop nuts.

**For a butter-based cake,** cream the butter according to the instructions on page 11. Beat in the eggs one at a time, being sure that each one is absorbed before adding the next, about 10 seconds after each addition. Now it's time to add the flour and any liquids (usually milk or buttermilk), but don't just dump them in. The flour and liquids need to be added gradually, or you will crush the air bubbles in the batter that you have worked to create. With the mixer on low speed, add one-third of the dry ingredients, mixing until they are blended in. Now add one-half of the liquid and mix just until smooth. Repeat with another third of the flour mixture, followed by the remaining liquid and finishing with the flour.

**For a foam-based cake,** it's all about whipped egg whites, which bring lots of air into the batter. The whites should be beaten until they form barely stiff peaks (see page 12). To keep their fluffy texture, the whites are then gently folded, not mixed, into the batter. Folding is a gentler way to combine the heavier batter with the lighter whites. Set yourself up with a large flexible spatula to help with the folding, as small ones literally don't cut it. Stir about one-quarter of the eggs into the batter to lighten the mixture. Now add all of the remaining whites to the batter. Using the spatula, cut through the batter, reaching down to the bottom, and bring the batter up and over to incorporate the whites. Turn the bowl a quarter turn and repeat until the batter is homogeneous, taking care to keep the whites as inflated as possible.

Once the batter is mixed, transfer it to the prepared pan(s). For a two-layer cake, divide the batter evenly among the pair of pans. You can eyeball the amount, but for the best results, weigh the pans with the batter on a kitchen scale to be sure they are equal. Do this, and you are already one step ahead to picture-perfect cakes. Spread the batter evenly in the pan with a metal icing spatula or a flexible mixing spatula.

## BAKING CAKES

Cakes should be baked on the center rack of the oven. If they are too close to the top or the bottom of the oven, they can burn. Stagger the pans on the rack, as close to its center as possible, so they do not touch each other or the sides of the oven.

There are a few signs that the cake is done:

- Insert a wooden toothpick (or in the case of large tube-pan cakes, a thin bamboo skewer) into the center of the cake. It should come out clean.

- The sides of the cake are barely shrinking away from the pan sides.

- The cake top is evenly browned (or in the case of chocolate cake, shows no wet spots), and it springs back when pressed in the center with a fingertip.

## COOLING CAKES

A large wire rack, large enough to hold two pans, is the best place to cool cakes. If air doesn't circulate around the cakes during cooling, steam can collect on the surface and you end up with a sticky cake. A second wire rack, preferably a small one, is a good tool for initially removing the cake from the pan, but a flat plate will work, too.

Transfer the cake pans to the wire rack and let them sit in the pan for 10 minutes to allow the cake to cool slightly and firm up a bit. For each cake, run a dull knife around the inside of the pan to loosen the cake. (For a tube pan, don't forget to loosen the cake around the tube, too.) Place a small wire rack or plate over the cake pan. Hold and invert the rack and pan together to unmold the cake onto the rack. Carefully peel off the paper liner and discard it. Now, flip the cake over so it is right side up and slide it off the rack onto the large wire rack to cool completely.

## FROSTING CAKES

Be sure the cake is completely cooled before frosting it. In fact, if you have the time, refrigerate the cooled layers for 30 minutes or so until they are actually chilled. Cold cake layers don't give off as many crumbs during frosting.

A metal icing spatula, especially an offset spatula, is the best tool for spreading the frosting. And if you have a rotating cake turntable, use it to elevate the cake above the work surface for much easier access to the layers. Even an upturned, wide-bottom bowl can stand in for a turntable if you are careful to keep the cake on the bowl balanced. Some batters bake into cakes with rounded domes (caused by too much baking powder or too many eggs) that need to be trimmed off to level the cakes for frosting. My recipes don't have this problem, so you can proceed without trimming.

Frosting is easiest to use if it is freshly made. Most frostings take only a few minutes to mix up, so you really don't gain much time by making them ahead. Place a dab of frosting in the center of an 8-inch cardboard cake round or the flat metal bottom of a tart pan. Place one cake layer, bottom side up, on the round. The frosting will help keep it from sliding.

If you want to frost the cake directly on its serving platter, apply the dab of frosting on the platter and add the cake layer. Tuck a few strips of waxed or parchment paper around the cake layer to protect the platter from the icing. The cardboard round is better than a platter simply because it takes up less room in the fridge if you want to chill the cake for whatever reason.

Transfer the cake on the round or platter to the turntable. Spread the top of the cake layer with about ¾ cup of the frosting. Add the second layer, bottom side down and top side up. Spread the top with another ¾ cup of frosting. Now gradually apply large dabs to the sides of the cake with the spatula and smooth the icing. Rotate the cake after each application, and before you know it, the sides will be frosted.

In some cases, crumbs may loosen from the cake and show up in the frosting. In that case, apply a thin "crumb layer" of the frosting, refrigerate it to seal the crumbs, and then finish with a thicker layer of icing. The technique is detailed in the recipes that use it.

## STORING AND SERVING CAKES

Finished cakes can stand at room temperature (covered with a cake dome if you have one, but otherwise uncovered) for 4 to 6 hours. Sugar is a preservative, so although the food safety rule is 2 hours, most people create their own rules. For longer storage, the cake should be refrigerated. Chill the cake uncovered until the frosting hardens, then lightly cover the cake with plastic wrap or a cake dome.

Cakes taste best at room temperature. This is because the butter in the batter and frosting hardens when chilled and cold cake has an unpleasant texture. If you refrigerate the cake, let it stand at room temperature for at least 1 hour before serving so it can soften.

To serve the cake, set yourself up with a thin-bladed, sharp knife, a tall glass of warm water, a serving spatula, and a plate with a folded paper towel. Dip the knife into the water before cutting each slice to keep the portion nice and clean. Wipe the frosting from the knife as it collects with the paper towel.

# Muffins and Quick Breads

## PREPARING THE PANS

The muffin recipes in this chapter call for a standard muffin pan with cups measuring about 2¾ inches across and 1½ inches deep. Shiny pans bake muffins more evenly than dark ones. If you use a dark pan, remember that the baking time will probably be reduced, so start checking about halfway through the estimated time in the recipe.

Note that none of these recipes make a full dozen, and average eight muffins. This is done on purpose, as I don't know about your house, but eight is sufficient for my family. If you want more, double the recipe.

While you could butter and flour the insides of the muffin cups, it is not anyone's favorite job. Paper muffin liners make the job much easier and cleaner. Sometimes you see advice to fill any empty cups in the muffin pan with water to help even out the heat in the pan, but I never do that extra step and my muffins bake just fine, thank you. I also spray the top of the muffin pan with cooking oil spray because if the batter puffs over the cup's edges, the muffin won't stick to the top.

For quick breads, there are three sizes of loaf pans readily available to the home cook: 8 by 4 by 3 inches, 8½ by 4½ by 2½ inches, and 9 by 5 by 3 inches. I use only the last two because the first pan makes a pretty small loaf. Check the recipe to be sure that you are using the correct size. You will probably be surprised to find out that there is a 2-cup capacity difference between the smallest and the largest pans.

Butter, line, and flour loaf pans according to the directions for round cake pans on page 236. In some cases, especially with tube or Bundt cakes that can be difficult to unmold, I use dried bread crumbs instead of flour to coat the pan.

This may sound odd, but the crumbs create a firmer coating that will not soak into the batter like butter and flour can.

## MIXING THE BATTER

The batters for quick breads and muffins are often made with melted butter or oil, making them softer than recipes using creamed butter. It is important not to overmix these batters because they don't have a lot of air beaten into them. If they are stirred beyond the point where the batter is just moistened and comes together, the gluten in the flour will activate accordingly, and the baked goods will be tough. Use a spoon or flexible spatula to mix the batter, not a whisk. The whisk may seem like a good idea, but the wet batter just sticks to the wires.

If the recipe calls for add-ins like raisins, they are gently folded in after the batter is mixed. But in that case, it is a good idea to slightly undermix the batter (with a few wisps of flour showing), dump in the add-ins, and let the subsequent folding finish the mixing.

## FILLING THE PANS

Here's a muffin secret passed down from professional bakeries: Use a **portion scoop** to transfer the muffin batter to the pan. Why? It's the best way to get that rounded dome on your muffins—the browned and slightly crusty top you can pull off and nibble before devouring the soft and tender base. So, for picture-perfect muffins, use a ⅓-cup-capacity spring-loaded portion scoop with a green handle. The handles have an industry-wide color coding so a worker can easily grab the correct size in a busy kitchen. The scoop that fits a standard muffin is officially known as the #12 scoop, meaning that 12 scoops will equal a quart. For example, the next size up, the beige #10, takes 10 scoops to make a quart.

These scoops are easy to find at restaurant supply stores and online.

For picture-perfect muffins, scoop out the batter, turn the scoop over, and release the batter into the cup so the domed side faces up. Do not spread the batter out—leave it intact. It will stand a little higher than the edge of the cup, which is what you want. Bake the muffins immediately after the cups are filled.

There's nothing to filling up quick bread loaf pans. Just remember that you never want to fill the pan more than three-quarters full or the batter could overflow during baking.

### BAKING AND COOLING MUFFINS AND QUICK BREADS

Muffins are baked at a slightly higher temperature (400°F) than other breads and cakes to ensure a browned top with lots of caramelized flavor. Quick breads are baked at a moderate temperature (350°F) so the bread cooks through before the outside is burned.

Always bake muffins and quick breads on the center oven rack.

One thing to remember about both muffins and quick breads: They are supposed to look homey. Don't worry if there is a crack running down the center of your quick bread or your muffin tops aren't perfectly smooth.

Cool muffins in the pan for about 10 minutes so they can cool slightly and set up a bit. At this point, thanks to the paper liners, they will be easy to remove from the pan. Most muffins can be served warm or cooled completely to room temperature. Quick breads should be cooled in the pans on a wire rack for about 10 minutes. Run a dinner knife around the inside of the pan to release the bread, and then invert it onto the rack and discard the paper liner. Turn the cake right side up to cool completely.

### STORING MUFFINS AND QUICK BREADS

Most of these baked goods are best the day they are baked. Wrapped tightly in plastic wrap and stored at room temperature, they will keep for a day or so more. Day-old muffins can be cut in half vertically and lightly toasted in a toaster oven to refresh them.

# Cookies

### PREPARING THE PANS

I have mentioned this earlier in the book, but it bears repeating: Cookies are best when baked on heavy-gauge half-sheet pans. If you use thin cookie sheets, the cookies could burn.

Remember the chore of buttering and flouring the baking sheets for cookies? That's gone the way of the transistor radio. (Disregard nonstick baking sheets, which are not recommended because they can overheat in the oven.) These days, you can make any baking sheet nonstick with parchment paper, which is now available at every grocery store. To help the rolled paper sit flat on the baking sheet, lightly grease the corners of the pan with a dab of butter or shortening. You can also use reusable silicone baking mats. See more about these items on page 8.

Bar cookies are baked in pans. For these recipes, I use either a 9 by 13-inch pan (a very common size) or an 11½ by 8-inch pan (sometimes called a brownie pan). Metal pans are preferred. If you have Pyrex baking pans, check the pastry carefully for doneness as these pans retain heat well and tend to bake a bit more quickly than the metal ones.

It can be a headache to keep bar cookies from sticking to the pan, and a chore to dig out that first bar. By making foil "handles" for the dough, you can lift the pastry out of the pan in a single piece and cut it into bars as desired.

Nonstick aluminum foil works best (it is sold with the standard foil) because it is easier to fold into shape than parchment paper. Or use regular foil, but be sure to grease and flour it well. If you use parchment paper, you may find it easier to cut two sheets of paper, and then crisscross them to cover all the sides of the pan.

To make foil handles, grease the pan with butter or shortening. Cut a piece of nonstick foil 5 to 6 inches longer than a long side of the pan bottom. Fold the foil lengthwise so it fits into the bottom of the pan, and run the excess foil up the two short sides of the pan. Fold the excess foil back to act as handles. Dust the exposed sides of the greased pan with flour and tap out the excess flour. Spread the dough in the pan and bake as directed. After the cookies have cooled, run a dinner knife around the inside of the pan to release the pastry, then pull up on the handles to remove the pastry in one piece. Cut away!

## MIXING COOKIE DOUGH

Many cookie doughs use the creamed butter and sugar method described on page 11, and all the usual rules apply. One thing to watch out for, however, is to not beat too much air into the creamed mixture, as most cookies should have a little density and not be too fluffy and cakey. You can cream the butter and sugar with either a hand mixer or a standing mixer. However, if you use a hand mixer, change over to a sturdy wooden spoon to mix in the dry ingredients, as its motor isn't strong enough. Standing mixers do a great job of mixing the dough from start to finish.

## BAKING COOKIES

For an even shape, the dough for drop cookies is often scooped up and rolled into uniform balls. A measuring tablespoon is a good tool to get equal portions, or use a tablespoon-sized food portion scoop made specifically for cookies. (This scoop does not have a color-coded handle like the larger portion scoops.) With bar cookies, it is just a question of spreading the dough evenly in the prepared pan.

For best results, always bake cookies in the center rack of the oven. If you are baking drop cookies on a half-sheet pan, you do have the option of baking the cookies on two racks, as long as you switch positions halfway through the estimated cooking time for even baking. Place the racks in the top third and center of the oven before preheating. Place the pans on the racks. About halfway through the baking time, move the pans from top to bottom, and rotate them 180 degrees from front to back.

For drop cookies, it is a good idea to bake a test batch to see just how much the dough will spread. It is not always easy to tell when these cookies are done, although this can be ascertained from the test batch. Usually the cookies will be just beginning to show a bit of browning around the edges. For chewier cookies, you might prefer slightly underbaked cookies; or bake them a little longer than the estimated baking time for crispier cookies.

Bar cookies can be tested for doneness with a wooden toothpick—stick it in the center of the pastry and it is done if the toothpick comes out clean. For brownies, the toothpick can have a few moist crumbs clinging, because if the brownies are baked too long, they will be dry.

## STORING COOKIES

Cookie jars are a romantic notion. But, unfortunately, they don't work very well because they allow in too much air, which can make the cookies stale. If you have a cookie jar that you want to use, put the cookies in zippered plastic bags first. (This wasn't a problem when we were kids because we ate the cookies too quickly for them to get stale.) For the longest storage, pack the cookies in airtight containers with waxed paper separating the layers.

If you bake more than one kind of cookie (during the holidays, for example), store each kind in its own container. Don't mix different types of cookies, because they can exchange flavors and textures: Crisp cookies can get soft, and vanilla cookies can pick up a spicy taste.

# Pies and Cobblers

## EQUIPMENT FOR PIES AND COBBLERS

Cobblers and crisps are cooked in baking dishes, usually the common 9 by 13-inch size. Because they are served right from the dishes, look for especially attractive pans, although transparent Pyrex dishes do a good job. To prepare the dishes, just give the inside a thin coating of softened butter (not bland shortening or cooking oil spray) to help keep the juices from sticking to the dish and to act as a bit of extra flavoring.

Pie pans (also called pie plates or pie dishes) are rarely buttered because there is enough fat in pie dough to prevent it from sticking. I use the standard 9-inch-diameter pie plate with 1½-inch-tall sides, which makes 8 decently sized servings. Watch out for the larger and deeper pie pans. If you use them, your crust and filling amounts, as well as baking times, will be off and need to be increased.

Pyrex and metal are the best materials for pie pans. Both are good conductors of heat and help brown the pie dough. A lot of pretty pie pans are made from ceramic, and it is acceptable, but crusts in these pans do not brown as well.

## MIXING PIE DOUGH

I usually use my tried-and-true pie dough recipe with butter-flavored shortening on page 151. Pie dough is made from flour (and salt) with small pieces of fat cut into it with a pastry blender or two knives. (You can also use a food processor to cut in the butter, but transfer it to a bowl for the final mixing because it is easy to overmix in the machine.) When the dough is rolled out, the fat is squished into thin flakes. When the dough is baked, the oven heat melts the fat and creates steam that separates the dough into thin, flaky layers.

There are many secrets to making pie dough. Some people swear that they can't make pie dough because their hands are naturally too hot, which seems like a crazy excuse (unless, of course, you're dealing with the menopause monster [see pages 161–162], in which case I totally feel for you). But the most important advice is to keep the dough as cold as possible at all times before it goes into the oven. All of the ingredients, especially the shortening, must be chilled and used straight from the fridge (or freezer). During the warm summer months, which is prime pie season, my aunts would sometimes put the flour in the refrigerator to chill it, too, but that probably isn't necessary unless you have a very hot kitchen. But the water should definitely be ice-cold.

Mix the flour and salt in a large bowl. Add the diced chilled shortening and toss it to coat with the flour. Using a pastry blender, quickly cut in the shortening, turning the bowl occasionally and scraping off the fat from the blades as needed, until the mixture resembles coarse crumbs with some pea-sized bits. Using a fork (which is wider than a spoon and helps mix the dough better), toss the mixture, adding enough of the ice water for the dough to begin to clump together. You may need more or less of the measured water because the ambient humidity in the flour affects the final amount of water. The dough may look a little crumbly and dry at this point. To check the consistency, pinch some of the dough in your hand—it should be malleable, like Play-Doh, and not break apart. If it is too dry, sprinkle in a teaspoon or so of water and try again.

Gather up the dough. For a single-crust pie, shape it into a thick disk about 5 inches across. For a double-crust pie, shape it into two disks, one slightly larger than the other. For the apple and peach cobbler, divide the dough into thirds, but shape each portion into a thick rectangle, as they are going to be fit into an oblong baking dish and not a round pie pan. Wrap the dough in plastic wrap or waxed paper.

The dough needs to be chilled for 20 minutes to 1 hour before it is rolled out. The rest period is necessary to relax the gluten in the flour, which has been activated during mixing. If you use the dough too soon, the gluten will make the dough shrink in the pan during baking. I've seen piecrusts shrink a good inch all the way around, so don't rush this step. Also, the fat must stay cold so it doesn't soften into the dough, which makes a greasy crust. Don't let the dough refrigerate until it is rock-hard (longer than 2 hours), or it will crack during rolling. If it gets too hard, soften it at room temperature for about 10 minutes before rolling out.

I love from-scratch pies, but some people find they don't have the time to make the dough and let it chill. If you like refrigerated piecrusts or frozen pie shells, by all means use them. Simply follow the package directions.

In addition to the piecrust cobbler that my family prefers, there are also biscuit and cake-based cobblers. These cobblers are dead simple and don't have any special tips beyond what you see in the recipes.

## ROLLING OUT PIE DOUGH

After the dough has chilled, you are ready to roll out the dough. If there is one baking technique where practice makes perfect, it is rolling out pie dough. But if you are a newbie to pies, don't fret—I am going to walk you through it.

Be sure you have a good, heavy, and long (at least 12-inch) rolling pin. Let the size and weight of the pin do some of the rolling work for you. I like ball-bearing pins because they roll smoothly over the dough.

Dust your work surface (which should be smooth and clean) with some all-purpose flour. Spread it out with the palm of your hand so you have a very thin layer of flour. Don't be afraid to use enough flour to keep the dough from sticking. Some bakers warn against using "too much" flour. I understand their concern, because the moist dough can absorb some of the flour, throw the whole thing off, and make the crust tough. But you can always brush off any excess flour with a pastry brush.

Here's a great tip to save you from guessing if the rolled dough is the right size for the pan. Place the pie pan in the flour. Use your fingertip to draw a circle around the pan, leaving a 2-inch border on all sides. Lift up the pan, and you now have a 13-inch circle in the flour to guide you in the rolling of the dough. (For the peach-apple cobbler, which uses three layers of pie dough, you can still use the bottom of the baking dish as a template, keeping in mind that you will be rolling the dough into a 9 by 13-inch rectangle and won't need extra dough to go up the sides.)

Unwrap the chilled dough (if you are making a double-crust pie, start with the larger portion of dough) and center it in the marked-off round on the work surface. Sprinkle some flour on top of the dough. (Dusting the rolling pin with flour to avoid sticking doesn't work at all.)

Roll out the dough in a methodical fashion, giving the dough a quarter turn after each pass. Too often, the baker "attacks" the dough and rolls it out every which way. That's how you end up with pie dough that looks like a map of Florida instead of a nice circle.

Put the rolling pin in the center of the dough. Using short strokes, and applying even pressure, roll the pin and the dough away from you to the edge of the dough. Now rotate the dough 90 degrees and roll it out again the same way. If the dough is sticking to the work surface, slip a long metal spatula (or even a ruler) underneath the dough to release it and scatter more flour underneath. Continue rolling and rotating the dough a quarter turn after each pass until you have rolled the dough to fill the template. The dough will be about 13 inches across and ⅛ inch thick.

If the dough cracks during rolling, it is probably too cold. In that case, cover the dough with a clean kitchen towel, wait a few minutes for it to soften slightly, and then try again.

To fit the dough into the pie pan, fold the round in half. Place the crease at the center of the pan and unfold the dough, being sure the dough fits snugly in the pan corners without stretching. The edges of the dough should hang about ½ inch or so over the edges of the pan; trim, if needed.

Now fold the edge of the dough under the rest of the round to make a double thickness of dough at the edge of the pan. The dough edge is now ready to flute to create a decorative edge around the circumference of the crust. The easiest way? Use a fork to press a pattern into the dough at the top of the pan. Or create the classic "pinched" fluted edge. Here's how you do it: Put your forefinger and thumb of one hand together in a "pinch" pose. Then put the "pinched" fingers on the outer edge of the dough. Got it? Okay, good. Now take the knuckle of your other hand, place it at the inner edge, and push the dough toward the "pinch" to create a pointed scallop. Finally, work your way around the circumference of the pan, pinching at intervals about 1 inch apart. That wasn't too hard, now, was it?

For a double-crust pie, do not fold or flute the dough edges. Add the filling to the bottom crust. Set the pie pan aside. Clean the work surface by scraping up any bits of dough and flour with a metal spatula. Dust fresh flour on the work surface. If you wish, make a 10-inch-round template in the flour. Roll out the second piece of dough into a 10-inch round about ⅛ inch thick, trimming off any extra dough. Center the dough over the filling. Pinch the edges of the rounds together or press them with fork tines. Or flute the dough now. Make a few slits with the tip of a sharp knife in the top crust.

For a lattice-top pie, do not fold or flute the dough in the pan. Add the filling to the bottom crust. Roll out the second portion of dough into a round about 9 inches in diameter and ⅛ inch thick. Use a ravioli or pizza wheel and a ruler to cut the dough into strips about ½ inch wide. Arrange half of the strips, spaced equally apart, vertically over the filling. Arrange the remaining strips running horizontally to the vertical ones. Fold the edge of the dough over to enclose the ends of the strips. Flute the dough edge.

At this point, the dough-lined pan needs to be chilled again. Freeze it for 10 to 15 minutes or refrigerate for 20 minutes. Freezing is best because it firms up the dough and helps reduce shrinkage.

## BAKING PIES

Soggy pie bottoms are the bane of the baker's existence. Steps must be taken to keep the crust crisp. There are a lot of easy fixes.

While the dough is chilling, position a rack in the lower third of the oven and preheat the oven to the temperature in the recipe. The location of the rack in the lower third of the oven is important to help brown the crust bottom. The lower part of the oven is a little hotter than the center, from the heat bouncing off the oven floor. Also, be sure to put the pie pan on a large baking sheet; the hot, wide, and flat surface will come into contact with the pan bottom and brown it better than the wire oven racks. And the sheet also serves to catch drips from pies with bubbly fruit fillings.

Some piecrusts are partially or even fully baked before adding the wet filling as further insurance against soggy crusts. (An empty, prebaked piecrust is called a *blind crust*.) To support the dough and keep it from slouching in the pan, it is lined with aluminum foil weighed down with dried beans, raw rice, or pie weights. While beans and rice work well, they eventually go rancid and need to be replaced. Pie weights, made from ceramic or metal, can be reused for years, even if they are a little pricey.

To prebake a piecrust, line the pan with the dough and pierce the dough all over (about 10 times) with a fork. Line the bottom and sides of the dough with a piece of aluminum foil (the nonstick kind works especially well) or parchment (not waxed) paper, with the foil extending about an inch above the pan edge. Fill the foil with 2 to 3 cups of beans, rice, or weights, being sure that some of them are pressed up against the sides of the foil (as the dough sides will slump first if not supported). Place the pan on a baking sheet.

Bake the lined pan in the preheated oven (usually 375°F to rapidly set and brown the crust) for about 15 minutes, or until the visible edge of the dough looks set and dry and barely beginning to brown. Remove the sheet with the pan from the oven, quickly lift up and remove the foil with the beans, and set them aside to cool for reuse. The bottom of the piecrust will still look a bit raw.

Return the sheet and pan to the oven and continue to bake. For a partially baked crust, bake until the bottom of the crust is very lightly browned, 5 to 10 minutes. For a fully baked crust, bake until the entire crust is a pale golden brown all over, 10 to 15 minutes longer. Cool the piecrust in the pan on a wire rack.

### SERVING AND STORING PIES AND COBBLERS

Cobblers are always best served warm from the oven. But be careful, because those sweet fruit juices can be as hot as lava! Let the cobbler cool for at least 15 minutes before spooning it up.

There are so many different kinds of pies that there are no hard-and-fast rules for cooling. Most fruit pies are best if they are allowed to cool completely so the fillings can set up. I warn you: This takes a long time, about 3 hours.

# Puddings and Custards

In the pudding and custard family of desserts, it is all about eggs, which help them to set, and, along with dairy products, give them that extra measure of creaminess. Be sure to use Grade A large eggs for these recipes. Other sizes have more or less egg and can easily throw off the recipe proportions.

Eggs are temperamental and cannot tolerate temperatures above 212°F. Puddings cooked on the stovetop usually don't curdle because the flour or cornstarch in the mixture insulates the eggs. But for the smoothest puddings, always strain the mixture through a wire sieve to remove the chalazae (the tiny cords attached to the egg yolk). These cords set at low temperatures, and unless they are strained out, you'll have little bits of what seem to be egg whites ruining the smooth texture.

Custard can be baked at 350°F, but if it actually reaches that temperature, the custard will curdle and become watery. This issue is solved by a **bain-marie,** which is no more than a hot water bath that insulates the custards as they cook. Information on how to set up a bain-marie is located below.

### EQUIPMENT FOR PUDDINGS AND CUSTARDS

Many custards are baked and served in individual serving dishes. Straight-sided, ovenproof dishes are often called **ramekins.** They can be made of ceramic or heatproof glass. The most useful size has a capacity of 6 ounces (¾ cup). I bake the large sweet potato flan in a 9-inch cake pan, as it will be removed from the pan. And the flan cake on page 157 is made in a standard Bundt pan.

For serving individual puddings, tall parfait or ice cream sundae glasses are pretty; parfaits usually aren't too large and help with portion control.

### PREPARING A WATER BATH

As I said before, if baked custard is overcooked, it will curdle. A hot water bath (sometimes called *bain-marie*) solves this problem. The custard-filled ramekins (or other cooking vessels) are placed in a large roasting pan and hot water is added to surround the ramekins. The water acts as insulation because even if the oven heat is 350°F, it takes a long time for the water to heat to the boiling point of 212°F (at sea level), and the custards are cooked before the water boils.

To set up a water bath, choose a large roasting pan that will comfortably hold the ramekins (or in some cases, the cake pan). Arrange the ramekins in the pan. For easier

access when adding water to the pan, slide the oven rack out of the open oven an inch or so. Put the pan with the ramekins on the rack. Pour hot tap water (it should not be boiling water) from a teakettle into a corner of the pan, taking care not to splash water into the custards. Add enough water just to come about ½ inch up the sides of the ramekins. The water is not actually cooking the food, so it doesn't have to be deep. Now carefully (to avoid splashing) slide the rack with the pan into the oven.

When removing the pan, slide the rack out again (with pot holders or oven mitts!) and then remove the pan from the oven. To take the hot cups out of the bain-marie, protect your hands with a kitchen towel or use a pair of kitchen tongs.

### STORING AND SERVING CUSTARDS AND PUDDINGS

Most custards and puddings are served chilled. First, let the custards cool to room temperature. Then cover each cup (or the baking dish) with plastic wrap. If the custards are wrapped before they cool, condensation can form on the wrap and drip onto the custard.

Allow plenty of time for individual custards and puddings to chill, at least 2 hours, or 4 hours if they are going to be unmolded (such as the panna cotta on page 233, or your own recipe for French crème caramel). Overnight refrigeration of at least 8 hours is best for large unmolded custards (e.g., Chocolate Flan Cake, page 157). Custards and puddings can be covered and refrigerated for up to 3 days.

The typical way to unmold chilled custards like flan and panna cotta is to run a knife around the inside of the mold to release the custard, and then invert the custard onto a plate: Place the dessert plate over the mold and hold the two together with your hands. Invert them together and give them a good shake to unmold the custard onto the plate. The main problem with this method is that you can cut into the custard, but it is the easiest way. As an alternative, use your thumbs to gently pull the custard away from the sides of the mold. Firmly rap the heel of your hand all the way around the mold. You can insert a knife in one spot down to the bottom of the mold to be sure that you have broken the air seal, but don't run the knife around the mold. Now try to invert and unmold the custard.

# Breakfast Treats

## EQUIPMENT FOR BREAKFAST TREATS

For the most part, these baked goods use the same familiar pans as the rest of the treats in the book. However, I prefer a 10 by 15-inch baking dish for the sweet buns because it holds a full dozen good-sized rolls. You can find this dish at just about any supermarket.

If you make a lot of pancakes, you will never regret purchasing a full-sized **griddle** that fits over two burners on the top of the stove. A griddle is so much easier to use than any skillet.

Heat the griddle over high heat. It is hot enough when a splash of water flicked from your fingertips onto the griddle immediately forms tiny balls that skittle over the surface. After this preheating, reduce the heat to medium. Do a test pancake to check the temperature—the pancake should take about 2½ minutes to cook on both sides and not cook beyond a golden brown color.

There a few different types of **waffle irons,** so it helps to know the differences. My recipe is for an American waffle iron that makes four 4-inch-square pieces. Extra-deep irons are for Belgian waffles, which use a special yeast batter, so don't use that iron unless a recipe calls for

one. Follow the manufacturer's instructions for heating the iron and adding batter.

Always grease a griddle or waffle iron with vegetable oil. Do not spray them with nonstick oil spray because the lecithin in the spray will eventually build up on the utensils' surfaces.

To keep the pancakes and waffles warm after cooking, place them directly on the racks of a preheated 200°F oven. Don't put them on a baking sheet or they will get soggy from the condensation. You want the air to circulate around the pancakes or waffles as much as possible.

## SERVING AND STORING BREAKFAST TREATS

For the most part, all of the items in the breakfast chapter are best served the day they are made. One thing to remember about pancakes and waffles is temperature control. Keep them warm as directed in the recipe, but also be sure to warm the syrup and have the butter softened to room temperature (or even use melted butter).

# Acknowledgments

Thank you to the Grand Central team: Jamie Raab (for always making me feel at home) and Karen Murgolo (for believing in this book from the start and taking it from proposal to publication with patience and skill).

Gail Ross: Thank you for your illuminating, spot-on advice and for skillfully shepherding this book through all of its stages.

Zuri Edwards: You are the manager every entertainer hopes for and the son every mother dreams of, as you (once again!) proved with your deft handling of this book…and me.

Armstead Edwards: Mad appreciation for your commitment to—and considerable skill at—making it all happen. But most of all for helping me show Gia and Ellington the meaning of family and friendship.

We had three wonderful photographers and a bunch of excellent stylists contribute to this book. Thanks to lead photographer Steve Legato and his team—Katrina Tekavec, Mariellen Melker, and Caitlyn Moore—for making the photo sessions in my hometown a pleasure. Thanks also to photographer Amy Roth and stylists Diane Vezza and Gwen Galvin for their fine work. And for the cover, hats off to Melanie Dunea and stylist Kristy Mucci.

Thanks to Byl Holte for sharing the technical expertise needed for the family photos, and for handling them with such tender, loving care.

Kristin Clark Taylor: Deep gratitude for your brilliant eyes and excellent edits. You've got a gift.

Norma Harris Gordon: Thank you for being there in good times and bad, but most of all for putting up with all of my Patti/Priscilla moods. We may not be blood, but we *are* sisters.

To the wildly talented Rick Rodgers: Serious and sincere appreciation for the many hours (not to mention blood, sweat, and tears!) you put into making every single recipe in this book nothing short of fabulous. (That goes double for the instructions for making them.) You are the man.

And last but by no means least, heartfelt gratitude to my friend and (dream) collaborator, Laura Randolph Lancaster, for her unwavering commitment to excellence and for magically morphing her voice into a smarter, wiser, better, cooler version of mine. I knew you had a rare and special talent from the moment we got together for my very first book.

# Index

# About the Authors

**Patti LaBelle** is one of the most successful and beloved entertainers of our time. She has earned numerous honors and accolades including multiple Grammy Awards and American Music Awards and is the only celebrity whose star on the Hollywood Walk of Fame was paid for entirely by fans. She continues to perform to sold-out concert halls around the world and is an award-winning author of five books, four of which were *New York Times* bestsellers: *Don't Block the Blessings, LaBelle Cuisine, Patti LaBelle's Lite Cuisine,* and *Patti's Pearls*. Patti hosts her own television show, *Patti LaBelle's Place*, on the Cooking Channel. She is also the creator and owner of a successful food and lifestyle line, Patti's Good Life, which introduced the worldwide sensation, Patti Sweet Potato Pie. She lives in Philadelphia.

**Laura Randolph Lancaster** is an award-winning author, nationally recognized journalist, and lawyer. She is the former managing editor of *Ebony*, where she created the magazine's popular column "Sisterspeak," and is the co-author of Patti LaBelle's three *New York Times* bestsellers.

**Rick Rodgers** is an award-winning cookbook author and cooking teacher. He is the author of *Kaffeehaus* and the co-author of *The Model Bakery Cookbook* and *Sarabeth's Bakery: From My Hands to Yours* among many others.